PROMISES I CAN KEEP

PROMISES I CAN KEEP

WHY POOR WOMEN PUT MOTHERHOOD BEFORE MARRIAGE

**KATHRYN EDIN +
MARIA KEFALAS**

UNIVERSITY OF CALIFORNIA PRESS
BERKELEY   LOS ANGELES   LONDON

University of California Press
Berkeley and Los Angeles, California

University of California Press, Ltd.
London, England

© 2005 by Kathryn Edin and Maria Kefalas

Library of Congress Cataloging-in-Publication Data

Edin, Kathryn
    Promises I can keep : why poor women put motherhood
before marriage / Kathryn Edin, Maria Kefalas.
        p. cm.
    Includes bibliographical references and index.
    ISBN 0-520-24113-4 (cloth : alk. paper)
    1. Unmarried mothers—Pennsylvania—Philadelphia.
2. Poor single mothers—Pennsylvania—Philadelphia.
1. Kefalas, Maria. II. Title.
    HQ759.45.E35 2005

                    2004022032

Manufactured in the United States of America

14   13   12   11   10   09   08   07   06   05
10 9 8 7 6 5 4 3 2 1

The paper used in this publication meets the minimum requirements of ANSI/NISO Z39.48-1992 (R 1997) (*Permanence of
Paper*).

CONTENTS

INTRODUCTION

IN SPRING 2002, the cover of *Time* magazine featured a controversial new book that claimed to "tell the truth" to ambitious young women hoping to have children. The book, *Creating a Life: Professional Women and the Quest for Children,* was written by economist Sylvia Ann Hewlett to "break the silence" about age-related infertility. Most professional women believe that female fertility doesn't begin to decline until after age forty, but Hewlett claims they are tragically wrong. Shockingly, she reports, the actual age is twenty-seven, and because of their misperception, large numbers of high-achieving women are left involuntarily childless. Having a baby "was supposed to be the easy part, right?" quips the *Time* cover story. "Not like getting into Harvard. Not like making partner. The baby was to be Mother Nature's gift. Anyone can do it; high school dropouts stroll through the mall with their babies in a Snugli. What can be so hard . . . ?"[1]

Hewlett's *Creating a Life* portrays involuntary childlessness as a tragedy for successful women who have played by the rules for the way a professional woman's life should unfold: get a college diploma, get even more education, get established in a career, get married, get more solidly established in that career, and then have a baby. But achieving these goals takes time—apparently more time for some than the biological clock allows.

Creating a Life didn't just make the cover of *Time*; it received extensive coverage in most major newspapers, including a three-part series in the London *Times*, and was named one of the ten best books of the year by *Business Week*. Hewlett appeared on *60 Minutes, The Today Show, Saturday Night Live, NBC Nightly News*, and *Oprah*. All this attention implies a great deal of public sympathy for the affluent highflier who inadvertently misses her chance to become a mother.

Our book also describes a crisis of fertility—one that occurs among a different population for very different reasons, and that draws a very different reaction from the general public. For those middle-class women Hewlett spoke to, the tragedy was unintended childlessness following educational and professional success. For the low-income women we spoke to, the tragedy is unintended pregnancy and childbirth before a basic education has been completed, while they are still poor and unmarried. How ironic that so many "Mistresses of the Universe" (as *Time* calls them) make all the right moves yet find they cannot have children, while those at the bottom of the American class ladder seem to have more children than they know what to do with.[2] And the plight of these poor women tends to generate not pity but outrage.

In 1950 only one in twenty children was born to an unmarried mother. Now the rate is more than one in three.[3] Having a child while single is three times as common for the poor as for the affluent.[4] Half of poor women who give birth while unmarried have no high school diploma at the time, and nearly a third have not worked at all in the last year.[5] First-time unwed mothers are also quite young—twenty-one on average.[6] And the situations of the men that father their children are not much better. More than four in ten poor men who have a child outside of marriage have already been to prison or jail by the time the baby is born; nearly half lack a high school diploma, and a quarter have no job. Thus it is not surprising that almost half of them earned less than $10,000 in the year before the birth.[7]

But there is another, even more pressing, reason to worry about the growing number of single mothers. Just when new legal and social freedoms, technological advances, and economic opportunities have given American women immense control over when (and if) they marry and when (and if) they choose to bear a child, social scientists have come to a troubling conclusion: children seem to benefit when parents get married and stay that way. Though many single mothers are admirable parents, it remains true that, on average, children raised outside of marriage typically learn less in school, are more likely to have children while they are teens, are less likely to graduate from high school and enroll in college, and have more trouble finding jobs as adults.[8] About half of the disadvantage occurs simply because their families have less money. Part of it arises because those who become single parents are more likely to be disadvantaged in other ways. But even when these factors are taken into account, children of single parents are still at greater risk.[9]

It is no surprise, therefore, that many Americans believe a whole host of social ills can be traced to the lapse in judgment that a poor, unmarried woman shows when she bears a child she can't afford. The solution to these problems seems obvious to most Americans: these young women should wait to have children until they are older and more economically stable, and they should get married first. Policymakers have been campaigning against teen childbearing for decades, and the downturn has been profound.[10] But because marriage rates for those in the prime family-building years have declined even more rapidly, nonmarital childbearing has continued to increase. Public concern over the rise in nonmarital childbearing cannot be dismissed as mere moralistic finger-pointing, since it is indeed true that if more of these mothers married their children's fathers, fewer would be poor.

In response, the Bush Administration resolved to restore marriage among the poor. Ironically, this controversial new domestic policy initiative has found encouragement in the work of liberal social scientists. A new landmark study of unwed couples, the Fragile Families and Child Wellbeing Study,[11] surveyed unmarried parents shortly after their child's birth. The results show that, contrary to popular perception, poor women who have children while unmarried are usually romantically involved with the baby's father when the child is born, and four in ten even live with him. More surprising still, given the stereotypes most Americans hold about poor single mothers, the vast majority of poor, unmarried new parents say they plan to marry each other.[12] But the survey also shows that their chances for marriage or for staying together over the long term are slim. It seems that the child's birth is a "magic moment" in the lives of these parents. And it is at this magic moment that Bush's marriage initiatives aim to intervene.

The "marriage cure" for poverty that the Bush Administration launched has infuriated many on the political left. The *Village Voice* exclaims, "It's as if Washington had, out of nowhere, turned into a giant wedding chapel with Bush performing the nuptials." A left-leaning columnist for the *Atlanta Journal and Constitution* insists, "Many of us don't believe that the traditional family is the only way to raise a healthy child. . . . A growing number of us will 'just say no.' And no amount of law is going to change that." The *San Jose Mercury News* editorializes, "It's impossible to justify spending $1.5 billion on unproven marriage programs when there's not enough to pay for back-to-work *basics* like child care." And on the web, a *Women's eNews* headline reads, "Bush Marriage Initiative Robs Billions from the Needy." Yet, a *Washington Post* editorial recently chided liberals for their "reflexive hostility" to the "not-so-shocking idea that for poor mothers, getting married might in some cases do more good than harm." "Why not find out," they ask, "whether helping mothers—and fathers—tackle the challenging task of getting and staying married could help families find their way out of poverty?"[13]

Even those who support the political agenda with regard to marriage acknowledge that if it is to succeed, we need to know why childbearing and marriage have become so radically decoupled among the poor. All policy should be based on a sound understanding of the realities it seeks to address. Since these trends first became apparent, some of the best scholars in America have sought answers, using the best survey data social science has at its disposal. They suggest several intuitively appealing answers—the extraordinary rise in women's employment that presumably allows them to more easily live apart from men, the decline of marriageable men in disadvantaged groups, or the expansion of the welfare state. Even taken together, however, these explanations can account for only a small portion of the dramatic break between marriage and child-rearing that has occurred (see our conclusion). So the reasons remain largely a mystery—perhaps the biggest demographic mystery of the last half of the twentieth century.

What is striking about the body of social science evidence is how little of it is based on the perspectives and life experiences of the women who are its subjects. Survey data can, of course, teach us a great deal, but surveys, though they have meticulously tabulated the trend, have led us to a dead end when it comes to fully understanding the forces behind it. Social science currently tells us much more about what *doesn't* explain the trend than what *does*, and it tells us next to nothing about what will make marriage more likely among single mothers.[14]

We provide new ideas about the forces that may be driving the trend by looking at the problems of family formation through the eyes of 162 low-income single mothers living in eight economically marginal neighborhoods across Philadelphia and its poorest industrial suburb, Camden, New Jersey. Their stories offer a unique point of view on the troubling questions of why low-income, poorly educated young women have children they can't afford and why they don't marry. *Promises I Can Keep* follows the course of couple relationships from the earliest days of courtship through the tumultuous months of pregnancy and into the magic moment of birth and beyond. It shows us what poor mothers think marriage and motherhood mean, and tells us why they nearly always put motherhood first.

These stories suggest that solving the mystery will demand a thorough reevaluation of the social forces at work behind the retreat from marriage, a trend affecting the culture as a whole, though its effects look somewhat different for the middle class than for the poor. But while members of the middle class delay marriage, they delay childbearing even more.[15] The poor also delay marriage—or avoid it altogether—but they have not delayed having children.[16]

The growing rarity of marriage among the poor, particularly prior to childbirth, has led some observers to claim that marriage has lost its meaning in low-income communities. We spent five years talking in depth with women who populate some of America's poorest inner-city neighborhoods and, to our surprise, found astonishingly little evidence of the much-touted rejection of the institution of marriage among the poor. In fact, these mothers told us repeatedly that they revered marriage and hoped to be married themselves one day. Marriage was a dream that most still longed for, a luxury they hoped to indulge in someday when the time was right, but generally not something they saw happening in the near, or even the foreseeable, future. Most middle-class women in their early to mid-twenties, the average age of the mothers we spoke to, would no doubt say the same, but their attitudes about childbearing would contrast sharply with those of our respondents. While the poor women we interviewed saw marriage as a luxury, something they aspired to but feared they might never achieve, they judged children to be a necessity, an absolutely essential part of a young woman's life, the chief source of identity and meaning.

To most middle-class observers, depending on their philosophical take on things, a poor woman with children but no husband, diploma, or job is either a victim of her circumstances or undeniable proof that American society is coming apart at the seams. But in the social world inhabited by poor women, a baby born into such conditions represents an opportunity to prove one's worth. The real tragedy, these women insist, is a woman who's missed her chance to have children.

THE STORIES THE MOTHERS TELL

Young women like Antonia Rodriguez, who grow up in the slums of Philadelphia's inner core, first meet the men destined to become the fathers of their children in all the usual places: on the front stoop, in the high school hallway, in the homes of relatives and friends. Romance brings poor youth together as it does their middle-class peers. But rather than "hooking up," carefully avoiding conception, or ending an unwanted pregnancy, inner-city girls often become mothers before they leave their teens. Chapter 1 tells of romantic relationships that proceed at lightning speed—where a man woos a woman with the line "I want to have a baby by you," and she views it as high praise; where birth control is quickly abandoned, if practiced at all; and where conception often occurs after less than a year together. Stories like Antonia's reveal why children are so seldom conceived by explicit design, yet are rarely pure accident either.

Mahkiya Washington, whom we introduce in chapter 2, illustrates how the news of a pregnancy can quickly put a fledgling romantic relationship into overdrive. How does the man who can do no wrong become the deadbeat who can do nothing right, even though his behavior may not change much at all? And how does he feel when his admiring girlfriend is transformed into the demanding woman who is about to become his baby's mother? The experiences of women like Mahkiya illustrate how an expectant mother uses pregnancy to test the strength of her bond with her man and take a measure of his moral worth. Can he "get himself together"—find a job, settle down, and become a family man— in time? What explosive confrontations result when he doesn't? Why do some men who once prodded their girlfriends toward pregnancy end up greeting the news with threats, denials, abandonment, and sometimes physical violence?

Yet the most remarkable part of the stories many mothers tell is of relational transformation at the "magic moment" of birth. Few couples escape some form of relational trauma during pregnancy, and for some the distress becomes extreme. So how does it happen that by the time the baby is ready to leave the hospital, most couples have reunited and committed themselves to staying together? The euphoria of the birth may suddenly resolve the tumultuousness of the previous nine months; even a father who has tried desperately to avoid impending fatherhood—by demanding that his girlfriend abort the baby or by claiming the child is not his, thus branding her as a "cheater" or "whore"—may feel a powerful bond with his newborn, so much so that he may vow to mend his ways. The mothers are all too eager to believe these promises.

Still, despite these young couples' new resolve to stay together, most relationships end long before the child enters preschool. In chapter 3, when we first meet Jen Burke, Rick, the father of her two-year-old son, has just proposed to her. Now, with a second baby on the way, he says he is ready for marriage. Surprisingly, when we run into Jen a couple of months later, Rick is no longer in the picture at all. What accounts for the high rate of relationship failure among couples like Jen and Rick? The lack of a job can cause strain, but it's seldom the relationship breaker. Sometimes, it's the man's unwillingness to "stay working" even when he can find a job—that was one of Jen's problems with Rick. Or he may blow his earnings on partying or stereo equipment. But most women point to larger problems than a lack of money, such as Rick's chronic womanizing. The stories these women tell uncover the real sources of relational ruin.

But what about the couples that stay together—why don't they marry? In chapter 4 we tell the story of Deena Vallas, who has had one nonmarital birth and is about to have another. She's in a stable relationship with the unborn child's father, a steady worker in a legitimate job who's off drugs, doesn't beat her or cheat on her, and eagerly plays daddy to her son, a child from a prior relationship. Yet there's no marriage. Is that a sign that marriage has no meaning in poor neighborhoods like hers? No. Her story doesn't indicate a disinterest in marriage; to the contrary, she believes her reluctance shows her deep reverence for marriage. So why does she feel she must avoid marriage for now?

Stories like Deena's show that the retreat from marriage among the poor flows out of a radical redefinition of what marriage means. In the 1950s childrearing was the primary function of marriage, but, as we show, these days the poor see its function very differently. A steady job and the ability to pay the rent on an apartment no longer automatically render a man marriageable. We investigate exactly what does.

Poor women often say they don't want to marry until they are "set" economically and established in a career. A young mother often fears marriage will mean a loss of control—she believes that saying "I do" will suddenly transform her man into an authoritarian head of the house who insists on making all the decisions, who thinks that he "owns" her. Having her own earnings and assets buys her some "say-so" power and some freedom from a man's attempts to control her behavior. After all, she insists, a woman with money of her own can credibly threaten to leave and take the children with her if he gets too far out of line. But this insistence on economic independence also reflects a much deeper fear: no matter how strong the relationship, somehow the marriage will go bad. Women who rely on a man's earnings, these mothers warn, are setting themselves up to be left with nothing if the relationship ends.

So does marriage merely represent a list of financial achievements? Not at all. The poor women we talked to insist it means lifelong commitment. In a surprising reversal of the middle-class norm, they believe it is better to have children outside of marriage than to marry unwisely only to get divorced later. One might dismiss these poor mothers' marriage aspirations as deep cynicism, candy-coated for social science researchers, yet demographers project that more than seven in ten will marry someone eventually (see chapter 4). What moral code underlies the statement of one mother who said, "I don't believe in divorce—that's why none of the women in my family are married"? And what does it take to convince a young mother that her relationship is safe enough from the threat of divorce to risk marriage?

Dominique Watkins's story illustrates why poor young mothers seldom view an out-of-wedlock birth as a mark of personal failure, but instead see it as an act of valor. Chapter 5 reveals our mothers' remarkable confidence in their ability to parent their children well and describes the standards they hold themselves to. As we explain, it is possible for a poor woman to judge her mothering a success even when her child fails in school, gets pregnant as a teen, becomes addicted to drugs, or ends up in juvenile detention. The women whose stories we share believe the central tenet of good mothering can be summed up in two words—being there. This unique definition of good parenting allows mothers to take great pride in having enough Pampers to diaper an infant, in potty training a two-year-old and teaching her to eat with a spoon, in getting a grade-schooler to and from school safely, in satisfying the ravenous appetite of a growing teenager, and in keeping the light on to welcome a prodigal adolescent back home.

Chapter 6 opens with the story of Millie Acevedo, who, like many of her friends and neighbors, believes that having children young is a normal part of life, though she admits she and Carlos got started a year or two earlier than they should have. Millie's story helps to resolve a troubling contradiction raised in our earlier account: If the poor hold marriage to such a high standard, why don't they do the same for childbearing? Shouldn't they audition their male partners even more carefully for the father role than they do for the husband role? Millie's experiences show why the standards for prospective fathers appear to be so low. The answer is tangled up in these young women's initial high hopes regarding the men in their lives, and the supreme confidence they have in their ability to rise to the challenge of motherhood. The key to the mystery lies not only in what mothers believe they can do for their children, but in what they hope their children will do for them.

Through the tales of mothers like Millie we paint a portrait of the lives of these young women before pregnancy, a portrait that details the extreme loneliness, the struggles with parents and peers, the wild behavior, the depression and despair, the school failure, the drugs, and the general sense that life has spun completely out of control. Into this void comes a pregnancy and then a baby, bringing the purpose, the validation, the companionship, and the order that young women feel have been so sorely lacking. In some profound sense, these young women believe, a baby has the power to solve everything.

The redemptive stories our mothers tell speak to the primacy of the mothering role, how it can become virtually the only source of identity and meaning in a young woman's life. There is an odd logic to the statements mothers made when we asked them to imagine life without children: "I'd be dead or in jail," "I'd still be out partying," "I'd be messed up on drugs," or "I'd be nowhere at all." These mothers, we discovered, almost never see children as bringing them hardship; instead, they manage to credit virtually every bit of good in their lives to the fact they have children—they believe motherhood has "saved" them.

EIGHT PHILADELPHIA NEIGHBORHOODS

As is the case for all Americans—regardless of their circumstances—people's beliefs about the meaning of marriage and children draw first from the family of origin. As children move into adolescence and adulthood, the hundreds of daily interactions they have both within and outside the family—with kin, neighbors, teachers, and peers—further shape their view of what "family" means. America's poor live in a wide array of communities, but since the 1970s, they have increasingly come to live in urban neighborhoods with people who are as disadvantaged as they are. It is these poor urban neighborhoods that have seen the most dramatic increases in single motherhood.[17]

The Philadelphia area, the setting for our story, has more than its fair share of such neighborhoods, and a brief glimpse into the colorful economic history of the region will show why. Early in its history, enterprising Philadelphians set out to make the growing metropolis into the leading industrial city in America and one of the most important manufacturing centers in the world. By the mid-1800s they had succeeded. Philadelphia's hallmark was the astounding diversity of its products. By the dawn of the twentieth century, the city that boosters had dubbed "The Workshop of the World" was the largest producer of textiles on the globe. It was also a leading producer of machine tools and hardware, shoes and boots, paper and printed materials, iron and steel, lumber and wood chemicals, glass, furniture, and ships, as well as a host of other products.[18]

Many neighborhoods produced a particular type of product, so that the city contained a number of areas that felt like specialized, industrial villages. One observer described Kensington, the city's leading industrial village, as "a city within a city, filled to the brim with enterprise, dotted with factories so numerous that the rising smoke obscures the sky. [The residents are] a happy and contented people, enjoying a land of plenty."[19]

To get a flavor of Philadelphia's rich industrial past, imagine the city at the dawn of the twentieth century. In the Spring Garden neighborhood, the fourteen-block-long Baldwin Locomotive Works, currently the city's largest employer, is turning out three times as many locomotives as any other firm in the world. In Brewerytown, Christian Schmidt is among the more than one hundred German entrepreneurs beginning to try his hand at brewing beer. In Kensington, an astonishing array of products, including the famous Stetson hat, flow from the textile mills. Just north of downtown along the Delaware River, the Cramps Shipyard makes its mark in the manufacture of both merchant and military vessels. The Southwark neighborhood, also on the banks of the Delaware but to the south, is home to the mammoth U.S. Naval Shipyard. In Center City, the Curtiss Publishing Company proudly publishes the *Ladies Home Journal* and the *Saturday Evening Post*. Across the Schuylkill River in West Philadelphia, the Breyers Ice Cream plant churns out delicious summertime treats. In Nicetown, the Midvale Steel Corporation refines steel. In the neighboring area called Tioga, the Budd Corporation manufactures transportation equipment. And across the river from Center City, in the humming industrial suburb of Camden, the Victor Talking Record Company makes records, while the Campbell's Soup Company is about to begin manufacturing a revolutionary new product, condensed soup.

Philadelphia is often known as a "city of firsts." But beyond its proud list of accomplishments (the nation's first capital, first bank, first hospital, first free library, and the first to provide all of its citizens with a public education) is a lesser known, less distinguished set of "firsts" that began to plague the city at the start of the twentieth century. Philadelphia was the first major American city to see the effects of job loss to the suburbs when Baldwin Locomotive Works made the decision, in 1918, to relocate twelve miles south of the city. It was also the first major city to suffer from competition with the nonunionized Sunbelt states and overseas trade as the 1920s saw the fortunes of the textile industry begin to fade.[20]

The city reached its zenith in the 1940s, when the grandparents of many of the mothers we spoke with were just about to come of age. And despite the losses of previous decades, half of its laborers still had industrial jobs.[21] But in the 1950s alone, the city lost one hundred thousand manufacturing jobs.[22] For much of the five decades since, Philadelphia and its inner industrial suburbs have been in an economic free fall. In these years, hundreds of other textile factories, breweries, and other specialized craft production shops shut down or moved elsewhere, and once-proud working-class neighborhoods lost thousands of residents, leaving behind those who were too poor to escape. [23]

As these neighborhoods hit the skids, most whites who could afford to fled to the suburbs, and the city's rate of nonmarital childbearing skyrocketed. The proportion of nonmarital births in Philadelphia increased from 20 percent in 1950 to 30 percent a decade later, to 45 percent in 1980, and to 60 percent by 1990. In 2000, this figure stood at 62 percent—twice the national rate (see figure 1).[24] Increases in some of Philadelphia's industrial inner suburbs, such as Camden, were equally dramatic. By 2000, in two-thirds of the census tracts that comprise the cities of Philadelphia and its poorest inner suburb, Camden, single-parent households were the rule rather than the exception.[25]

America's fifth-largest city entered the twenty-first century with almost a quarter of its citizens, and nearly a third of its children, living in poverty.[26] This is precisely why it was a perfect site for our research. Because of the high rates of poverty there, we found poor whites, blacks, and Latinos living in roughly similar circumstances. Though racial minorities often live in high-poverty neighborhoods, cities where whites

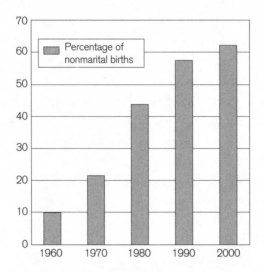

Figure 1. Nonmarital Childbearing Rates
in Philadelphia, 1960–2000. (Source: Webb 2000)

live in the same circumstances are rare. The white urban poor usually live
in mixed-income neighborhoods, and thus have considerable advantages
over the minority poor—better schools, better parks and recreational fa-
cilities, better jobs, safer streets, and so on. But in Philadelphia, the high
poverty rates in several former white ethnic strongholds—those once-
proud industrial villages—create a rare opportunity for students of race
and inequality to study whites, Latinos, and African Americans whose social contexts are quite similar. This unique feature of our study may explain why we found the experiences and worldviews of these groups to
be so similar, and why class, not race, is what drives much of our account.

We share the stories of the residents of eight hardscrabble neighborhoods across Philadelphia and its inner industrial suburbs: East Camden,
Kensington, North Camden, North Central, PennsPort, South Camden, Strawberry Mansion, and West Kensington. The white neighborhoods of Kensington and PennsPort (see figure 2) are located along the
Delaware River separating Philadelphia from Camden. Kensington was
a flourishing eighteenth- and nineteenth-century manufacturing village,

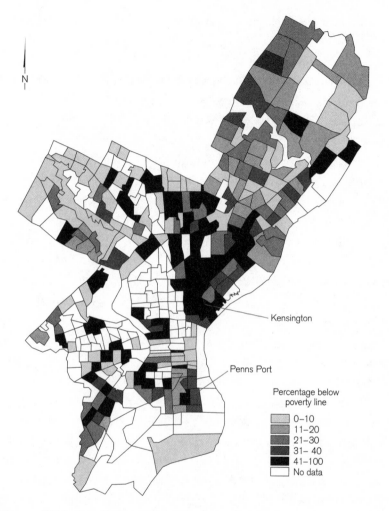

Figure 2. White Female-Headed Household Poverty by Census Tract, Philadelphia, 1990.

which Philadelphia annexed in the 1850s.[27] The village was never affluent, so the blocks of row homes are both modest and plain. Once the world epicenter of textile production, by 1980 only a handful of mills remained. The famed Cramps Shipyard, another major Kensington employer, stopped operating shortly after World War II. Perhaps the only vibrant sector of the local economy in these neighborhoods today is the drug trade.[28]

Several neighborhoods away, below the city's center, is PennsPort, on the eastern edge of the area formerly known as Southwark, whose tiny rowhouses have housed waves of poor immigrants from across Europe. In this area, the U.S. Naval Shipyard to the south had provided many of the jobs. The workforce of this industrial giant, founded before the revolutionary war, grew to nearly fifty thousand during World War II, and it continued to flourish until the 1970s, when the navy decided to get out of the business of building ships, causing this working-class white neighborhood to fall on hard times.[29] Now PennsPort's most notable feature is the famous Mummers, or New Year's, Clubs—the bars and practice halls of the marching string bands, comics, and fancy dress brigades that have competed each New Year's Day for over a century, featuring working-class white men parading down Broad Street decked out in Mardi Gras–like costumes.[30]

Just west of Kensington is the North Philadelphia neighborhood of West Kensington, once part of the same industrial village as its neighbor to the east. Today, the neighborhood is home to the city's small but growing Puerto Rican population (see figure 3). Here, the bleak rowhouse facades are occasionally brightened by a vividly painted bodega, a fluttering Puerto Rican flag, or a colorful mural of tinted glass shards.

Strawberry Mansion borders the Schuylkill River and stretches eastward on either side of Diamond Street. Further east along Diamond Street and across Route 1 is the very poor community of North Central, which ends at Broad Street where the campus of Temple University begins (see figure 4). The histories of these two primarily African American neighborhoods are closely intertwined. They were not industrial villages but opulent streetcar suburbs in the 1800s and 1900s. Strawberry Mansion was populated by well-off Jews who built the handsome twin homes along Thirty-second Street (colloquially known as Mansion Row), and North Central residents were affluent, white Protestants who built imposing brownstones along Diamond Street.

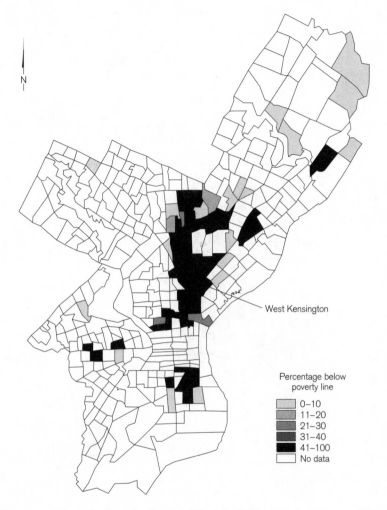

Figure 3. Hispanic Female-Headed Household Poverty by Census Tract, Philadelphia 1990.

Elsewhere in these neighborhoods, the avenues offered an exuberant display of Victorian style—bay windows, corner turrets, sprawling gingerbread porches—while the side streets were lined with the humble row homes of the largely black servant class.

As Jews began migrating across the new Strawberry Mansion bridge to

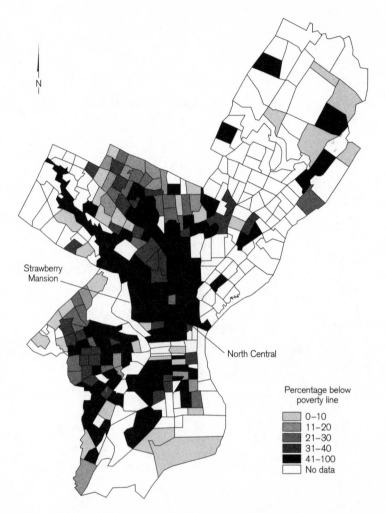

N

Strawberry
Mansion

North Central

Percentage below
poverty line

0–10
11–20
21–30
31–40
41–100
No data

Figure 4. African American Female-Headed Household Poverty by Census Tract, Philadelphia, 1990.

West Philadelphia, around 1890, many of the city's African American luminaries began moving in, and the neighborhoods enjoyed something of a heyday, emerging as areas of unprecedented residential opportunity for middle-class blacks. But when the local real estate market collapsed in the 1940s, largely due to Federal Housing Administration and Veterans Administration policies that favored the purchase of new suburban construction over older city homes, many of these dwellings were converted into multi-unit dwellings to accommodate the avalanche of African Americans who were arriving from the Carolinas and Georgia. Rapid factory closures soon created an epidemic of black unemployment. What vibrancy was left in the retail trade of its main arteries ended in the riots that erupted in the summer of 1964, as surely in Philadelphia as they had in Watts. White owners of businesses apparently targeted by looters no longer felt comfortable doing business there and closed their doors. In the wake of these events, these once-charming neighborhoods became two of the most blighted in the city.[31]

LISTENING TO POOR SINGLE MOTHERS

In the summer of 1995, the William T. Grant Foundation generously agreed to fund our efforts to untangle the story of marriage and childbearing, allowing us to listen to the stories of poor single mothers living in the Philadelphia area's devastated urban core. Given the difficulties other researchers had had in getting the full story, we decided to start by taking a lesson from our anthropologist friends, and one of us rented an apartment in East Camden.

In the two and a half years she and her family lived there, Edin built connections with families by joining a local church and volunteering at an after-school and summer youth employment program. She struck up dozens of conversations with owners of local businesses, talked with teachers, social workers, public health nurses, police officers, and other county and city bureaucrats, and sought the advice of community leaders such as aldermen, clergy, and grassroots community organizers. She shopped at local stores, ate at local restaurants, taught Sunday school, and attended community events.

Sharing in the local routine of daily life yielded dozens of opportunities to observe the lives of neighborhood residents and to experience personally some of the stresses of neighborhood life. She learned to carefully monitor her inquisitive three-year-old, as the sidewalks were strewn with broken glass or the occasional used condom, hypodermic needle, or tiny plastic heroin bag. Her observations soon taught her what virtually every neighborhood man knows, that the best way to woo a single mother on the rebound is to court her children as well. The immediacy of death that so many neighborhood residents felt became real to her as well when two of her five young Sunday school charges lost their fathers to gun violence in the space of a month. She watched as a sunny middle school girl, who initially was active in the local church she attended, suddenly became a sullen, uncommunicative adolescent who dropped out of school and ran away, returning to her distraught family when her pregnancy was several months along. And then she saw how the birth of that baby wrought a startlingly positive transformation in the young mother.

Edin's most telling encounter in the neighborhood occurred while walking to the local Chinese takeout with her younger daughter in tow, a two-year-old, biracial child. On the way, she greeted a local drug addict she'd become friendly with who went by the name "Chicago" (he generally wore a red sweatshirt bearing that legend). On this occasion, Chicago was clearly too high to have any memory of their previous encounters, and upon seeing Edin's daughter, he exclaimed in stricken tone, "Is she mine?" Chicago's alarmed response to Edin's innocent greeting brought home the realization that a casual encounter such as this was precisely how some fathers learned about their progeny.

Camden, directly across the Delaware River from downtown Philadelphia, has three major divisions, East, North, and South Camden, and contains substantial numbers of poor African American and Puerto Rican families (see figures 5 and 6). It is the poorest small city in America and one of the five poorest cities overall, but was once the proud home of dozens of important manufacturing concerns, including several giants: Campbell's Soup, the New York Shipbuilding Company, and RCA Victor. From 1950 to 1980, however, nearly all of Camden's industries moved south or overseas. The effects of job loss were com-

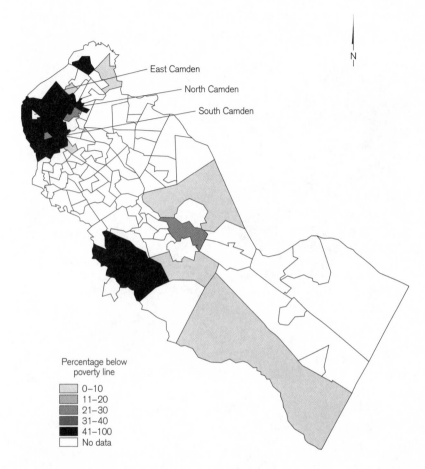

East Camden

North Camden

South Camden

Percentage below
poverty line

0–10
11–20
21–30
31–40
41–100
No data

Figure 5. Hispanic Female-Headed Household Poverty by Census Tract, Camden County, 1990.

pounded by the mass exodus of whites to the suburbs, leaving highly segregated and grossly depopulated neighborhoods in their wake. When Edin moved to Camden in 1995, its population was only half of what it once was and provided only a tiny fraction of the jobs that were once available.[32]

In 1998 we added the five Philadelphia neighborhoods to the study.

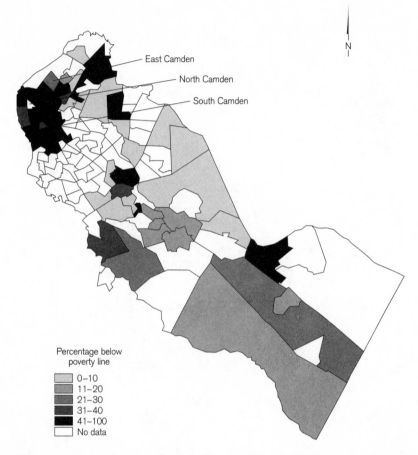

N

East Camden

North Camden

South Camden

Percentage below
poverty line

0–10
11–20
21–30
31–40
41–100
No data

Figure 6. African American Female-Headed Household Poverty by Census Tract, Camden County, 1990.

Kefalas, who had just spent five years studying a white, working-class Chicago neighborhood, began to recruit white mothers from Philadelphia's Kensington and PennsPort neighborhoods. Although census data identified these as the neighborhoods where low-income, white single mothers could most easily be found, local leaders and community groups seemed more interested in denying that single mothers even existed in these tight-knit, predominantly Catholic neighborhoods than in helping to identify them. The unique challenges posed by these social realities meant that finding low-income, white single mothers and convincing them to entrust their stories to her took several years.

Kefalas's efforts led her to a GED program for teenage mothers, several local Head Start centers, and some after-school programs. Once she was "in" with a small group of mothers, she spent time hanging out in their front rooms and kitchens, gathering clues as to how to recruit others. During her second year in the field, Kefalas became pregnant with her first child, and this new common ground provided just the entrée she needed. Residents' reactions to her pregnancy were almost as informative as the interviews themselves. Most assumed she'd had difficulty getting pregnant, as she was already thirty, and one described the pregnancy as a miracle. Another proclaimed with gleeful delight "that the doctors were proved wrong, right?" Most couldn't believe that any woman would postpone childbearing into her thirties by choice.

One teen mothers' GED program on the edge of the neighborhood, with a mostly African American clientele, provided some especially good opportunities to observe local life. Kefalas heard secondhand that the group had once debated whether the very pregnant "Miss Maria" was married. They were not sure, since so few of them could name anyone their age who had gotten married before having children. But she was nearly twice the age of many of them, so they reasoned that, for her, it might be like it was "back in the day," when their own mothers and fathers, or "grandmoms and grandpops," got together. She also had the chance to accompany the group to the downtown Galleria as they went window-shopping for the brand-name baby "coaches" they dreamed of buying.

In the course of Kefalas's fieldwork, she was invited into more than a dozen living rooms that displayed a "prison Polaroid," sometimes held to the wall by a thumbtack or tucked into a framed family portrait on the television set. Prisoners, she learned, can have these taken for only a few dollars at the prison commissary and usually pen cheerful inscriptions such as "Happy Birthday" or "I love you" on the back. When family members come to visit, the commissary photographer will, for a fee, commemorate the occasion with a keepsake Polaroid. One mother showed Kefalas a photo album of Polaroid photographs taken in the prison's visiting area—each commemorating one of the few times her daughter and her child's father had been in the same room together over the course of the six-year-old's life. The photos typically feature the inmate in his fluorescent orange Department of Corrections jumpsuit against a backdrop of a tropical beach scene, perhaps to give the illusion to the loved ones back home that their father is not in prison, but taking a much-needed vacation.

In each of these neighborhoods, we followed the tack we had taken in Camden and spent time talking to local business owners, representatives of grassroots neighborhood organizations and institutions, and private social services agencies to get some sense of the range of families who lived there. These contacts led us to an initial group of low-income single mothers of black, white, and Puerto Rican descent who were willing to share their lives with us. These mothers then introduced us to others in similar situations. We aimed for 50 to 60 mothers from each racial and ethnic group, and talked in depth with 162 mothers in all.

We limited our sample to mothers who had earned less than $16,000 in the past year, an amount about equal to the federal poverty line in those years. We wanted to capture both welfare-reliant mothers and mothers working at low-wage jobs. And because of the unusually strong economy at the time, women leaving welfare for employment were averaging $8 per hour in earnings, an annualized income of $16,000 for a full-time worker.[33] All of them lived in neighborhoods where at least 20 percent of the residents were poor. Each had at least one child under eighteen living at home, and though some had been married, all were now single, at least in the legal sense, although most did not live on their own or apart from male partners: only about three in ten maintained their own households. Nearly half were doubled up with relatives or friends, but a smaller yet significant number were living with men.[34] Some of these men were the fathers of at least one of their children, but others were boyfriends who had not yet fathered any children with the mother (see appendix A).

Mothers ranged in age from fifteen to fifty-six, but were twenty-five years old on average. Forty-five percent had no high school diploma, but 15 percent had earned a GED. A surprising number, nearly a third of the total, had participated in some kind of post–high school educational activities such as college, nurses- or teachers-aid training, or cosmetology school. Nearly three-quarters (73 percent) had borne their first child when they were still in their teens. Mothers under twenty-five had 1.6 children, while those twenty-five and older had 3.1 children on average. Almost half had collected cash welfare at some point in the past two years, and almost half were neither working nor in school when we met them. Forty percent held low-end service-sector jobs at the time, working as telemarketers, childcare workers, teacher's aids, nurse's aids, factory workers, cashiers, fast-food workers, waitresses, and the like.[35]

Aside from our informal interactions, we sat down with each mother for at least two in-depth conversations that we taped and transcribed. These focused exchanges typically lasted two to three hours and usually took place in the mother's own home, often around the kitchen table. When we could, we drove mothers to work or accompanied them on errands. Sometimes we were lucky enough to be invited to family gatherings such as birthday parties, christenings, sixth-grade graduation celebrations, and even a wedding or two.

Our goal was to give poor single mothers the opportunity to address the questions so many affluent Americans ask about them: namely, why they so seldom marry, and why they have children when they have to struggle so hard to support them. In the course of our conversations, we learned something of their life histories, including how they met their children's fathers, what happened in the relationship as they moved

dian price of a home in the neighborhood was about $5,000.[2] After we settle around the table in her newly remodeled kitchen, Antonia tells us she is the youngest of three children from her mother's first marriage and the black sheep of her Catholic family. Antonia's older brother and sister both graduated from high school and have stable jobs, one in the military and one at a mortgage company. Her sister also has a child, but she is married to the father. Antonia describes her sister as her "very best role model."

Unlike her siblings, Antonia became a parent very young—at fourteen—and left high school at fifteen. She's been unemployed and on welfare ever since, except for a brief stint behind the counter at McDonald's. Yet Antonia sees herself as bright and ambitious and believes she will go somewhere. She is sorry she didn't graduate from high school with her peers and "march down that aisle, have all those memories." She also regrets that the pregnancy prompted Emilio, whom she describes as very smart, to drop out just one month shy of graduation so that he could work full time and support his new family.

Antonia met Emilio when she was eleven and he was sixteen, about to enter his sophomore year at Edison High. "I always liked him," Antonia recalls. "I thought he was handsome. But he never paid no mind to me because I was young." She soon found out that his aunt, whom he often visited, lived next door to her own family, so Antonia spent much of the summer between the sixth and seventh grade camped out on her front stoop hoping to capture his attention. "I always told [his aunt], 'Tell him to just stop by to say hi. I'm not gonna bite him.'"

Two summers after she developed her crush, Emilio "walked by, he stopped, and we started talking ever since." In Philadelphia's poorest neighborhoods, "talking" is a handy euphemism for anything from casual flirting to sex. Antonia's problems at home and the frequent angry confrontations with her mother, whom she describes as verbally abusive, took her relationship with Emilio to the next level with breathtaking swiftness. When Antonia's mother evicted her at age fourteen, Emilio convinced *his* mother to let Antonia live with them. Soon after moving in, Antonia started "feeling kind of sick and hungry." Since they were not using any form of birth control, she immediately thought she knew the cause. "I said, 'Oh my God, I think I'm pregnant.'" After a positive home pregnancy test, Antonia and an older cousin did what many other low-income young women in her position do: they quickly made a furtive trip to Planned Parenthood to confirm the results. When the test "came out positive," Antonia was "happy, but then again I was scared because I was only—what?—fourteen years old."

Despite their youth, Antonia insists she and Emilio had already planned to have children before she got pregnant, but had agreed to wait a year or two so both could get further in school. In the half-year before the child was conceived, Antonia says she and Emilio spent hours imagining, "If in the future we have kids . . . I wonder who he'll look like. Yeah that'll be great . . . " Yet neither anticipated that the first pregnancy would occur less than six months into their relationship. The pair nonetheless dealt with the situation in what they deemed the only responsible way: "I didn't think I was gonna have a child at [such] an early age, but I faced it. We faced reality, and we moved on." Emilio faced it by looking for an apartment where they could set up housekeeping on their own. Shortly thereafter, he dropped out of school and began working two jobs to finance the move—a weekend job at Checkers, a local fast-food joint, and a weekday job as a mechanic in his uncle's garage.

- - - -

Pregnant by fourteen, a high school dropout at fifteen, and already a mother performing all the tasks of a wife—just when other girls her age are merely hoping to get a learner's permit to drive a car—Antonia is no neighborhood success story. But in poor neighborhoods like West Kensington, where Antonia has lived all her life, the haphazard way she and Emilio embarked upon family life is hardly unusual. Across the city of Philadelphia, more than six out of ten births are now outside of marriage, many to couples whose circumstances are no better than Antonia and Emilio's. And though Antonia may have been younger than most single mothers when she had her first child, nearly half of all first nonmarital births are to teens.[3]

What forces compel childbearing among the poor at a time in the life course when most of their affluent peers probably worry about whom to invite to the prom? To answer this question, we share parts of the hundreds of in-depth conversations held on front stoops and in the kitchens of these bleak urban neighborhoods. The stories of those we spoke with offer an intimate look into the private moments of courtship, as well as the drama of how relationships unfold during the often tumultuous experience of pregnancy and childbirth. Women's voices tell the stories; the perspectives of the men who father their children are not heard.[4] But as you will see, these women have their own theories of why the men in their lives behave as they do.

"I WANNA HAVE A BABY BY YOU."

Like Antonia Rodriguez, young women who come of age in poor communities like West Kensington usually meet the men who father their children in their neighborhoods: on their front stoops, at the corner store, in their school hallways, or through mutual friends.[5] Yet once a young pair begins casually flirting, or "kicking it," the relationship often moves at lightning speed along the trajectory that culminates in the delivery of a shared child. Kimberly, a twenty-seven-year-old Puerto Rican mother of two children, ages six and three, provides an excellent example: "There's this bridge in Puerto Rico that he took me to [on our first date]. That's where he asked me to be his girlfriend. That's where we had our first kiss. . . . It was really nice. I got pregnant *quick* though. We started [dating] April 1, and by May I was pregnant."

Romance and dreams of shared children seem almost inevitably to go together for Madeline, an eighteen-year-old Puerto Rican mother of a four-month-old, who casually explains, "In the beginning, when you first like a guy a lot, oh, you wanna have his baby."[6] And young women are not the only dreamers. Lisa, white and thirty-two, now a mother of two teenagers, recalls that her children's father announced his desire to father a child by her almost immediately after they met. "From day one . . . I'd say within a week . . . of being with him, he wanted to have a baby by me. He talked about how pregnant women are beautiful and it'd be beautiful if we had a baby."

To the outside observer, begging one's girlfriend for a baby just days or weeks after initiating a new romance might seem to be little more than a cynical pickup line, and that is certainly how it is sometimes used. But in the social world of young people like Antonia and Emilio, nearly everyone knows that a young man who proclaims his desire to have a baby by a young woman is offering high tribute to her beauty, for this avowal expresses a desire for a child that will have *her* eyes and *her* smile. The statement's significance extends beyond praise for her physical charms, though. A man who says these words with sincerity bestows an even higher form of flattery: she is the kind of woman he is willing to entrust with the upbringing of his progeny, his own flesh and blood. Yet expressing the desire to have a baby together is far from a promise of life-long commitment. What it does reflect is the desire to create some sort of significant, long-lasting bond through a child. Lena, a white mother of a one-year-old, who is only fifteen when we talk with her, says her boyfriend told her he "*wanted* to get me pregnant . . . so that I won't leave him. So that I'll stay with him forever. Then he said [to me], 'When you have kids by somebody, they'll always go back to you.'" And when Lisette, an eighteen-year-old African American mother of two toddlers, discovered she was pregnant, "[The father] said to me, 'You know, I got you pregnant on purpose because I want you *in* my life for the *rest* of my life.'" For Lena and Lisette and the men in their lives, marriage is both fragile and rare, and the bond that shared children create may be the most significant and enduring tie available.

The heady significance of the declaration "I want to have a baby by you" is also fueled by the extraordinarily high social value the poor place on children. For a lack of compelling alternatives, poor youth like Antonia and Emilio often begin to eagerly anticipate children and the social role of parents at a remarkably tender age. While middle-class teens and twenty-somethings anticipate completing college and embarking on careers, their lower-class counterparts can only dream of such glories.[7] Though some do aspire to these goals, the practical steps necessary to reach them are often a mystery. We return to this theme in chapter 6.

African American, sixteen-year-old Brehanna conceived a child when she and her boyfriend Jason were only fourteen. Her sister too had her first child young, and Brehanna says she wants to be just like her. This high school dropout from East Camden, now a telemarketer, tells us that from the early days of their courtship, "We was always going out to the mall and going [window] shopping for [baby things]. We always talked about having a baby. We used to *always* talk about having kids and everything."[8]

Thoughts of children—when to have them, who with, what they'll be like—often preoccupy the hopes and dreams of Brehanna, Jason, and their peers throughout adolescence and into the early adult years. Visions of shared children stand in vivid, living color against a monochromatic backdrop of otherwise dismal prospects. An unabashed confidence that they're up to the job of parenting feeds the focus on children that most poor youth display, and this is at least partly because they've already mastered many of its mechanics. This point was brought home when one of us (Edin) was asked to speak about urban poverty to a group of several dozen Camden middle school youth in a summer employment program. While she talked, her daughter Kaitlin, then three, toddled around in the middle of the room. Suddenly, the child tripped and fell. Almost instantly two-thirds of the youth were on their feet, ready to spring into action on her behalf. While she'd been talking, most of her young audience had been listening with one ear while at the same time closely monitoring the child, and they were doing so out of habit—something she could not imagine herself having done at the same age. Inspired by this insight, she asked, "How many of you help take care of younger siblings or cousins?" Almost all raised their hands. Then she asked, "How many of you know how to change a diaper and make up a bottle?" Again, dozens of hands shot up in the air. "I didn't know how to do either until I was thirty and had a baby!" she admitted to the group.

A childhood embedded in a social network rich with children— younger siblings, cousins, nieces and nephews, and the children of friends—creates the illusion of a near Dr. Spock-like competence in childrearing. Tatiana, a twenty-two-year-old African American mother of two preschoolers and a first grader, brags, "My sister used to make me have my niece all the time. I *really* had experience. . . . I had a *lot* of experience." Sonia, a twenty-three-year-old Puerto Rican with a three-year-old son, says the prospect of becoming a mother at eighteen didn't scare her because, "I was the responsible one. I was *already* a mom. . . . I would cook, clean, do everything else. . . . I've *always* been a mom. That's why it wasn't nothing new to me." Destiny, an eighteen-year-old white mother of two toddlers, explains, "When we were living with my mom, I was taking care of my little sister and my little brother anyway. She was working two jobs, so I was taking care of them mostly. I got patience, a *lot* of patience. It wasn't like I wasn't able to take care of no kids anyway!"

"MY DAUGHTER WAS DEFINITELY PLANNED. I WANTED A KID!"

Children come early to couples in West Kensington and other decaying neighborhoods in Philadelphia's inner core—in fact, most conceive their first child within a year of being together. As talk of shared children is part of the romantic dialogue poor young couples engage in from the earliest days of courtship, this is not surprising. Nonetheless, for these mothers, only one in four children is conceived according to an explicit plan—about one in five for our African American and Puerto Rican mothers, and one in ten for our whites (see appendix A).

Some youth decide to begin trying to get pregnant so they can escape a troubled home life. Roxanne, a white mother of an adult child, a teenager, and a one-year-old, now in her early forties, recalls the first time she and her boyfriend had sex. "We went down to the shore. I remember we had sex eight times in a row without using anything. He agreed [to try and get pregnant, and it worked the first time]. I got pregnant to get out of my house, to get away from my father, to get away from my mother. I couldn't *stand* living there any more." Young women like Roxanne hope that motherhood will somehow free them from the trauma of difficult personal situations, though they're not always sure exactly how the rescue will be accomplished.

But children are no mere escape from strained familial relationships. Young women also hunger for the love and intimacy they can provide. Aliya, a twenty-seven-year-old African American mother, who got pregnant at seventeen with her one child, passionately exclaims, "Some people may say it was for the wrong reasons, but it was like too much around me going on. . . . I guess that was my way out of all these situations. [But] I wanted a child because it was *mine*. It was [for] love." For those like Aliya, pregnancy offers the promise of relational intimacy at a time few other emotional resources are available.

Trust among residents of poor communities is astonishingly low—so low that most mothers we spoke with said they have no close friends, and many even distrust close kin.[9] The social isolation that is the common experience of those who live in poverty is heightened for adolescents, whose relationships with parents are strained by the developmental need to forge an independent identity. The "relational poverty" that ensues can create a compelling desire to give and receive love.[10] Who better to do so with, some figure, than a child they can call their own? Pamela, a white middle-aged mother of seven children, ranging in age from fourteen to twenty-eight, reflects, "I think [I got pregnant] mainly because I wanted to be loved. I went through my childhood without it. Somehow, I knew that . . . I would grow up and have kids, and it was something that was *mine*. Nobody could take it away from me. It was something that would *love* me. I would be able to love it unconditionally. There was no strings attached to it." Pamela concludes, "I just *knew*, growing up, 'Oh, you're gonna have your kids. . . . The kids are still gonna love you. They're *yours*.' "

The desire to conceive can become so compelling that some young couples begin trying as soon as they feel it is minimally feasible to care for a child. Gianni, a seventeen-year-old African American mother of a one-year-old, says, "I was *happy* [when I found out] because I *wanted* a baby. [My baby's father lived with my mom and me] and we had a good relationship. We *both* wanted a baby. Everything was cool, and I could go to school and everything because I had help [from my mom]. It was me *and* him [planning it]. He was eighteen and I was fourteen." Deena, featured in chapter 4, now twenty, a white mother who conceived her child at seventeen in similar circumstances, explains, "I *wanted* to have a baby. It wasn't like because everybody *else* had a baby. I really wanted to have a family. I wanted somebody to take care of. I wanted a baby."

While older and wiser parents and kin may—and do—encourage the young to wait, to "live their lives" first, many young women come to see parenthood as the point at which they can really start living. When Pepper Ann's mother learned she was planning to get pregnant at fifteen, she tried to put an end to her daughter's scheme. Now forty-seven, this African American mother of two grown children and a twelve-year-old remembers vividly how her mother wanted her to get a diploma first and "live her life." "But to me," she explains, "that [baby] *was* life!"

Poor young women decide they're going to try to conceive for other reasons as well. Some want to express gratitude to a boyfriend who has shown them kindness. Others want to seal a new and hopeful romance. Some feel obligated because their boyfriends have other children they're barred from seeing because they've lost touch, the children have moved away, or the children's mother refuses them contact. A few use pregnancy to steal a man from another woman or to trap a man they're losing. The desire to bear children early—to "get it out of the way" before beginning a career—also compels some to make pregnancy plans. While most poor young girls don't plan to become mothers at fourteen, they almost all agree that no reasonable woman would postpone childbearing into her thirties. Tatiana, introduced earlier, exclaims, "We definitely was like, 'I'm ready. You ready?' We went for it. It happened. I didn't want to have one at *thirty!* I wanted to get it out of the *way!*" And once the first child is born, many have another child or two quite quickly to get the early childhood years "over with," for there is nearly universal agreement that all children ought to have a sibling or two to play with.

But attempts to get pregnant aren't always motivated by the mother's desire. Listen to the stories of four young mothers with newborns. Celeste, a white twenty-one-year-old, says she and her boyfriend James, who fences stolen goods for a living, had been together for just three months when she conceived. "He just kept saying, 'I wanna have a *baby*, I wanna have a *baby*,' just out of the blue. I kept saying, 'Not yet, not yet.' And it wound up happening." Alexis, also white, conceived her child at sixteen with her boyfriend, age thirty-three. She relates, "He wanted to, but I told him I wasn't ready. So it was like he got his way." Champagne, an African American mother, says, "He was sixteen when I first met him. I had to be about eleven, twelve—something like that. He said that he wanted kids, and I said I wasn't ready for no kids. I wasn't even having *sex!* He waited for about two years until I got old enough to do what [he] wanted to do, but I still wasn't ready for kids. . . . He just had to wait. When I turned fifteen, we [conceived] the baby . . . but it wasn't something that I wanted to do [that soon]." And fifteen-year-old Zeyora, a white mother, recalls asking her boyfriend Tom, age nineteen, "'What do you want for your birthday?' And he was like, 'For you to be pregnant.'"

From the young woman's point of view, any boyfriend who begs for a baby ought to be man enough to promise support too. An exasperated Cherry, an African American who is sixteen and just about to give birth to her first child, says her boyfriend Joe didn't initially seem to realize that being ready to have a baby means being ready to support it as well. "[Joe wanted to be a father. When I asked him why], he said 'I [am just] *ready* to have a *baby*.' He sees everybody with their baby and he's thinking he's the right age and stuff [even though he] still wasn't out of school. . . . I was like, 'Well, I'm too young. . . . ' He said, 'I'm ready to . . . start a family.' . . . He's like, 'I wanted a baby by you.' I'm still saying that's not a good enough *reason*. But then he [finally] clears it up and says that he's ready to support us."

Eighteen-year-old Lisette, introduced earlier, also worried about the ability of her boyfriend Shawn, age seventeen, to support a family, but was eventually worn down by his insistent pleas for a child. She explains, "That's all he kept talking about is having a baby. . . . I actually [got pregnant, even though I was only in ninth grade,] on *purpose* . . . because *he* wanted a *baby* so bad." Seventeen-year-old Natasha, an African American mother of a one-year-old child whose boyfriend Martin was still a junior in high school when he got her pregnant, had also tried and failed to negotiate for more time. "He was like, 'Oh, well, I want you to have my baby.' I'm like, 'Well,' you know, 'its okay for you to want me to have your baby but we can't have no baby right now because we both in school and we gotta graduate and we gotta do this and that.' He was like, 'All right,' you know, 'We gonna be together for *that* long anyway, so we can wait.'" In the end, however, she gave in to her boyfriend's demands. "That was May," she remembers. "By August I'm pregnant."

"IN A WAY I DID, IN A WAY I DIDN'T."

Though pregnancy by design is by no means rare, in neighborhoods like West Kensington it is more the exception than the rule.[11] Nevertheless, most conceptions are hardly pure accidents. Typically, young women describe their pregnancies as "not exactly planned" yet "not exactly avoided" either—as only a few were using any form of contraception at all when their "unplanned" child was conceived.[12] Nearly half (47 percent) of the mothers characterized their most recent birth as neither planned nor unplanned but somewhere in between (see appendix A). The whites were the most likely to characterize their births in this way (56 percent) and Puerto Ricans the least likely (34 percent), with African Americans falling in between (46 percent). Most of the rest—roughly four in ten—described the birth as "accidental," and Puerto Ricans were especially likely to do so. When probed, however, roughly half of the women with accidental pregnancies said they were not doing anything to prevent a pregnancy at the time. Yet most knew full well the facts of life and realized that unprotected sex would almost inevitably lead to conception.[13] So why do nothing to avoid pregnancy?[14]

One reasonable guess is a lack of access to contraception. But Planned Parenthood, area hospitals, and Philadelphia's network of free clinics all offer family planning services, and these institutions are so well known in these neighborhoods that few have to look in the phone book to find the address. Furthermore, most say they used birth control—usually the pill, a condom, or both—at the beginning of the relationship with the baby's father.[15] But once there is an understanding that they've become an exclusive pair, he often abandons condoms because continued use would signal a lack of fidelity and trust.[16] And the same young woman who initially took a birth control pill each day, wore the patch each week, or visited the clinic for the "depo" (Depo-Provera) shot every three months suddenly decides that these practices are not worth the trouble.[17]

Sometimes women stop using birth control even when they are not sure a relationship has really reached "the next level." They complain that the pill, patch, or shot makes them sick, lose their hair, or feel depressed or irritable, and they have not yet found a more palatable method. Still others simply say they tired of the required routine. Lori, a thirty-one-year-old Puerto Rican mother of a two preschoolers, remembers, "Their father used condoms. That was our way of birth control. And he did that for a whole year, so he was tired [of using them]. He was like 'Come on, the baby's already a year! Let's try without. I'm *tired* of using these things! You probably won't even come out pregnant that fast.' So as soon as we tried without, I came out pregnant like *that!* Really quick." Abby, a white twenty-five-year-old with a three-year-old daughter, tells us she "didn't plan on . . . getting pregnant," but then admits, "Well, [I] more or less did. I just stopped taking my birth control pills, [thinking] 'If I get pregnant, I get pregnant.' I got pregnant." Irene, an African American mother in her early forties, with five children ranging in age from thirteen to twenty-five, didn't plan for any of her pregnancies in advance, but admits that her lackadaisical use of the pill practically guaranteed her five "accidents." She shrugs, smiling, and says, "You forget to take one pill and then you miss three. . . . Hey, next thing you know, you are having another one!"

One way or another, most of these women drifted into the Russian roulette of unprotected sex. The lack of a clear plan does not mean there is no desire to get pregnant, yet those who admit—even to themselves—that they're trying to have a baby invite public contempt and self-reproach, for they know that the choice to bear children while young and unmarried is, in many ways, absurd. At the same time, though, they wonder if their circumstances will ever be "right." The potent mix of social shame, self-doubt, and compelling desire leads to accidents *waiting* to happen.

Some, like Abby, begin to take chances on purpose and leave the outcome to fate. But others are so deeply engaged in a high-risk lifestyle that they simply aren't thinking about where their actions might lead. Depression and despondency spawned by difficult life situations sometimes stop them from caring whether they become pregnant or not. Monica, a twenty-nine-year-old white mother of two, ages five and nine, explains, "It wasn't like I cared if I did or didn't. It wasn't like a matter of, 'Oh my God, if I get pregnant, I'm *dead*.' It was just—if I did, I did."

Twenty-one-year-old Sam, a white mother of a four-year-old son, was living with her drug-addicted father and had just seen her best friend murdered in a drug-related incident when she became pregnant. Both she and her boyfriend were also using drugs at the time. On top of that, the Kensington neighborhood she lived in had become so crime-ridden that most owners of the row homes there had switched from aluminum to plastic screen doors so that drug addicts wouldn't steal the metal and sell it for scrap. She says that with all the "negativity" pressing in upon her, neither she *nor* her partner cared whether they got pregnant. "I think he just didn't *care* if I got pregnant or not. I was pretty much [thinking] the same thing. . . . If I was pregnant, I *wanted* to be pregnant, but if I wasn't it didn't *matter*. It's like I wasn't *planning* to have a kid [but] I wasn't doing nothing to *stop* it from happening neither. I was *ready* if I wound up getting pregnant."

Conception without planning is most common among the young, yet even the very young—like Antonia Rodriguez—usually say they got pregnant only a year or two before they'd hoped. Sherry, a Puerto Rican mother who is twenty-four and has three children under the age of six, says her first baby—conceived at sixteen—came only about a year too soon. "As soon as I found out [about the pregnancy] I got happy, because I wanted a kid. . . . I was trying to get pregnant, but not so *fast* as I did. I at least wanted [to wait] a year. We talked about it, and he was willing. We both agreed with [the idea of having] a kid." Tasheika, a twenty-year-old African American mother of a kindergartener and two younger children, has a similar story. "I was fourteen. I wanted to get pregnant because his father treated me right. . . . And I was like, 'Well, *he* want a baby, *I* want a baby—we're gonna have a baby!' He was planned. . . . Well, we planned it, but he didn't *come* when we planned, [he came a little sooner]."

The vigilance and care that most birth control methods require are hard to maintain when women like Tasheika see so few costs to having a baby. These young women often reject the idea that children—or at least the first child—will damage their future prospects much. Most believe that becoming a mother only gets in the way if a girl lets it. Nikki, an eighteen-year-old African American mother who gave birth just weeks after graduating from high school, explains, "I was supposed to go to college, but [having a baby] don't mean you don't want go to *college*. You can *do* this! Some girls just get lazy and their potential will get real low, or whatever. That's why most of them, they just stay home and don't do nothing." Ebony, an eighteen-year-old African American mother, conceived her first child in her freshman year of college. She defends her choice to bring the pregnancy to term by telling us, "I *wanted* it. I wanted to keep it. I felt as though I was out of school—out of high school—and I thought I could manage. I had started having sex when I moved in with [the baby's father, but we didn't use protection]. He was saying, 'You can have a baby and still go to school.' I thought, 'Okay, I'm gonna have my baby. . . . I'm still gonna be able to go to college. . . . It's gonna be fine.'"

At first it is puzzling how any young woman could maintain this belief while living in a neighborhood that seems to offer nothing but evidence to the contrary. But our mothers have a different point of view. While they often struggle to name one happily married couple, they can easily rattle off the names of dozens of women who, in their view, are "good" single mothers. And many of these local heroes have, in their view, succeeded against great odds. So though their neighborhoods and schools offer plenty of examples of young mothers who had to leave school and face extraordinarily hard times, they still provide an ample supply of counterexamples—young unmarried women who have succeeded in doing well by their children, ensuring that they're clean, clothed, housed, fed, and loved. Armed with these role models, they insist that it doesn't take a college education, a good job, a big house, matching furniture—or a marriage license—to be a good mother.

Thus, most are ambivalent about—though not opposed to—the idea of having a child when the conception occurs. When we ask Violet, a white sixteen-year-old mother of a five-month-old, if she'd planned to get pregnant, she answers, "No, not really. In a way I did, in a way I didn't. I was confused. I *wanted* to be a mom and I did *not* want to be. It was back and forth. I don't know, I just wanted a baby, I guess." Seventeen-year-old Aleena, a white mother of a two-year-old boy, tells us, "As I got older, like around fourteen, [I went on the pill] so I couldn't get pregnant, [but] I was confused. I wanted to have a baby, but just not at that time, you know. [But] I always loved kids. . . . I would [go through a time where I would] try [to get pregnant]. But then . . . I would figure, 'Well, how am I gonna *raise* this baby?' . . . I didn't know whether this week I wanted to try or next week I didn't. [But] I was always thinking about it. Always."

Once a young pair has been together for a while and feels the relationship has advanced to the next level of commitment, the conception of a child often seems like the natural next step. Even if children seem to just "happen," most believe they were meant to be. Jasmine, a Puerto

Rican mother of two adult children and a four-year-old she conceived in her mid-thirties, tells us, "I never used anything [when] I got pregnant. *God* is in control. And [my kids] was *meant* to *be*. . . . I feel like, if it happens, it happens." Forty-three-year-old Susan, a Puerto Rican mother of one adult child and a preschooler, says her most recent pregnancy was "a surprise" too. Yet, she counters, "It wasn't like I could just *plan* things. Things happen, and so you just go ahead. Some things happen you just can't plan!"

As a new romance deepens, young women who are "not exactly planning" to have children may nonetheless begin to look for signs of their partner's willingness to "do the right thing" if they were to "wind up pregnant." A boyfriend's mere willingness to engage in unprotected sex is sometimes the only green light a young woman requires, though her judgment is sometimes in error. Marilyn, a twenty-four-year-old white mother of a preschooler and a kindergartner she is raising alone, made this mistake. Just before they conceived, he'd proposed marriage. She told him, "'Yeah, sure, but let's wait and see. I want a diamond ring, and let's get a house.' He worked on [that] part and I just got pregnant. I was [*open* to getting pregnant]. I figured, '*This* is the man I'm going to *marry!*' We were having sex for a long time, sometimes protected, sometimes [not]. I *trusted* him. I figured, 'He's not *stupid*. . . . When we're having unprotected sex he must *know* that something can happen!'"

"IF I DIDN'T WANT TO GET PREGNANT, I SHOULD HAVE DONE SOMETHING TO PREVENT IT."

Even though most pregnancies are not planned, happiness is the mother's typical response to the news that she's conceived, at least once she recovers from the initial shock. Madeline, a Puerto Rican eighteen-year-old with a four-month-old whose father deserted her and the child, told us, "To be honest, I was happy [when I found out]. Like at first, I was scared, I was all scared, I cried at the same time, but I was crying *happy* tears *too*. All I could think of was that I'm too young to have a baby, I didn't finish *school!* But then I thought, 'I got the father with me, [it will be okay].'" Lenise, a thirty-six-year-old African American mother of two, ages eleven and seventeen, says her second pregnancy "wasn't planned, but I was just *too* happy. I was happy *every day*. I didn't know I could *be* so happy!"

Children, whether planned or not, are nearly always viewed as a gift, not a liability—a source of both joy and fulfillment whenever they happen upon the scene. They bring a new sense of hope and a chance to start fresh. Thus, most women want the baby very much once the pregnancy occurs.[18] This is partially a reflection of neighborhood norms about how a young woman ought to respond to a pregnancy, as the few mothers who admit a less favorable reaction often express shame about it. While everyone knows that accidents happen—and these youth say that not everything, especially children, can or should be planned—the way in which a young woman reacts in the face of a pregnancy is viewed as a mark of her worth as a person. And as motherhood is the most important social role she believes she will play, a failure to respond positively to the challenge is a blot on her sense of self. Rasheeda, a nineteen-year-old African American mother of a one-year-old, tells us that when she learned she'd conceived a child unintentionally, and in the midst of very difficult personal circumstances, "I was happy. I'm *proud* of that." But Denise, an eighteen-year-old white mother of two-year-old twins, guiltily admits, "I felt bad about myself in a way because, like, I didn't really want them. I was like doing so good in school and [I felt] I [had to] throw everything away."

When the pregnancy is confirmed, most take a fatalistic view that it is meant to be, just as Antonia Rodriguez did. They also believe that it is unjust to penalize an unborn child for its parents' poor planning, so they nearly always conclude that the "responsible" reaction is to "deal with it" and have the baby rather than seek an abortion.[19] Michelle, a thirty-one-year-old African American mother of three, a seven-year-old and four-year-old twins, tells us, "I don't believe in having abortions. . . . If I didn't want it to happen, I would have *protected* myself better. It's here. I have to deal with it. So that's what I did, I dealt with it. Because if I didn't want to get pregnant, then I should have done something to prevent it." Brenda, a twenty-six-year-old white mother of a seven-year-old, has just learned she is pregnant again by Derrick, the same man who fathered her first child. She demonstrates what she feels is her high moral standard by telling him, "We're gonna get through this and do it the right way because I'm against abortion." Amber, a twenty-three-year-old white mother of a four-year-old and a newborn, was abandoned by her boyfriend after she found she was pregnant with her second child. She too, however, believes she has made the self-sacrificial choice to "struggle" rather than go through with an abortion or "give the child away." "Four months into the relationship I wound up pregnant. I was like, 'Oh no, I don't believe in abortion.' I was talking about giving the baby away, but I couldn't do it. I couldn't do it. I was like, 'I'll struggle, I don't care, I'll do it by *myself*.'"

As sociologist Kristin Luker shows, many middle-class women view abortion as a personal choice arising from a woman's right to control her body and her life. Yet most mothers who live in the Philadelphia area's bleak core typically share a radically different view. Though most concede there are circumstances desperate enough to warrant an abortion, most still view the termination of a pregnancy as a tragedy—perhaps unavoidable but still deeply regrettable. Virtually no woman we spoke with believed it was acceptable to have an abortion merely to advance an educational trajectory. Something else, they say, must be present to warrant that decision—the desertion of the child's father, an utter lack of support from the young woman's own mother, rape or incest, an uncontrollable drug or alcohol addiction, homelessness, or impossible financial straits.

The irony here is that a substantial number of the mothers we spoke to willingly admit that they themselves have had abortions in the past—about a quarter of the total. In absolute terms, the poor have more abortions than the middle class, but that is because they also have more pregnancies. Affluent youth are far more likely to terminate any given pregnancy than those raised in poor, minority, or single-parent households. Even among the most disadvantaged, it is those youth who are performing poorly in school who are least likely to respond to a pregnancy by seeking an abortion. The class contrast is even starker when we look at only those with "unplanned" births. Affluent teens faced with an unplanned pregnancy choose abortion about two-thirds of the time, while their poor counterparts do so only about half of the time.[20] Still, a large number of youth from poor backgrounds do have abortions.

The lack of correspondence between belief and behavior presumably arises because poor youth raised in impoverished contexts are simply quite likely to find themselves in desperate straits. Most believe that abortion is "the easy way out." To them, "doing the right thing" or "taking care of your responsibilities" means bringing the pregnancy to term. And adoption is, to almost all, simply out of the question—it is generally viewed as "giving away" your own "flesh and blood."

In choosing to bring a pregnancy to term, a young woman can capitalize on an important and rare opportunity to demonstrate her capabilities to her kin and community. Her willingness and ability to react to an unplanned pregnancy by rising to the challenge of the most serious and consequential of all adult roles is clear evidence that she is no longer a "trifling" teenager. Nikki, introduced earlier, graduated from high school just weeks before the birth of her child. She says that anyone who is mature enough to "handle stuff" ought to be able to handle a child. "[The doctor] threw all these papers in my face real quick. [She was] like, 'You have two options: you can terminate the pregnancy, or you can keep the baby.' So I looked at her and I was like, 'I'm keeping it.' Even though I didn't *plan* for it or whatever, I can *handle* stuff. . . . Just by the way I am, I can *handle* stuff."

Twenty-eight-year-old Allison, a white, recovering drug addict with a nine-month-old child, explains that though her pregnancy wasn't exactly planned she could find no reason *not* to take the pregnancy to term. "I'd say my first thought was to take the *easy* way out, and then, once I had thought it, I realized that was [not] what I wanted. The way I kept looking at it was that if I do this now and I never have a chance to be a mom again, I would never be able to live with myself, because I'd always wanted to have children. . . . Like I'm twenty-eight, I have a good job where I could support her, and I felt like . . . there was really no good excuse *not* to have her."

Brehanna, the sixteen-year-old African American mother of a child she conceived when she was fourteen, explains, "I had stopped taking birth control. . . . I didn't really care [whether I got pregnant or not]. . . . [But when I found out,] the first thing I thought about was school. [Then] I was like, 'Oh my God, what am I gonna . . . tell my *friends?* Oh my God, what are people going *think?*' Then it hit me that it shouldn't matter what [other people] thought because it was *me*, *I* was pregnant. . . . It was *my* problem, *I* had to deal with it, and it shouldn't have been anybody else's business. . . . Even though it was a mistake, I didn't want to take it out on the baby and be like, 'Oh, I'm gonna get an *abortion*, he's a *mistake*.' That's just not *me*, you know, that's just not the way I go about things."[21]

"TO ME, THIS BABY *WAS* MY LIFE."

Romance these days leads quite rapidly to sex among poor and middle-class teenagers alike.[22] But for a disadvantaged woman, a sexual relationship often leads to conception, and the fact of the pregnancy defines the arc of her young adulthood. Unlike their wealthier sisters, who have the chance to go to college and embark on careers—attractive possibilities that provide strong motivation to put off having children—poor young women grab eagerly at the surest source of accomplishment within their reach: becoming a mother.

Poor kids dream of future glory just like their well-heeled peers in the suburbs. But while the offspring of the middle class envision the professional kudos and chic lifestyles that await them, the dreams poor men and women share with each other often center on children. The men seem at least as eager to dream as the women. Yet this does not mean that the pregnancies that so often follow result from clear planning. Few say their children are the result of *either* an overt plan *or* a contraceptive failure. Rather, the large majority are *neither* fully planned *nor* actively avoided. Most often, the young women are well versed in the use of birth control prior to conception. In fact, many practiced contraception in the early days of their relationships with their children's fathers. However, when the relationship moves to a higher level of trust and commitment, they typically abandon these practices or begin to engage in them inconsistently.

Whether the pregnancy is planned, accidental, or somewhere in between, most are eager to have the child once the conception occurs. This is because they value children so highly, anticipate them so eagerly, and believe so strongly they can do a good job of mothering even when young and in difficult circumstances. A poor girl who gets pregnant just a year or so sooner than planned reacts far differently than a middle-class girl who gets pregnant a decade or two before she'd intended to. Most of those who grow up in the urban slums of metropolitan Philadelphia also believe strongly that those not actively avoiding pregnancy by using birth control have no business "getting rid of" an unwanted child or "giving it away" after birth. Even mothers who conceive despite careful contraception do not often escape moral condemnation for having abortions or putting their children up for adoption, as they ought to have known where sex can lead.

While abortion is sometimes accepted as necessary—when a young woman's situation is deemed truly desperate—most do not view their own circumstances as dire enough to qualify. Mothers who choose abortion when they have the means to avoid it are viewed as immature at best and immoral at worst, unable or unwilling to face up to the consequences of their own actions. But beyond the confines of this moral landscape is the fundamental fact that, for these disadvantaged youth, a pregnancy offers young women who say their lives are "going nowhere fast" a chance to grasp at a better future. Choosing to end a pregnancy is thus like abandoning hope. Whereas outsiders generally view childbearing in such circumstances as irresponsible and self-destructive, within the social milieu of these down-and-out neighborhoods the norms work in reverse, and the choice to have a child despite the obstacles that lie ahead is a compelling demonstration of a young women's maturity and high moral stature. Pregnancy offers her a unique chance to demonstrate these virtues to her family and friends and the community at large.

Middle-class beliefs about the right way to start a family are conditioned by a social context that provides huge economic rewards for those who are willing to wait to have children until a decade or more after attaining sexual maturity. For a white college-bound adolescent raised on Philadelphia's affluent Main Line, each year of postponed childbearing will likely lead to higher lifetime earnings. In fact, if she can hold out until her mid-thirties, she'll likely earn twice as much as if she'd had a child right out of college.[23] Just imagine how her economic prospects would plummet if she brought a pregnancy to term at fifteen! From this privileged vantage point, a disadvantaged young woman's willingness to bear a child well before she is of legal age is beyond comprehension.

Even in the most impoverished of communities, most youth understand that bearing children while young, poor, and unmarried is not the ideal way of doing things. Yet they also recognize that, given their already limited economic prospects, they have little to lose if they fail to time their births as precisely as the middle class does. And though most single mothers readily acknowledge that having a child before establishing a stable two-parent household or landing a well-paid job may not be the best way of doing things, their sense of when the right time might be often seems quite vague. In the meantime, they typically perceive little disadvantage to bearing a child while unmarried or still in their teens or early twenties. Thus, in the heat of romance and sex, many simply fail to take the steps that could prevent them from becoming pregnant

The young people who live in these neighborhoods—whether they play by society's rules or not—share the same dismal prospects for lifetime earnings.[24] So, for Antonia Rodriguez and Emilio and others like them, having a child while still in their teens is hardly the end of the world. Granted, Antonia didn't get to graduate from high school—to "march down that aisle, have all those memories"—but she plans to go back for her GED soon. And Emilio needs no high school diploma for his job as a mechanic in his uncle's auto repair shop, nor does he need one to achieve his dream of owning and operating his own garage.

Of course, children aren't free—Emilio had to take on two jobs to pay for a place for his young family to live, and buying diapers, formula, clothing, and the other things the baby needs takes a large share of the couple's meager resources. But Antonia and Emilio have few regrets. They planned on having children in a "year or two" anyway. Like their neighborhood peers, each firmly believes that life without children is meaningless and concludes that it really doesn't matter all that much whether they accrue these costs early on or later in the life course.

The centrality of children in this lower-class worldview of what is important and meaningful in life stands in striking contrast to their low priority in the view of more affluent teens and twenty-something youth, who may want children at some point in the future, but only after educational, career, and other life goals have been achieved. Putting motherhood first makes sense in a social context where the achievements that middle-class youth see as their birthright are little more than pipe dreams: Children offer a tangible source of meaning, while other avenues for gaining social esteem and personal satisfaction appear vague and tenuous.

TWO

"WHEN I GOT PREGNANT . . ."

MAHKIYA AND MIKE

Mahkiya Washington, age twenty, her boyfriend Mike, and their seventeen-month-old daughter Ebony live with her sister in an apartment across the street from her mother's house. Though their building is not perfectly maintained—the door buzzers don't work, the screen door is broken and boarded over, and the apartment's drop ceiling is missing tiles in several places—it's clean. This young African American couple's North Philadelphia neighborhood, Strawberry Mansion, was once an opulent streetcar suburb on the leafy outskirts of the city. But that was a more than a century ago. Now the neighborhood is one of the city's poorest, and its only claim to fame is that John Coltrane's boyhood home sits on its western boundary. On Mahkiya's block, however, the unkempt physical environment masks a web of close social relationships: nearly all of the other residents here are members of Mahkiya's extensive kin network, and most, like Mahkiya, have lived in the neighborhood all their lives.

Mahkiya is the third of five children born to stable, married, working-class parents. Her father died when she was ten, and her mother supported the children through her work as a community organizer and the Social Security Survivors Insurance benefits the family received as a result of her father's death. Mahkiya and Mike were high school sweet-hearts and graduated together from Strawberry Mansion High School near the top of their class. During high school, Mahkiya says, her relationship with Mike was idyllic. "We went out, no arguments; wonderful, beautiful . . . it was no problems." After graduation, Mike enrolled in a college located in a small central Pennsylvania town. He could only stomach the "country living" for a few months, though, and decided to take a year off to work. Mahkiya enrolled in a historically black college an hour southwest of the city, majoring in accounting.

When Mahkiya was nineteen and living in the freshman dorm, the couple began to occasionally have sex without a condom during weekends back home. Mike expressed concern that these "slip-ups" might result in a pregnancy that would derail their college plans. Mahkiya told Mike not to worry, assuring him she'd seek an abortion if she got pregnant. But the positive result on her home pregnancy test near the middle of the school year created a crisis in her relationship with Mike. Almost immediately, she says, she felt a strong desire to bear the child. Her grandmother fed this desire, warning her granddaughter that she might "never have another [chance to] have a baby, so you enjoy this."

Whereas Antonia Rodriguez's boyfriend Emilio greeted the news of her pregnancy with a kind of stoic acceptance followed by joy and anticipation, Mike campaigned hard to avoid fatherhood. "He called me on the phone at school to say, 'Get an abortion. . . . If you don't get an abortion, we aren't going to be together.' Then he would just call up and say I was cheating on him, it wasn't his baby. . . . If I wasn't in my room, he'd say, 'You must have been with somebody else.' And I was like, 'I don't need this. I am trying to stay in school and still manage to be pregnant.' It just stressed me out."

But the news of the pregnancy soon reached Mike's mother, who initiated a campaign of her own to convince Mike it was immoral to "force someone to get rid of their baby." This tactic apparently worked. "So then he calls me back in the middle of the night, 'Mahkiya, I think we should keep the baby.'" Even after Mike's capitulation, though, "It was like he hated me for [being pregnant]. I still cared for him and loved him, but every day . . . he'd [call] and say, 'It ain't my child. Don't put my name on the birth certificate.'"

Mike's occasional bouts of "wild" behavior, which became more frequent during the pregnancy, also caused tensions in his relationship with Mahkiya. Prior to pregnancy, she says she might have joined Mike in some of the fun. But the practical realities of pregnancy meant that her behaviors were suddenly constrained in a way that Mike's were not. Like so many others, Mahkiya spent the last trimester of her pregnancy on the couch at home, bored and lonely, while Mike was out partying, clubbing, and "ripping and running the streets."

Mahkiya's relationship with Mike was also strained by dramatic changes in the expectations she placed on him once pregnant. Mike financed his romance with Mahkiya with a weeknight shift at McDonald's. Even this minimum-wage job provided ample money to purchase the right props for the romantic partner role. But when she got pregnant, this expectant young mother quickly did the mental math and realized Mike's meager earnings didn't add up to what it would take to buy the crib, the stroller, the diapers, clothing, and other things the baby was going to need. Worse still, the couple was nowhere close to having enough money to set up the independent household she believed a new family should have. Thus, though Mahkiya deemed Mike a "perfect" boyfriend prior to pregnancy, he became "nothing" when the pregnancy failed to prompt him to respond the way Emilio had—to "get off his butt" and land a "real job."

Mike and Mahkiya were one of the few couples we met who had been on their way to what might have been a bright economic future. Their local high school produced more dropouts than graduates, and despite the appallingly low test scores of its students, this young pair's high grades were sufficient to earn them admission to college. Though both wanted children together eventually, they had agreed that the first year of college was not the time to start. Mahkiya's strong desire to bring the pregnancy to term, in spite of the clear costs to her relationship with

Mike and her educational career, surprised even her. But the most surprising part of the story Mahkiya tells is how the news so profoundly transformed Mike's behavior. She cannot fathom why the boyfriend who adored her could begin to treat her with such contempt.

"I'M PREGNANT."

The story of courtship and conception told in chapter 1 is only the first act of a dramatic tale ending in childbirth. For poor youth like Antonia Rodriguez, Emilio, Mahkiya, and Mike, the news of a pregnancy can dramatically transform the relational dynamic. Two young people who have only been "kicking it" for a short period of time—often less than a year—suddenly realize they've ignited a time bomb. Most young women respond as Mahkiya and Antonia did—they attempt to get serious about life for the sake of the baby. Some of the young men do likewise, though few can manage to launch a business and purchase a home in such short order as Emilio did. Many young men, however, react on some level as Mike does, attempting to deny the new reality.

Once the dream of shared children becomes real, young couples moving at lightning speed along the relational trajectory leading to parenthood quickly learn that the imagined child is very different from a rapidly developing fetus. An expectant mother's experience of pregnancy almost always radically changes her sense of herself—she is transformed in her own eyes from an irresponsible youth to the solemn custodian of the priceless next generation. Overnight, her behavior must alter dramatically "for the sake of the baby." Even if she does not have the internal drive to make this transformation, the physical evidence her own body provides soon activates a powerful set of social expectations. Suddenly, the penalty for indulging in a drink at the neighborhood bar or a night spent hanging out on the corner with friends is steep, for she must endure the piercing social censure contained in the disapproving glances and contemptuous whispers of acquaintances and strangers alike. For these neighbors and friends, any expectant mother with a shred of decency ought to be home taking care of herself, not "ripping and running the streets."

Young men are not subject to the physical changes that announce to the world they're about to become fathers. Strangers do not look askance at them if they continue to party or hang with the boys on the corner. They get no special attention because of their "condition," nor are they the guests of honor at the baby shower. Only their girlfriends and some-times their kin chide them to grow up, get serious, and begin taking care of their responsibilities. Their male peers, on the other hand, may well be encouraging them to celebrate their freedom while they can.[1]

Pregnancy and birth test the mettle of the soon-to-be mother and fa-ther. Some rise to the occasion; others do not. The advent of pregnancy quickly divides the committed from the fickle, but over the course of nine months, even men who show initial devotion may falter.[2] Thus, few cou-ples emerge from this turbulent period unscathed. Yet the magic moment of childbirth often has at least momentary power to heal these fractured relationships. Optimism and hope may return, and couples may again make promises to one another that they fervently hope they can keep.

"WELL, I GUESS IT'S THE POPE'S, RIGHT?"

Despite the dreams of shared children that young couples so often in-dulge in before conception, men are as likely to respond with shock and trepidation—or even outrage and denial—as with pleasure. Like Mahkiya's boyfriend Mike, some immediately attempt to deny the child is theirs and accuse their mystified girlfriends of being "cheaters" or "whores." Others try to force the expectant mother to have an abortion, threatening to break up with her and have nothing to do with the child unless she complies. Still others simply abandon their pregnant girl-friends when they hear the news.

These responses provoke both heartbreak and anger, and even some-times a lust for revenge in the would-be mother. A twenty-seven-year-old Puerto Rican mother of three named Millie, whose story continues in chapter 6, tells how she got retribution when her boyfriend tried to force her to get an abortion the third time they conceived, though its sweetness was short-lived. "He was harassing me from the moment he found out that I was pregnant. . . . 'Take it out, take it out, take it out.' I was like, 'All right, you give me the money and I'll do it.' So he got me the $600 and I [was so angry I] went on a shopping spree! So he flipped! And right there, he went to my house and actually beat me up that day." At the time this mother of a ten- , eight- , and seven-year-old had already lived with her boyfriend for nearly a decade in a stable, marriage-like relationship. She concludes her story in this way, "He wanted me to get an abortion, [and said he would leave if I didn't]. And I felt as though, 'It's there, I don't believe in abortion.' So I was like, 'If you wanna leave me, go right ahead. . . . I'm not gonna kill something that's mine.'"

The nineteen-year-old boyfriend of Aleena, a white seventeen-year-old mother of a toddler, heard rumors from friends that she'd been seen with another man right around the time their child was conceived, providing an easy excuse for him to deny paternity. "He went home and told his mom and dad that I cheated on him and that he knew it wasn't his child . . . and ever since then, you know, they always denied the baby. Then . . . they wanted to take me for the DNA test. . . . He's the only guy I've been with in the last three years! I never cheated on him. I never even hugged another guy when I was dating him. . . . [They] believed all his friends over me." Though young women usually claim their boyfriends' accusations are completely groundless, youth in these neighborhoods do move quickly from one relationship to another, and the rapid onset of sex means that there is sometimes legitimate reason for doubt. Brielle, a thirty-two-year-old African American mother of four children under the age of eleven, tells us, "Now my first pregnancy, I was shocked. . . . We only went together like six months, and I had . . . broken up with him [because I had] met somebody else. . . . I was wondering why my period didn't come on. [So] two months later I had to make this phone call, 'Guess what? I'm pregnant.' So of course I knew there was going to be doubts about whether it was his."

Abandonment is perhaps the most painful response to the news of a pregnancy from the mother's point of view. Madeline, an eighteen-year-old Puerto Rican mother of a four-month-old, told us, "He said he wanted the baby from me, but I guess that was just words to get me to bed. Because that's one thing I was really afraid of—getting pregnant at a young age. And he told me, 'If anything happens, don't worry.' That's why I was confused when he said he didn't want to have nothing to do with me. Because he talked about it. . . . We didn't actually plan . . . like, 'Oh, it's time to have a baby,' but we talked about what would happen if I would be pregnant. He was like, 'If you were ever to get pregnant, don't worry because I will be there for you. You won't [have to take care of it] by yourself. I will be there anytime you need anything.' After I found out how he felt [about the baby], I felt like killing myself."

Denial, threats, and abandonment sometimes even occur when the pregnancy is not accidental but planned. Denise, a white eighteen-year-old mother of two-year-old twins, told us that although she and her boyfriend "decided together" to have a child, he nevertheless "totally denied [my twins]. The first words that . . . came out of his mouth when I told him I was pregnant [were] 'It's not mine.' So I said, 'All right. Well, I guess it's the pope's, right?'" Denials and threats are sometimes backed with physical violence. In the most extreme cases, the violence seems to be aimed at the fetus itself. Twenty-seven-year-old Millie, the Puerto Rican mother of three we introduced above, says her children's father "hit me all over . . . hit me in the belly" when she refused his demands for an abortion after their third child was conceived. "He was like 'You don't wanna take it out, I'll take it out through your mouth.'"

Even when a young man does not immediately deny the child is his or demand that his girlfriend have an abortion, pregnancy often puts the romantic relationship into overdrive. The woman hopes the pregnancy will spur her boyfriend to become a responsible adult. She wants him to get serious about employment, stop hanging around his friends, and share in the pregnancy by attending doctor's visits. She also wants him to lavish a particular type of attention on her, helping to relieve her physical discomforts and cravings by rubbing her ankles or running to the 7-Eleven or the Wawa (a local convenience store) at midnight to buy the proverbial pickles and ice cream.

Most men just don't seem to understand these desires or are not prepared to fulfill their girlfriends' growing expectations.[3] Joanne, a sixteen-year-old Puerto Rican mother of a nine-month-old, said of the fifteen-year-old father of her child, "Before I was pregnant, when we first went out . . . everybody's all lovey-dovey and everything. [Then] I got pregnant. That was the most miserable part of my life. You would think that . . . your boyfriend . . . would baby you and everything." Eighteen-year-old Elaine, an African American mother of an eight-month-old, says, "[Our relationship] changed when I was pregnant. . . . I went through a lot of mood swings and stuff, and he wasn't there. He was *there* but he didn't support me, you know, comfort me and stuff. He just like, 'We having a baby,' and that is it. And I was like, 'Well, we got planning do to.' He ain't wanna sit down and talk and stuff."[4]

In response to the new pressures she begins to place on him and the growing disappointment she begins to express, he may become resentful. For the soon-to-be father, spending time with the soon-to-be mother can mean little more than constantly having to face his failures. This was certainly the case with Mahkiya's boyfriend Mike who, despite his achievements in high school, was a college dropout without a full-time job when the child was born. Men who once fantasized about having a baby with their admiring girlfriends sometimes aren't so sure they want to face the months and years ahead with the demanding woman who is about to become their baby's mother.[5] For their part, women believe that the response to a pregnancy is the measure of a man, and hope the crisis will force their partners to move toward maturity.

Many men do not cope with the stress of a pregnancy well. After he learns that his girlfriend has conceived, some level of regret and doubt often creep in. What seemed like an enchanting possibility in private moments of courtship can become a terrifying responsibility in the harsh light of day. Even fathers-to-be who initially greet the news eagerly may

With the flight of jobs and stable, working-class homeowners, abandoned buildings have afflicted our eight neighborhoods. In the past few years, city officials have begun an aggressive campaign against blight. The strategy focuses on securing such buildings to prevent them from being used for illicit purposes such as drug use or prostitution. The neighbors have transformed this house into a makeshift basketball court for neighborhood kids.

A boy stands in front of his family's nail salon along Kensington Avenue. The commercial arteries of Kensington and Allegheny Avenues, known around Kensington as simply "K and A," sit underneath the elevated train tracks. The business district is the kind one expects to see in a depressed inner-city neighborhood. The only mainstream businesses are the fast-food chains; the rest of the strip is a mix of enterprises that reflect the neighborhood's problems and limited opportunities: bars, strip clubs, auto dealerships, thrift stores, storefront churches, check-cashing businesses, liquor stores, and local nonprofits.

Walking home in Kensington means making your way past drug dealers and corner boys, who often use the front stoops of abandoned buildings for their activities.

This young mother with a college degree and a good job and her bright, cheerful daughter offer a striking contrast to the troubled block behind her in Strawberry Mansion, where her grandmother lives and where she is raising her own family.

Walking home from school.

One of the many drug outreach programs operated out of a storefront in Kensington.

To remember those who have lost their lives to the violence of the streets, friends and family commission local graffiti artists to create murals like this one, in the section of West Kensington known as "the Badlands."

An abandoned storefront in Kensington, near Kensington and Allegheny Avenues.

This recreation center, just beyond Kensington's borders in the neighborhood called Fishtown, is a popular hangout for kids from the neighborhood. The mural in the background honors a local white youth named Freddy Adams who was beaten to death on the playground in 1989.

A young mother poses with her three children in the rowhouse she shares with her fiancé and three other members of the extended family. Using her childhood bedroom as their bedroom, the mother, her fiancé, and the older children sleep on couches, while the baby sleeps in a portable crib. Living arrangements where several generations of a family inhabit a two- or three-bedroom house are quite typical.

This mother, shown with her oldest son, shares this subsidized apartment with her fiancé and two children. She is now five months pregnant with her third child. To get the housing voucher that allowed her to move out of an apartment with lead paint, this mother spent time in a homeless shelter to prove her "need" to housing officials.

Other men may react in the opposite way and try to exercise an almost maniacal control over their baby's mother. As we show in chapters 3 and 4, the sexual mistrust that is so palpable in the relationships of many poor couples fuels both women's suspicions and men's possessiveness. For example, Dominique, featured in chapter 5, a thirty-four-year-old African American mother of three school-aged children, tells us, "When I [got] pregnant with my oldest daughter . . . that's when, all of a sudden, [he started to become abusive]. He was always really jealous and possessive. . . . One day we were coming from the supermarket, and he [thought I'd been looking at other men, so he] just started hitting me."

Pregnancy can sometimes bring a couple closer together, though, which is how most mothers believe things are supposed to work. This was true for Antonia and Emilio, and it has worked out that way for Kimberly, a twenty-seven-year-old Puerto Rican mother of two, ages six and three. Her relationship with her boyfriend was rocky from the start, as he was repeatedly jailed for petty crimes and parole violations; however, each pregnancy has solidified the relationship and has helped keep him out of further trouble. She tells us, "If anything, [my getting pregnant] made us get closer. With his first daughter, he calmed down a lot. We got closer. The second kid united us more." Deborah, an African American mother of two, ages eight and twelve, who is now twenty-six, says, "[Our relationship] became stronger because [of the pregnancy]. He cared more because he had to protect me and my baby. That is the way he felt. He was worried about us . . . that was his every thought."

Sarah Lee, a twenty-two-year-old African American mother of a seven-year-old and an infant, also claimed that pregnancy drew her boyfriend and her closer. "During the pregnancy we was just going out to the comedy shows, eating, and always being together. Sometimes I may get cranky in my moods and don't want to be bothered, but other than that we have a nice time together. I say he is a real sweet man." These happy outcomes are not uncommon, though many of these relationships still falter after childbirth. We'll pick up on the stories of couples in these more stable unions in chapter 4.

"ALL OF A SUDDEN, HE WANTS HIS NAME ON THE BIRTH CERTIFICATE!"

Though pregnancy brings the presence of the child closer to reality, nothing is more real than the birth itself. And though many fathers respond with denial and threats when dreams of shared children translate into an actual pregnancy, the advent of a child is a compelling reality that few can respond to with indifference. Young women often believe men's claims that they value children and desperately want to be part of their lives. Once a man knows he can no longer do anything to prevent the birth, the child becomes something of great potential value for him, for in these communities, young men's lives are at least as aimless and relationally impoverished as those of young women. A child is one of the few things a young man can say he has created and one of the few ways he can make an early mark on the world. And men believe a child's love is easier to win and hold than its mother's.[6] While mothers say they find it hard to deny their connection to a man they've had a child by, fathers believe it is even more difficult for children to deny the bond with the man who gave them life. But the rewards of having a child come with risks as well. Unmarried fathers who "step off" of their responsibility to their children—as they often do—are still the subject of contempt in these communities.[7]

For these reasons, despite the heartbreaking behavior that some men subject their baby's mothers to during pregnancy, many reluctant fathers seek and find redemption in the magic moment of childbirth. Listen to how Millie describes her relationship with her child's father during her most recent pregnancy: "He left me [when I wouldn't have the abortion he wanted]. He said he fell out of love. He couldn't deal with it, and he left. And he was with a couple of girls out there. After the whole pregnancy by myself, he came back after the baby was born. He wanted to be with me again."

Aleena, whose boyfriend denied responsibility for the pregnancy, tells how he changed his attitude when the child was born. "All of a sudden, he believes that my son is his. My son looks just like his father, the olive skin, and everything, the dark eyes, all of it, same birthmark and everything. There is no way he can deny that baby." Children, once born, can exert a strong pull on a father's emotions. Yet not all attempt to reconnect with the mother at the magic moment of the birth. A man who fails to show up at the hospital to witness the birth or at least visit the child in the maternity ward shows that he is unwilling to accept responsibility. Of her oldest two children's fathers, Irene, a forty-four-year-old African American mother of five (three adults and two teens), tells us derisively, "They didn't even came to the hospital, let alone try to hang in there, try to buy Pampers."

Surveys show that in seven of ten cases unmarried fathers do come to the hospital and may even be there for the delivery itself.[8] Often the euphoria of the birth temporarily calms the tumultuousness of the previous nine months. Lee, a white twenty-four-year-old mother of four (all under the age of five), said she had trouble with her children's father before their first child was born. Things got even worse after she conceived again, just months later. Yet here is her description of his emotional reaction to the birth of their second daughter and her twin, a son: "He was there. He watched everything. It was funny. When [my daughter] first came out—you know how their head is—he was really upset, I mean ready to cry. 'My baby's a cone head!' He was really upset. He didn't know [it was normal]. I really knew then that he really cared about this baby. I knew he loved her. He was just really excited [the twins] were there."

Men are typically delighted by a new baby and often vow to mend their ways. Because new mothers almost universally believe that a child is better off with both a mother and a father, they often desperately want to believe this promise to change. Shawndel, a twenty-five-year-old African American mother of two, ages five and three, explains her decision to reunite with an abusive boyfriend after the birth: "I want my kids to have a father even if he ain't a good father. . . . I don't want them to grow up without a dad like I did." Forty-year-old Carol, a white mother with three children, ages twenty-one, nineteen, and seven, also reunited with her youngest child's father for a time, though during pregnancy he denied paternity and then deserted her. He "showed up the day I came home from the hospital. I have no idea [how he found out she'd been born.] He was just there. He always showed up at the most important moment. . . . He wanted to hold her. He seen how she looked [like him], and his eyes just started beaming. Oh, you could tell by looking at him [he knew] whose baby she was!"

Some women, though, greet these hospital-bed conversions with skepticism. Twenty-five-year-old Cheyenne, a white mother of two school-aged children, says she was too jaded by the time her first child was born to be much impressed by the father's visit. "I wasn't together with him for the pregnancy at all. The pregnancy was by myself. . . . After she was born . . . he came up to the hospital, brought a big teddy bear or whatever. . . . [He told me,] 'I love you. She's so beautiful. Yadda, yadda, yadda.' You know, bullshit, bullshit, bullshit, lies, lies, lies."

Kensington resident Denise says her boyfriend cheated on her during pregnancy, gave her gonorrhea, then denied paternity and kicked her out of their apartment—all within the first two months of the pregnancy. She was forced to move in with her aunt and her three children, in a tiny row home that was also housing a cousin and two other friends. After the birth, he wanted to reunite, but she refused. "He called me after I had the babies, and it really blew me [away] because I hadn't heard from him in like seven months. And then he was like, 'Congratulations!' and, 'I want to come see them.' And I was like, 'No. What do you want to do with them after you denied them? You said they're not yours and you just kicked me to the curb.' That's the last time . . . I heard from him."

"WHY SHOULD I GIVE HIM THAT TITLE?"

One of the most reliable barometers of the state of the couple's relationship just after a child's birth is how the mother decides to name the baby. Lola, a twenty-four-year-old Puerto Rican mother of a two-year-old daughter, tells us, "I know one of my friends decided not to give the father's name to the child . . . because he said, 'It's not my baby.' But in the hospital, during labor, he showed up, and then she gave her his last name. At one point, I wanted to take Alice's [last] name off because I figured I'm the one—I supported her for a year before he decided to help me. I was like, 'If I'm the one supporting her, if I'm the one playing the role of the parents, then she should have my name. . . . Why have a name [of a father] that's not there for her?' At the time, I wasn't getting no child support, no visits for her. I was like . . . 'Why should I give [him] that title?'"

Danielle, a white mother in her mid-twenties with two children (ages five and nine), also punished her second baby's father, who had deserted her during the pregnancy, by denying him the privilege of giving the baby his last name. "After I had her, I called his work . . . to let him know that he had a baby girl. So early Monday morning my phone rang, and it was him. He was like, 'Can I come and see her? What is her name?' He wanted to know why I didn't give her his last name, and I said, 'Well, you wasn't around. You're lucky you are on the birth certificate!'"

Men clearly read the failure of the mother to give the child their name as a signal that they have failed her during pregnancy. Sometimes, however, the meaning goes deeper. One nineteen-year-old African American mother named Tyhera, with a three-year-old daughter, tells of her boyfriend's heartbreak and shame when his first baby's mother gave the child her own last name, thus signaling that she would give him no role in the child's life. "The first one, he didn't even get a chance to take care of her. The girl had another boyfriend, so the boyfriend took on that responsibility for the child. The little girl has the mom's last name. . . . She didn't even name her after the real father. She didn't give her his last name."

Mahkiya Washington refused to give Ebony Mike's last name because he denied the child was his throughout much of the pregnancy. After she was born, Mike's rejections turned to enthusiasm. "He was happy, and it was [his] child then, and he said, 'Put my name on the birth certificate!'"

But his new attitude was too little, too late. "I was like 'No, her last name is mine's!'" Mahkiya knows full well that her refusal to give her child Mike's last name is a public slap in the face.

This isn't to say that fathers can't sometimes still redeem themselves. Mahkiya and Mike broke up during the pregnancy but reunited a year after Ebony was born, when he finally landed a full-time job. "In the end, it turned out real good because he got a job, and I got a job, and we [got back together and] manage to take care of [our daughter] very well." This couple is not thinking of marriage yet, but they share an apartment with her sister while saving for the security deposit that would allow them to live on their own.[9]

Other mothers also tell of boyfriends who "came around," at least temporarily, after their child's birth. Chanel, a white thirty-three-year-old mother of three, ages fifteen, nine, and three, has recently gotten back together with her youngest child's father after a pregnancy marred by severe violence. When her daughter turned seven months old, "He started changing . . . he started coming around. Now you can't take them two apart. Her dad's her favorite." She has forgiven her child's father, who no longer beats her. Of the beating during her pregnancy she now says, "It's a man thing. They're scared [of the responsibility]."

"THEY WERE DISAPPOINTED, BUT EXCITED TOO."

When young women learn they are pregnant for the first time, they are typically terrified of their own parents' response. Many fear that their own mother or father will throw them out of the house or try to force them to abort the child, and this does occasionally happen. Most of these parents have campaigned hard for years to get their children to stay in school and avoid early pregnancy, and some are enraged when their children ignore these dictates. Parents who have been down that road themselves are often desperate to keep their children from doing the same. We deal with this theme among our own mothers in chapter 5.

Victoria, a white sixteen-year-old mother of a one-year-old child whose own mother had her while still in her teens, said her first thought when she found out she was pregnant was "my mom—how my mom was gonna react. That's the only thing that went through my head. . . . She said if I ever got pregnant she would make me get an abortion. Before I told her, I called hot lines and stuff to see if she could make me have an abortion. They told me that she could not because I had to sign the paper myself. [Finally,] my [older] sister . . . told [my mother that] if she makes me have an abortion, she's gonna take me and she's gonna leave, and she's never gonna talk to her again." Elaine told us, "When I first found out I was pregnant . . . I was scared to tell my mom. . . . I thought she was gonna put me out. . . . I wasn't afraid of having a baby, I was just afraid of her."

Everyone, including the poor, acknowledges that having children while young and not yet finished with schooling is not the best way to do things. This is why the kin of these poor youth usually react to the news with disappointment or, more rarely, anger.[10] Even in poor communities where nonmarital childbearing is the statistical norm, most still view early pregnancy as something of a tragedy, and girls in this situation may face censure from teachers, preachers, neighbors, and kin. But a pregnancy also often galvanizes those same adults to help and support her—if not for her sake, then for the unborn child's.

It is not the news of the pregnancy itself that provokes the greatest regret, but the realization that one's child will not be the rare exception to the neighborhood rule—the one who avoids early pregnancy, finishes high school, completes college, gets married, moves to the suburbs, and has children—in that order. Virtually every prospective grandmother would like to be the mother of that neighborhood superstar, and a pregnancy that comes first, rather than last, on that list ends the dream. But a pregnancy that occurs "out of order" offers another, alternative route to respectability—albeit a slightly tarnished one. For if the prospective mother can somehow manage to "struggle and strive," she may still achieve some of these goals. And the harder the struggle, the higher the social reward the community bestows.

While mothers' own mothers may mourn what might have been, they know the odds that their child would jump the class divide were never good, baby or no baby. Thus, the sense of loss an early pregnancy brings is, in many cases, purely hypothetical. Mahkiya's story offers a powerful example of these tensions in a would-be grandmother or great-grandmother's response. Her kin may have hoped the young honor student from Strawberry Mansion High would succeed in her bid for a middle-class life, and they do mourn the loss of this dream. Yet they recover rapidly from their disappointment. When Mahkiya finds herself pregnant, they staunchly support her decision to have the baby. In fact, her grandmother advises her not to end the pregnancy, cautioning that Mahkiya—at eighteen years of age—may never have another chance.

Denise recounts a similar story. Unlike Mahkiya, she chose to end her first pregnancy, conceived at the age of fifteen, in the wake of a boyfriend's desertion. She tells us her kin are still scandalized by that decision. When, at sixteen, Denise informs her mother, aunt, and grandmother that she is pregnant once again, they successfully pressure her to "go through with it." Denise then investigates another way out of her situation—adoption—but they firmly reject this option as well, characterizing it as "giving the baby away" and assuring her that they, her family, will help get her through this.

The African American grandmother has always played a powerful social and symbolic role in the lives of her grandchildren. But in the impoverished white and Latino neighborhoods we studied, where help from a child's own father is often in short supply, the mother's own mother is often an integral part of the parenting team as well. Poor single mothers across the racial and ethnic spectrum rely on their own mothers and grandmothers for much more than free babysitting or child-rearing advice. Mothers' own mothers will sometimes put up the money for the crib and the stroller, especially when a child's father cannot or will not offer support. But a mother's parental or grandparental home also serves as a haven when relationships go bad, a job is lost, and the rent cannot be paid. Mahkiya moved back to her grandmother's home when she finally evicted

Mike from her life. Jen, the pregnant, seventeen-year-old white mother of a toddler (profiled in chapter 3), moves back in with her stepmother when the bottom falls out of her relationship with her baby's father. And after Deena's relationship with her first child's father goes sour, this pregnant, white, twenty-one-year-old mother of a two-year-old (featured in chapter 4) finds herself back on her grandmother's living-room couch with her baby and new boyfriend in tow.

Thus, the tiny row homes of these crowded urban neighborhoods often house a revolving cast of characters that spans three, sometimes four, generations. In fact, nearly half of our mothers live in such households (see appendix A). Naturally, relations between the generations are not free of conflict. Many mothers complain about the grandmotherly tendency to meddle, the disagreements over childrearing strategies, and the sharp words over the men they choose to include in their lives. Thus, mothers tend to see their own mothers' homes as a temporary refuge, a chance to regroup while they figure out a way to reestablish their own independent households.

A grandmother's show of support should not be interpreted as a desire for her daughter to be pregnant. But just because her daughter's life is not A-plus perfect doesn't mean that she still cannot achieve a solid B-plus in life by coping successfully with the challenges life has laid at her feet. And given the tragedies that befall other neighborhood youth, how bad is a B-plus anyway? The pragmatic assessment of the probable losses and gains seeps into the accounts of the young, who so often insist that the pregnancy turned around their lives. Yet the persistent belief in the American dream and the sequence of steps "everyone knows" to follow in order to get there is reflected in a young mother's hopes for her own offspring. This is why young mothers also insist that they are going to teach their children to follow a different path. Starting a family young may have saved her own life, but no mother wants her daughter to end up with so little to lose that motherhood becomes her salvation too.

A young man's parents may react in much the same way as the young woman's do, though for them there is less of an immediate impact. And overall, the promise of practical support is far less sure. The mother of Antonia Rodriguez's boyfriend Emilio offered a great deal of assistance, harboring her son and his baby's mother until the couple could afford the row home they now occupy. Mike's mother lent Mahkiya support by convincing her son it was "immoral" to force Mahkiya into an abortion she didn't want.

But other would-be "mothers-in-law" join their son's campaign to pressure the young woman to have an abortion, or wholeheartedly back their son's efforts to deny paternity, sometimes even planting the initial doubt of her fidelity in his mind. Sons and their mothers are very much afraid of becoming saddled with the responsibility of children who are not their biological offspring. Some are constantly on guard for "trifling" girls who might take advantage of their sons in this way, despite the fact that many of them presumably faced similar doubts when they were younger.[11] And while sometimes a young man's kin may take responsibility for supporting the girl he has impregnated even when the boy does not, this is the exception rather than the rule.

"TAKING CARE OF HIS RESPONSIBILITIES"

The reactions of women and men to the reality of pregnancy often stand in startling contrast to one another. Young women often admit to being overwhelmed by the responsibilities that lie ahead. Yet they express willingness, and even eagerness, to embrace the new challenges. Though some, like Antonia and Mahkiya, may regret that the timing or the circumstances are not ideal, most seem hopeful and even confident that mothering is something they can do and do well. Many of these young women believe that children, not jobs or relationships with men, are their life's work, and they face pregnancy with the strong determination to "do the right thing"—to have the child and embrace the role of mother—even if it means giving up other opportunities.

The responses of young men run the gamut from Emilio's eager acceptance of the father role to Mike's denials and his campaign to get the young mother to end the pregnancy against her will.[12] Other men take the news well initially but later behave in destructive ways, cheating on or beating their pregnant girlfriends, or partying all night with friends. Some men manage to behave well throughout the pregnancy but fall apart as soon as the child appears. Zeyora, a white fifteen-year-old mother of a six-month-old, remembers that her nineteen-year-old boyfriend "was happy [about having the baby], buying baby things all the time when he had money. He wanted a boy. He was in the delivery room with me. [But] that's when things started changing. . . . I think it's because of the baby, that he's not ready to be a father."

The pregnancy test, the ultrasound pictures, the swelling belly—all indications of the tsunami wave of changes ahead—cause a lot of anxiety and fear in prospective fathers who are often at first eager for the experience. Even in poor communities, expectant fathers are still supposed to provide, to "straighten up," and to deepen their commitment to the mother, even though they are not legally bound to her. Pregnancy forces these young men to confront their limited ability, and sometimes their lack of willingness, to pay the full price of parenthood.[13] Emilio was both able and willing to do so, while Mike was neither, at least at first.

This is not simply because the young men in these communities are chronically irresponsible, though some of them certainly seem to be. Failure to take paternal responsibility has real consequences for these unmarried men, for if a father does not meet the mother's standards, the state steps in. The specter of child support is very real among young men in Philadelphia and Camden: Pennsylvania and New Jersey have two of the toughest child-support enforcement systems in the nation. Lola, a twenty-four-year-old Puerto Rican mother of a two-year-old daughter, whose child's father was twenty-three and stably employed at a legitimate job when she conceived, tells us, "First he thought it wasn't his. [Then] he was like, 'Now you are going to put me in child support, aren't you?' I was like, 'Well, we are not back together . . . of course I'm going to put you on child support!' He was furious. . . . [Then] he didn't wanna give the baby his last name. . . . I later got the truth out of him. I said, 'You're not really concerned about whose child this is. . . . It's about [the] $90 or $40 [a week you'll have to pay]!' They turn really rebellious, they really do. They feel they don't have a life as long as they are supporting [the children]."

Couples who remain together usually manage to avoid child support, unless she claims welfare and is thus forced to participate so the state can reimburse itself for her benefits.[14] But if the couple breaks up, the child-support system will appropriate a considerable portion of the father's income. If he doesn't pay, the police will visit him on his job and harass him in full view of his employer and coworkers. Then his driver's and other professional licenses can be revoked, and he may be imprisoned for the debt on a contempt of court charge or fined. And if he flees across the state line to avoid paying support, he can be jailed on a felony charge. More important, the mother will retain almost complete control over the child, regardless of whether he pays child support or not. Meanwhile, she can, on a whim, block his access to his child. Even worse, from his point of view, she can introduce another man into the child's life, one who may take the father's place.[15]

Young men are aware that once they are out of the mother's life, they may find themselves out of their children's lives as well, even though they might be required to bear the burden of an eighteen-year financial commitment. Though we did not interview fathers for this study, this scenario surely runs through a young man's head when he learns of the pregnancy. Ironically then, while pregnancy may ignite his fear that fatherhood means the end of his life as he has known it, his girlfriend sees it as the point at which her life has just begun.

THREE

HOW DOES THE DREAM DIE?

JEN AND RICK

When we first interview Jen Burke, this white seventeen-year-old and her year-and-a-half-old son are living with her stepmother and ten-year-old sister in a rowhouse just inside of Port Richmond—which Jen considers a big step up from the nearby Kensington neighborhood where she grew up. She waits for us outside a social service agency where she attends an alternative high school program for teen mothers. Jen is of average height and weight and has regular facial features. On this brisk fall day she has pulled her ash-blond hair into a ponytail and wears a kelly green sweatshirt announcing her Irish ethnicity in bold white lettering. Jen leads us down the agency's main corridor to a vacant classroom, a setting that affords more privacy than does her stepmother's small home. Though she is soft-spoken, her emotions are close to the surface as she begins to tell her story.

Rick, the father of Jen's son Colin, was a friend of a friend who first showed an interest in her when she turned fourteen. Jen was flattered by the attentions of twenty-one-year-old Rick but was "scared to go out with him at first because he was just one of those people who would just *be* with girls, then he *wouldn't* be with them anymore." Jen "got with" Rick in January, about six months after they'd first met. She thought Rick would be different with her than he had with past girlfriends because, "He said he wanted to have a baby by me. He didn't want to have a baby by any of them others." By April Jen was pregnant, a situation she blames on Rick's insistence that they try to conceive right away and his refusal to wear condoms. Rick was elated by the news of their pregnancy, though he was nervous about her parents' reaction and feared they might have him arrested for statutory rape.

Yet only two months after Jen's pregnancy was confirmed, her worst fears about Rick were proven true as well. She heard from friends that Rick was cheating on her with a girl named Nancy, who was now pregnant too. Although Jen says she chose to believe Rick's easy lie that Nancy's child was not his (a paternity test has since shown otherwise), Rick had begun to spend more time with "that wild crowd of his" and less with her. Seven months into Jen's pregnancy, he was picked up on a carjacking charge. Fortunately for Rick, the police never recovered the car, and he was released from jail just days before she gave birth to their son.

From the beginning, Rick was a bad bet for a lifetime partnership. He had been in and out of juvenile detention centers since he was eight years old, sold drugs, drank excessively, and "did coke and all that stuff." Jen was furious that he continued to do "the stupid things with his friends" that had so often gotten him in trouble after he found out that she was carrying his child. Still, upon his release from jail, Jen let him move in to her stepmother's house. But it was soon clear to her that "nothing had changed at all." In fact, "It just got worse. He cheated on me again when he got out. He drank again when he got out. He always wanted to be with his friends." As a result, Jen kicked him out just three months after the baby was born.

It wasn't until their son was over a year old that Rick finally began to "stop all of that" and settle down. He moved back in with her and her stepmother, and three months later, when their child was fifteen months old, a home pregnancy test confirmed that she was expecting again. She had not wanted a second child so soon and had been taking birth control pills, but when she told Rick the news, he set out to convince her to carry the pregnancy to term. "When he found out I was pregnant [again], he was telling his [family], 'It's time for me to get married. It's time for me to straighten up. . . . This is the one I wanna be with. I had a baby with her. I'm gonna have another baby with her.' Before I even got pregnant [again], we used to joke about [how he was going to straighten up when I got pregnant with the second one]."

We met Jen just as she and Rick had told their families about their second pregnancy. Though the situation prompted Rick to talk seriously about marriage, she expressed considerable doubt because of his wild past and chronic infidelity. "He wants me to marry him. I'm not really sure. . . . If I can't trust him, I can't marry him." When we caught up with Jen again several weeks later, she claimed she had broken up with Rick for good. Once again, he had taken up with his friends and resumed the heavy drinking, drug use, and petty crime. But the last straw was her discovery that he was having yet another affair. Now, completely fed up with Rick's behavior and convinced that he would never change, Jen broke things off once again. Soon afterward we heard that Jen had lost the baby. Discouraged and depressed, she would later describe this period as the worst time in her life.

- - - -

Mahkiya Washington's story (told in the preceding chapter) demonstrates the potency of the "magic moment" of a child's birth—the defining event for men and women making the transition from merely being "together" to becoming a family. A baby is the living, undeniable proof of a couple's bond, and its arrival is a powerful reason for staying together that is more tangible than a fleeting crush or even a rapidly swelling belly. Because of this, it can turn around a damaged or broken relationship like Jen and Rick's.

Young fathers like Rick who misbehave during the pregnancy—and even during the first months after the birth—often come around and beg for a second chance, promising to change. An angry and wounded young mother may forgive, as Jen did Rick, and may cautiously allow her expectations of his behavior and commitment to rise again, especially if she sees that he is growing attached to the child. Even couples who found it nearly impossible to stay together during the pregnancy will often, in the aftermath of the birth, try to mend their relationship for the good of the baby.

But despite their best intentions, few of these fragile relationships survive for long. A large national survey shows that when poor unmarried women give birth, eight out of ten are still romantically involved with their child's father, and four in ten are even living together, either with his or her kin or out on their own. Thus, women labeled "single mothers" in government statistics are rarely truly so at the moment of birth. When asked about their long-term prospects, almost all of *both the mothers and the fathers* predict that they will stay together and eventually marry. However, in the weeks and months after the mother leaves the maternity ward, these bright outlooks quickly become clouded, and surveys show that few of these couples stay together long enough to watch their children enter preschool. Twelve months after the birth, half will have split, and by the time the child turns three, fully two-thirds will have done so.[1]

How does the dream die so quickly? How does a young couple's optimism that they will be the ones to beat the odds turn into the bitter realization that they will not? As we will show, these mothers haven't given up on the dream of a loving life partnership; even in these communities, where lasting relationships are rare, young women still hope that the fathers of their children will mature into men who will be there over the long haul. The "one man for life" ideal may no longer be the statistical norm in America, yet young, disadvantaged women, whose prospects for lifetime partnership are far dimmer than most, still cling to the hope that it can be achieved. Denise, a white eighteen-year-old mother of two-year-old twins, feels a sense of accomplishment because she's only had children by one man. "I'm glad I only have *one* father of my sons. . . . My aunt . . . *her* three kids are by *different* guys." Angela, an African American twenty-two-year-old with a two-year-old son, has just broken up with her son's father because he's had a child with another woman. Her main regret is that now she faces the prospect of having to complete her family with another partner. "It was hard to deal with breaking up with him, because I only wanted to deal with one person," she says. "He was my first, and I just wanted to stick with one man."

Most social scientists who study poor families assume financial troubles are the cause of these breakups.[2] After all, these young people grow up in a context of extreme disadvantage, at least by American standards, and they come of age with little education, few skills, and not many future prospects. Lack of money is certainly a contributing cause, as we will see, but rarely the only factor. It is usually the young father's criminal behavior, the spells of incarceration that so often follow, a pattern of intimate violence, his chronic infidelity, and an inability to leave drugs and alcohol alone that cause relationships to falter and die.

"HE WANTS TO LIVE HIS LIFE OF LUXURY."

Job insecurity is endemic among workers in the eight neighborhoods we studied, even when the rest of the country may be enjoying an economic boom.[3] Many women tell stories of male partners who lost a succession of jobs and had trouble finding others as yet another manufacturing concern moved south or overseas, or another large city hospital closed its doors. Perhaps because job loss and unemployment are so common, most mothers are usually sympathetic to boyfriends who can't find work or can't work full time because they are still in school. Tasha is a nineteen-year-old African American with a three-year-old son who lives rent-free with her mother and pays her other bills by babysitting full time. We ask her about the baby's father, who is seventeen and still in school. She replies, "He had a job, but it's off and on. He's trying to find a job, [but] I ain't really rushing him to get one though, because *I* make money. I mean, I know [my baby's] dad . . . feel he *wanna* give him something. He gets [the baby] something every month. He buys him sets [of clothes] and stuff. Get him a set [or] a pair of shoes [every month]. That's all I ask for. . . . I don't ask a lot from him, because I know people don't got a lot. But he takes care of him. He'd *better!*"

Over time, however, a chronically unemployed father proves too much for most mothers to bear. Yolanda, a twenty-six-year-old Puerto Rican mother of two children, ages three and four, from East Camden, had been a stay-at-home mother because her children's father had a steady and well-paid factory job. A year ago, however, the plant closed down as the company's operations moved overseas. The economic strain on the family—now forced to rely on the meager $424 in cash and the $284 in food stamps she can glean from welfare—has been tremendous. Though she says she knows that in some sense he is a victim of circumstances, she can't help feeling angry and resentful that this steady breadwinner has turned into nothing more than an economic drain. A few months before we interviewed her, she kicked him out. "He would go all over and telling me he would look but he couldn't find anything," she recalls. "It's like a tug of war [was going on] inside of me. [I was telling myself] 'You gotta make him get a job!' and 'This can't continue!' Then the other side of me was like, 'You gotta have patience. You *know* it's hard out there.'"

Conflicts over money do not usually erupt simply because the man cannot find a job or because he doesn't earn as much as someone with better skills or more education. Money usually becomes an issue because he seems unwilling to keep at a job for any length of time, usually because of issues related to respect. Some of the jobs he can get don't pay enough to give him the self-respect he feels he needs, and others require him to get along with unpleasant customers and coworkers, and to maintain a submissive attitude toward the boss.[4] Thirty-five-year-old Nell, an African American mother of three children aged fifteen, twelve, and two, says her relationship with her younger child's father faltered for this reason. "Whenever he got a little decent job, something negative would happen you know? And next thing I know, he would come home [saying],

'I don't have a job no more' because of something somebody said or something somebody else did."

Other mothers say that their boyfriend's inability to "stay working" can be attributed to sheer laziness. Mariah, an eighteen-year-old Puerto Rican mother of a four-month-old, recalls, "I used to tell him, 'Get a job! Get a job! Get a job!' He always said, 'Oh, *I* don't *work* no *9–5*.'" Twenty-year-old Tasheika, an African American mother of three young children, gripes, "He want[s] to be in the fast life and do things. He don't want to have a steady *job* or nothing. I said to him, 'That's what a family *is*—you have to bring a *paycheck* home!'" Caroline, also a twenty-year-old African American with a four-year-old son, relates, "When [Hassan's father] was here I felt like I was taking care of him *and* Hassan too! After a while I thought I could do better by myself." Chanel, a white thirty-three-year-old with three children, ages fifteen, nine, and three, broke up with her youngest child's father just after we met her for the first time. When we ask about him later, she says dismissively, "He's not around no more. I got rid of him. . . . He was only here to sleep—didn't want to pay no bills, didn't want to do nothing. When he was here all he did was fight and argue and drink. I had to get rid of [him]." But Chanel clearly feels his absence is a loss. "We would have been together this April *eight years*," she says, and expresses shock that he has become as financially reckless as other neighborhood ne'er-do-wells she knows. She purses her lips in disgust as she tells us such men are unworthy of the children they father. "That's the men of the nineties now—they just make their *name* out there and that's *it*, that's *it*. It's all it is—it's only a name they passing around."

Sometimes, though, the issue is how much of a man's income his partner believes he is sharing with the family. Monica, a twenty-nine-year-old white mother of two, ages five and nine, told us, "[My baby's father] was my first [boyfriend]. I was in love [and didn't think about money]. But then, after I had a baby and I had these responsibilities, . . . I started to realize it wasn't enough—it's not *enough* to hand me five dollars once a month. I started to realize *I* was taking care of *him!* I was doing for *both* of them! I was taking care of him, Big Danny, [like] he was a baby—like making sure he had food, making sure he had clothes. I shouldn't have had to do that. He wasn't taking care of me and the baby. He wasn't even taking care of his *own child!*" Lola, the twenty-four-year-old Puerto Rican mother of a two-year-old daughter, tells us how the father's failure to share all of his income led to bitter conflict. "I would get his pay stubs and I was like, 'Where is the rest of this money going?' And he would never have an explanation for me. I was like, 'Hmm.' Something was fishy. I would confront him, and that's when the big fights would come. . . . He . . . was bragging, 'I got all this money,' but he didn't wanna waste it on bills. He didn't wanna waste it on my daughter."

Young mothers regularly rail against young fathers who squander too much of their earnings on alcohol, marijuana, new stereo components, computer accessories, expensive footwear, or new clothing, while the needs of the family are, in their view, not adequately met. Amy, a white thirty-year-old mother of three, ages six, five, and three, had a boyfriend who worked steadily but insisted on spending on selfish pursuits. This is what eventually broke the young couple up. "He wouldn't spend money for the kids' food. I had to send my kids across the street to my *mom's* to feed them and stuff. That's what I got fed up with. I shouldn't have to live like that. . . . I said it's time for *him* to support these kids instead of [me] being on [assistance], and he didn't like it. He wouldn't take care of the kids, and I just said [to myself], 'It's time to get out of here.' He was there for them, and then all of sudden he didn't want to be. He always wanted to go out bowling, playing softball, be at the [Mummers] Club. . . . [He] wouldn't let me get off food stamps because he couldn't be *bothered* [with their needs]."

Lola says that just when she and her baby's father had finally managed to make a down payment on a row home, "He went crazy buying luxury stuff, like clothes and jewelry and all this. I didn't see anything for me or my daughter. [Then] I couldn't even get anything for my daughter because everything [I earned] was going on the bills. [I said,] 'I'm that type that my bills are first and . . . then my daughter and then you.' Then he got jealous. He got jealous of that. He was like, 'You never buy *me* anything, you are buying *her* everything.' I'm like, 'Don't compare yourself to my *daughter!*' It was like all this arguments all at once. I couldn't take it anymore." Lola concludes her story, "Yeah, that was basically our downfall, the money. He would just spend it. I don't know what he spends money on, it's ridiculous. He goes out and he'll just spend $20 in a day, with no problem or nothing and not come home with anything. That was our biggest problem."

Megan is still with her child's father, but complains that he repeatedly charges computer equipment to their credit card even though their budget leaves no room for extras. This twenty-seven-year-old white mother of two, ages four and nine, explains the effect of his spending habits on their precarious economic situation. "I try to get everything together with the financial stuff, and *he* wants to live his life of *luxury!*" Kyra, a seventeen-year-old African American mother of a child nearly two, fought bitterly with her baby's father when he spent $70 on a pair of designer boots for their son when he needed clothes instead. "The last time he bought him something was some boots, which he didn't need. . . . [The baby] could have used some clothes, but *he* wanna spend like seventy dollars on a pair of baby [Timberlands]. . . . I guess he feels as though that was his money, and he do what he want with it. It was stupid because like what he gonna wear the boots with? He ain't got no *clothes* to wear with them. So what is he gonna [do]? Just walk around with a diaper and some new boots on? It just don't make no sense. . . . Plus too, he bought *himself* the *same pair!*"

These disagreements over the father's work effort and spending habits cut right to heart of the couple's relationship because, for the new mother, his behavior with regard to money is an emblem of his dedication to the family. Financial responsibility is often the yardstick by which she measures his love for and commitment to her and the child. For young and impoverished mothers working to establish a stable environment for their children, the making and spending of money is much more than a matter of income and expenses, of budgets and balance sheets: it is a morality play. Few women expect their baby's fathers to be the sole breadwinners, but they believe that good fathers should at least try to stay employed, work at a legitimate trade, and turn over most of their earnings to the family.

Fathers often take a very different view of what mothers should expect from them. If the mothers can be believed, their men often prefer to maintain, at least to some degree, the casual approach to work and the carefree consumption patterns of their bachelor days, believing that not everything has to change with the advent of a child. While she wants to spend the money on a brand-name stroller or a trip to the Sears portrait studio, he thinks he deserves an occasional night out with his friends. The clash between these two outlooks often becomes a blame game. Monica says, "We used to fight about money. [He would say that] I was money hungry, [that] I was a money hungry bitch and stuff like that. We would fight mostly about the [money he always seemed to have for drugs]. He would tell me I turned into a dud. I'm like, 'No, I didn't. I turned into a *mom*. I became *responsible*. I had to grow up. You didn't have to. You got to stay a kid still. You got to do whatever you wanted. I became responsible.' That was a lot of the fighting."

For many couples, the opening act in the drama involving money is her desire for the baby to start life with the best of everything. Though a used crib or stroller will do in a pinch, mothers feel that fathers should find a way to make sure their children don't have to sleep on hand-me-down mattresses and can ride in strollers fresh from the factory. Whereas a young father may think it is perfectly okay to skimp and buy inexpensive diapers, the mother expects him to buy Pampers or Huggies, claiming that the name brands absorb more and are better at preventing diaper rash. Fathers who spend more on themselves than on their kids are not worth much in the mothers' eyes. This is especially true when the child is small and the mother is looking for visible demonstrations of his commitment to the young family. Some fathers do try to meet these expectations, but others begin to view mothers who make such demands as "money hungry bitches."[5]

When financial problems become chronic, most mothers do conclude, "I can do bad by myself," especially when effort and spending habits are in question. When men become a drain to the family's meager resources, the rational response is for the mother to go it alone. Though empathy for the child's father is not entirely lacking, few mothers are willing to endanger the resources they and their children desperately need just to keep the baby's father around.

Yet, while money troubles certainly contribute to the tensions between poor unmarried young couples, money is seldom the primary reason mothers give to explain why they and their children's fathers are no longer together. Although a lazy or spendthrift boyfriend is certainly an aggravation, especially for a family living close to the economic margin, the mother usually points to far more serious offenses as the prime forces that pull their young families apart. It is the drug and alcohol abuse, the criminal behavior and consequent incarceration, the repeated infidelity, and the patterns of intimate violence that are the villains looming largest in poor mothers' accounts of relational failure.

About one in three mothers we talked with said that crime, usually drug dealing, and the almost inevitable spell in jail or prison were what broke them apart.[6] More than a third blamed their partner's alcoholism or drug addiction for the strain on the relationship. Four in ten say their relationship broke down because their child's father couldn't manage to stay faithful. An even higher proportion—nearly half—say that they could no longer take the chronic abuse they suffered at his hands. Taken together, fully two-thirds of the mothers say they've had a relationship disintegrate for one or more of these reasons, and about half have encountered these problems with more than one man.

"I'M GOING TO LOSE HIM
ONE WAY OR THE OTHER."

In the poorer neighborhoods of Philadelphia and its inner suburbs, the street corner offers a quick apprenticeship to any enterprising young man who's bold enough to flaunt the law. A young woman may forgive a little drug dealing in the dating phase and even during her pregnancy, and she sometimes even puts up with it when the child is very young and the father spends the money on a bassinet, not a high. Young fathers who are otherwise quite law-abiding sometimes enter the drug trade temporarily to cover the startup costs of having a baby—the crib, the coach (stroller), and the dozens of other things a new baby needs. Mothers, however, seldom consider this a legitimate, long-term alternative to a "real" job in the formal economy.

Twenty-one-year-old Celeste, a white mother of a five-month-old, says she is desperately trying to find a way to convince her baby's father to stop robbing houses and stores, and get a "real" job. "I want him to get a legal job and do it the right way. He gonna be twenty-five years old— it's time to grow up. He always blames it on his mom and dad [who didn't provide for him when he was a kid]. He says, 'Well that's why I stole, to support myself and all.' I say, 'Okay, maybe *then*. But *now* you're twenty-five years *old*—it's time to stop all that! Grow *up*—be an *adult*.' That's what I always say to him. '*I* changed, now *you* have to change.'" Cherry, the African American sixteen-year-old mother of a newborn, has noticed her boyfriend spending more and more time hanging out with friends on a nearby drug corner. She says she warns him, "Joe—if you're selling drugs I can't be in this relationship. Because I don't want you selling drugs and stuff like that. You know that's not the right thing to do." Twenty-three-year-old Mickey, a white mother of two, ages one and seven, reacts similarly to the street-corner activities of her baby's father. "The baby came home, and he was still selling drugs. I kept on telling him, 'Well it's time to get a *job*. We have a kid—it's not on the way anymore. The kid's *home* now, and it's time for you to get a *job*. I can't do it by myself. The baby can't live off love, it's gotta live off money, we need money. [You need a job] where you're not going to get hurt or you're not going to get locked up.'"

Young mothers reject drug dealing for both symbolic and practical reasons.[7] On a symbolic level, residents of even the poorest communities believe that a good father must earn his living by respectable means. While drug money may substitute for legitimate pay at times, mothers agree that it ought to be a stop-gap measure during financial crises, not a long-term career.[8] Practically speaking, dealing drugs is simply not a family-friendly activity. For starters, most mothers believe that life in the trade will land their baby's father in a cell or a casket—not the ideal scenario for the man they are relying on to "be there" for them and the child.

Fathers are pulled in opposite directions when it comes to the easy money that drug dealing brings. Most try to stay employed at legitimate jobs, but if they lose them or are temporarily laid off, the continuing pressure to bring in money makes the street corner hard to resist.[9] Mickey, mentioned above, tells us that the problems between her and her boyfriend started "when he lost his job. They closed down. There goes his job, there goes the income. I still had my assistance, which wasn't doing too much, . . . so he started selling drugs on the corner. . . . I was scared because people were getting killed around there and stuck up and locked up. I'm thinking, you know, in my mind I'm thinking, 'I'm gonna lose him one way or the other, either to jail or to death.'"

Mickey's fears are not unfounded, as incarceration and death rates for men in these neighborhoods, especially drug-related arrests and murders, are extraordinarily high. Though only a few have actually lost one of their children's fathers to street violence, many know someone—a relative or childhood friend—who has. Thirty-six-year-old Lenise, an African American mother of two, ages eleven and seventeen, was in a loving, decade-long partnership with her baby's father but left him when he turned from legitimate employment to crime. "We broke up because he started doing things that I didn't wanna live with. And that's how he died. . . . [I left because] I couldn't sleep wondering when I was gonna get that call. . . . He bought me a diamond, he bought me a ring, [and even though] I had to . . . pawn it when I needed food and stuff, I always said we got to get married because . . . I'll never find another person like him that love me [like that]."

Drug dealing poses a number of other risks to the family as well. First, no mother wants her baby's father to stash drugs or guns in the house, possibly incriminating her and opening the way for her to lose her children to foster care. Though middle-class mothers are only rarely investigated for child abuse or neglect, the poor are much more likely to be under the scrutiny of Child Protective Services, whose workers are sometimes derisively called "baby snatchers" by mothers in the communities we studied.[10] Second, mothers also know that dealers often become "their own best customer," and "druggies" make poor parents as well as poor partners. Mickey told us, "The drugs he was selling he started doing, which was cocaine." Finally, even those raising children in the worst of urban neighborhoods want desperately to teach the right values. Thus, the only thing worse than a baby's father who is trying to make a living on the corner is a son or daughter who ends up doing the same.

"FIVE YEARS IS A LONG TIME TO BE WAITING."

Celeste, who is determined that her boyfriend take a "legit" job, is cautiously optimistic that he will do so. He's given up robbery for an under-the-table job at a back-alley garage, a somewhat shady operation in her estimation. The fact that the job is not legal and that some of the activities that go on there may not be aboveboard clearly scares her, because she and her newborn endured hardships the last time he went to prison. "He's doing OK, I guess. He's been working at a garage. But I'm not sure if it's all legit. I keep telling him, 'If you get locked up again, I'm not waiting for you.' The judge already told him if he gets locked up again, he's going upstate for a couple years. I don't know, I keep telling him he has to get a job on the *books*. I don't want to go through it again. It wasn't easy at all. If it wasn't for my family and friends, I don't know where I would have been."

Corinda, a twenty-six-year-old Puerto Rican mother of four, ranging from three to eleven in age, blames the breakup with the father of her older two children on his failure to give up the illegal activities that had already landed him in jail when her children were young. "My kids' father, my two oldest—he's a bad father because . . . when he first came out [of jail] and they were babies, he should have tried to stay away from the drugs and get a good job to take care of them instead of going back to the corners and selling and getting locked up." Corinda goes on to say, "When he [comes] out, I don't even want him to come *near* my baby. I did [it] this far, I could do it the rest of the way."

Elaine, an African American eighteen-year-old, was similarly furious when the father of her eight-month-old ignored her warning to stop selling drugs. She told us, "[My son's] dad is in jail for some drugs. I told him before [our son] was born, 'If you get fired or whatever . . . ' I was like, 'I don't want you selling no drugs.' Soon as I had [my son], he got fired or laid off, or whatever, and he started selling drugs. I told him, '*Marv*, . . . look for a *job!* It's not that hard!' I was like, 'You got that *[other]* job easily! It's not that hard! Now *find a job!*' He wanted to sell drugs, so I was like, 'I hope you get locked up.' And he got locked up [when our son] was three months old." Monica shares similar sentiments. After her children's father was jailed again, she relates that as "time went on, I'm like, 'What does he do for me?' He's in jail, I have two kids, I'm raising them, I'm working, I'm doing this, I'm doing that. What was his *purpose?* I started thinking, 'I don't need him.' He was just like an extra burden. It was actually easier without him."

Michelle, a thirty-one-year-old African American mother of a seven-year-old and twins who are four, is, unlike most, still holding on to her relationship with her children's father, despite a substantial second-offense prison sentence for drug dealing, an activity he was only pursuing temporarily when he was between legal jobs. Her oldest child, Tacoya, can barely remember the father who went to jail when she was only two, and the twins don't know him at all. "Right now he's incarcerated, so that's why he's not here. He *was* cleaning and helping and letting me get a break. But it's been so hard because he's been in for so many years and I've been doing everything *myself.* He's been in for four years now," says Michelle. "He was here for two years with Tacoya, [but] most of the years with the youngest he's missed." In the meantime, Michelle valiantly tries to keep her baby's father connected to her and her child. "I try to take them up to the prison to see him, but it's so expensive. . . . It costs $87 for the bus to come and take the kids and I up there. . . . What can I really do? It's my mother's house, but I still have to pay her rent, and I still have to pay the bills! The kids still need clothes and shoes! He says he understands, and he says when he comes home he's going to look for a job to help to do the things so we can get married and live, hopefully, happily ever after. Especially since we've both been through a lot with him drug dealing and he [being in prison]. Hopefully, he worked his stuff out. We'll see."

Even the most steadfast can be done in by a man who is in and out of jail repeatedly or commits an offense serious enough to warrant a long sentence. Seventeen-year-old Champagne, the African American mother of a six-month-old, laments, "I'm so fed up with him going in and out of jail I couldn't take it no more. Five years is a long time to be waiting. . . . I waited for a year and a half the first time, when we first started going together before I had my son. . . . He got out, he was doing fine. I got pregnant, and then he was just in and out of jail the whole pregnancy. [Now he's in for five years]." Deborah, an African American twenty-six-year-old with two children, ages twelve and eight, tells a similar story. Their father ended up repeating a pattern her own father had set. "My father is not a part of my life. I know who he is, I seen pictures of him, but I don't *know* him. . . . My kids are going through the same thing, . . . they father is just not *here*. He is in jail. He is in jail for *killing* somebody, so I am a single parent basically." For women like Deborah, there is really little point in waiting.

As everyone knows, a prison record is an ongoing handicap for a man struggling to be a responsible father and support his children.[11] Tasheika, introduced earlier, tells a particularly poignant tale about the employment problems her baby's father had because of his criminal record and the effect on their family life. "He was there [for me until after the baby was born,] but he got incarcerated. He got mixed up in his other life, and all of that stopped. [After he got out,] he had a lot of issues, you know? He was trying to take care of the family, but he didn't have a job because he been in and out of prison. . . . And then he wasn't able to take care of the child, and he just gave up." She concludes, "Me and him were so *close* . . . [but] it wasn't worth *nothing*, and here I go again. Had to start all over again and do things differently, meet the different guys, and things like that."

"HE LOVED HIS DRUG MORE THAN HE LOVED HIS FAMILY."

Rose, an African American mother of four children ranging in age from two to fourteen and now in her early thirties, says her relationship with the two younger children's father broke down when his return to his "street" associations led to a pattern of heavy drinking and an addiction to drugs. "After Charles was born, we was doing fine. We still remained in the relationship. [But] he loved to associate with different friends on the street. . . . To me they were strays. You bring a stray home [because it] is out in the street and no one else want it. . . . Then he started to associate more [with them], like hanging out in the bar drinking and carrying on like that. I was never one for hanging out in bars or drinking, you know. . . . [Then] I come to find out he was a *druggie!* He does *drugs* and I didn't *know* it."

It is impossible to overemphasize the devastating impact of drugs and alcohol on the lives of the men in the eight communities we studied. Outside observers often find it impossible to ignore the public displays of these addictions, the men with bloodshot eyes drinking "forties" on the stoops, the strung-out addicts huddled in doorways or weaving down the sidewalks. But the destruction these toxins wreak inside of the family is equally profound. Drugs and alcohol can quickly transform men who are valued partners and fathers into villains who threaten the well-being of the family.

Thirty-one-year-old Toby, a white mother of two children, ages one and nine, recalls a "wonderful" relationship with her younger child's father before he became addicted to cocaine. She tells us, "I tried so much, but there was nothing I could do or say [to make him stop]. I *had* to throw him out. I almost lost my apartment [because he started spending all our money on drugs]—I had a very nice little apartment, and that was my home. I wasn't going to lose it for him. That was my and my daughter's *home*, and I told him that he needed to leave." "He's out of control," she finishes. "There's nothing I can do for him. He's not going to take food out of my daughter's mouth for [drugs]. I always told him, 'My daughter comes first—she will always be first.'"

The first evidence of an addiction to alcohol or drugs is often a startling change of personality, a dramatic reshuffling of priorities that results in draining precious economic and emotional resources from the family as the addiction "takes him over." We asked twenty-two-year-old Tatiana, an African American mother of three, ages six, four, and two, how her children's father changed over time. She replied, "I think he's gotten worse. . . . When I first met him he did drink like a beer or two a day [or] he would smoke a joint. . . . Now he's smoking blunts, and he can drink a case of forties by himself a day.[12] That's a lot of beer. . . . He doesn't think about my kids. If he has a dollar and they don't have any juice, he'll put that dollar [toward] buy[ing] a beer instead of . . . buying them juice. I can't deal with that." Twenty-one-year-old Cindi, a white mother of two toddlers, tells a similar story of callous behavior on the part of her youngest child's father, who watched the children when she worked the night shift. "Once the baby was getting older, I would come home from work, and he would look weird. I started flipping out on him because he was getting high. The kids were upstairs sleeping, but *still*, he was *watching* them and *using* at the same time. . . . Angel dust, PCP, and like taking pills!"

Tatiana relates the incident that was the last straw for her. "Some men think a lot about their kids. A lot of men, their kids are their world. I'm not saying he doesn't love my kids, I'm just saying he doesn't know responsibility. I think the beer is taking [him] over. Like I said, when I first met him, we had *everything*. Now, I [am] lucky [to get a] Mother's Day [gift]. As a matter of fact I got a Twix [candy bar] for Mother's Day [this year]! I mean I'm *serious*, I got a *Twix* for *Mother's Day!* I mean it hurt me. I still throw that up in his face." Tatiana then relates how the next morning her boyfriend ate the candy bar himself, leaving the empty wrapper on the table for her to clean up. Tatiana sums up the effect his addiction has had on the family: "It's his . . . *attitude* [that's changed]. He [just] thinks about himself. He's constantly telling me that *I* should think about *me*. But if I get like him, who would my kids have?" Twenty-five-year-old Cheyenne, the white mother of two, ages five and eight, tells us, "I stayed with [my boyfriend] till [our daughter] was a year old. We [even] looked at rings a few times. . . . [But] last year he sold [my older daughter's] Christmas presents [for drug money]."

For a young mother who aspires to raise her children right and not lose them to the state, pregnancy and birth make an ongoing devotion to an addiction difficult, if not impossible. Not so for fathers, who are seldom the legal custodians of their nonmarital children. In fact, some mothers attribute their boyfriend's free fall into drug or alcohol addiction to the birth of the child. Francine, a white thirty-year-old mother of three children, ages five, seven, and eleven, tells the following story. "Then I . . . . gave birth. No sooner had that happened than it really started to fall apart with his father. He was just really a drunk. . . . It was like *all the time*—no consideration [for me or the baby]. Like, 'There's a *child* in the house now! You can't invite all your buddies over and be smoking all your marijuana in the *parlor!*'" Jackie, a thirty-three-year-old white mother of three children who are four, six, and eight, watched her children's father get off and on drugs several times before she left him, each new cycle seemingly provoked by the birth of one of their children. "He was more into his drug than he was into his family." She tells us, "It would even get worse once the baby was born because he would . . . tell me he would feel the pressure of taking care of his family. I said to him, 'Well . . . you *wanted* kids, and now we *have* kids, and now you telling me this is a *pressure* for you?' I'm like, '*Hello!*'"

The heartbreak of addiction lies not only in the threat to the family, but in the destructive effect on the addict himself. Raven, forty-three, a white mother of two children, eleven and seventeen, vividly describes the seizures, disorientation, and behavioral deterioration her children's father suffers after years of a "really bad" drug addiction. Her first clue to the severity of the addiction was his rapid weight loss. "He wore a pair of shorts underneath his jeans so that no one would know how skinny he was when he was out in public. But I would see the ribs." Tatiana, who got the Twix for Mother's Day, describes frightening physical manifestations of her partner's alcoholism. "He refuses to go to the hospital because he's scared that it's the drinking that's doing it. He doesn't want to stop drinking. He goes through the whole side of his body being numb and all. He can't breathe. . . . I gotta watch him go through that. I got [life] insurance on him—I'm not lying. I went and got insurance because if he [dies] at least my kids will have *something* . . . they'll still have *something* from their dad."

"HE PLAYED ME THREE TIMES."

In neighborhoods where few couples wear wedding bands, and unmarried couples seldom manage to stay together for long, virtually everyone is, in some sense, still "on the market."[13] On the one hand, poor unmarried couples try hard to keep it together for the baby. Yet they borrow their notions of commitment from the broader culture, and most middle-class couples who are still in the dating phase, even those who cohabit, believe that as long as they are not married, it is acceptable for either partner to walk away at any time, and for virtually any reason.[14] Of course, middle-class couples who date or cohabit only rarely have children together.[15]

Because society has not yet adjusted to the new reality that many non-marital births are to couples still romantically involved and even cohabiting, the cultural norms regarding this family form are still evolving. Thus, unmarried parents must borrow from the norms most close-at-hand. On the one hand, they adopt expectations of financial responsibility and, as we shall see, sexual fidelity, as couples in marriage do. But on the other, walking away from a nonmarital union is not viewed as a betrayal of a vow, and it is more or less okay to hold oneself open to a better option, should one come along. The very fact that the couple remains unmarried implies that one partner, or both, is ambivalent about whether the other is truly "the one." Yet both middle-class cohabiters and their poor counterparts view cheating as unacceptable.[16]

Added to the ambivalent nature of the relationship itself is the fact that the sex ratios in these neighborhoods are out of balance, women usually outnumbering men, especially in the African American neighborhoods.[17] This means that a young father who is struggling to become a family man has ready access to scores of willing sexual partners who will not impose substantial burdens, at least at the start of a new romance. Twenty-two-year-old Angela, an African American mother of a two-year-old son, explains her view of the state of affairs in her East Camden neighborhood: "I'm just saying it's a shortage of men, so they think, 'I can have more than one woman.' And, you know what I'm saying, 'I'm going to go around to this one or that one, and I'm going to have two of them, or three of them, . . . a main one and a sidekick.'" So that's sort of what [my son's] dad was doing. He had a main one and a sidekick. *I* was the main one, but he had a *sidekick.*" Later, she reflects, "I really trusted that boy, for real. . . . I like a man who can control himself as far as temptation and stuff like that. If he can't control himself . . . then he's not the one for me."

It is thus not surprising that infidelity is much more common among men than among women.[18] The poor mothers we spoke to seldom deem infidelity acceptable. Yet some mothers do admit that as long as he wasn't "in my face with it," they were willing to ignore the telltale signs for a time. A few others say they "discovered" flagrant affairs only after being "in denial" for months about what was so obviously going on. Some are also, for a time, willing to take back a partner who has strayed, as twenty-year-old Amanda, a Puerto Rican mother of a three-year-old, was: "I was so blinded by everything. He'd come back and I'd go back with him; [then] he'd leave me and be with someone else. And [now] he has a baby two months older than [my son]. So I really went through a lot of stuff with him."

But turning a blind eye to signs of unfaithfulness is the exception rather than the rule. More often, suspicious mothers become amateur detectives, checking out a telltale slip of paper with an unknown phone number scrawled on it or tracking down a neighborhood rumor by calling or visiting the alleged "other woman" to confirm or deny the story. Jessica, fifteen, a Puerto Rican mother of a two-year-old, tells a typical story in this regard. "When [my daughter] was about ten months old, that's when [her father and I] broke up. [But only after] he played me three times." When we asked her how she found out about his affairs, she explained, "I used to go with his mom to wash his clothes. I'd look into his pockets to see if he had anything in it. That's when I [would find] the phone numbers [or] the napkin with the lipstick on it. When I went to go ask him about it, he said, 'Oh, that's my friend.' Then I went to go call the girl, and the girl said, 'Oh, that's my boyfriend.' I said, 'Do you know that I have a child by him?' They'd be like, 'No.' So we broke up."

Many of the mothers are clearly disgusted with the seeming inability of "grown men" to remain faithful. Sixteen-year-old Brehanna, the African American mother of a one-year-old, chose a much older man because she assumed he'd be mature enough to live up to the commitments that being "together" demands. "He's like thirty, thirty-one. A *grown man*, and he *lie*, right? Like we were supposed to be seeing each other, whatever, [but] I [always] had to track him down. [One time] I took his car and tracked him down, and he was at another female's house. I stood outside until he came around, and then he lied and told me he had *kids* by her. He doesn't have any kids by her! He said, 'I'm over here visiting my kids.' He did *not* have kids by this woman. . . . Guys make me so sick—they're just pitiful!"

The worst-case scenario is when a "side" relationship produces a child, because this creates an alternative family with equal claim to the man's income and loyalty. Tyhera, a nineteen-year-old African American mother of a three-year-old daughter, says the relationship with her child's father ended for this reason. "Now . . . he *really, really* did something that is like *unforgivable!* He had another *child* on me. [How it happened was that] I had had an abortion . . . and he was really kinda heartbroken about that. . . . She was talking to him about it and so on and so on. He got drunk, and this, that, and the other, and had that one-night stand with her. I don't care *what* type of one-night stand you had! You didn't have to be *careless.* I did [things, and] said things in the past, but I didn't bring no baby . . . into our future. What if *I* was to pop up pregnant by someone? You would *really* be upset." Lenise, the thirty-six-year-old African American mother of two, offers another story in this vein. "We were doing really well, but . . . he was younger than me. I [felt] like I had stolen his youth, because he came right out of school and became a family man. . . . A lot of girls wanted him. [Then] he got somebody else pregnant, which broke my heart. He didn't even *like* the girl that much."

Infidelity is so common among couples in these neighborhoods that over time, some come to question any man's ability to remain sexually faithful, and at some level, young women like Jen Burke may almost expect it to happen. Still, it devastates them when it does. Not only is the infidelity itself a blow, but so are the layers of dishonesty and betrayal that accompany it, particularly when the other woman is the mother's own friend. Marilyn, a white twenty-four-year-old mother of two preschoolers, tells us, "It's my eighth month of pregnancy, and my brother comes over at 11:00 at night. He says to me, 'Brace yourself, I know you're eight months pregnant, and I don't want you to get worked up, but you have to know this. I feel I have to tell you this.' I'm saying, 'What?' He said, 'It's about Tom.' I said, 'He is cheating on me.' I just knew right then and there. He says, 'But *who with*, you're gonna have a problem with.' I said, 'Who . . . ?' It was my cousin's cousin. I used to play with her when I was little. I was just so upset."

Young mothers are often appalled by the astonishing callousness men show not only regarding who, but when and where they conduct their side liaisons. Jennifer, a twenty-three-year-old Puerto Rican mother of six, all under the age of seven, who broke up with her children's father before the youngest, now one, was born, tells us, "He was cheating on me for three years out of the five we were together. One time he even brought the girl to my home when I was [out] baptizing our son!"

There are practical as well as emotional reasons why women refuse to tolerate infidelity. First, mothers are now well aware that a secret side relationship poses serious risks to their health. Angela tells us, "I mean I don't know *nobody* who is just going to [say its okay for their boyfriend to] go out there and mess with anybody, because that's trifling with AIDS and syphilis." Second, when a boyfriend's casual infidelity turns into a full-blown affair, his money begins to flow out of the household and into the new woman's pocketbook, as these new girlfriends expect the men to "do for them" as well. The final straw for Raven came when she realized that her children's father's bank account was depleted because he was spending money on another woman. "I was eating *hot dogs* with my kids, and he [was taking her] out for *steak dinners!*"

"ONE DAY HE GRABBED ME ON MY NECK . . ."

Physical abuse can be just as corrosive of trust as repeated infidelity, and though it occurs across class lines, it occurs more often among the poor.[19] Such violence not only bruises her body but also violates her sense of self. Mickey had just broken up with her children's father when we first met with her. Their six-year relationship had been abusive from the start, had gotten better with time, and then abruptly changed for the worse. This white twenty-three-year-old mother of two told us, "He abused me a month ago—gave me a black eye. Then a week later he gave me another black eye. . . . So the last time, I couldn't take it no more. I felt like I was going to die—felt like I would rather be dead. I wanted to kill myself—I really wanted to kill myself, but my children is what's kept me alive."

Carmelita, a nineteen-year-old Puerto Rican mother of a preschooler and a seven-month-old, has been able to sustain her relationship with the father of her children, but only by convincing him she'd leave if he hit her again. "He beat me to where I was afraid of any man" she says. "When I finally got that pride back to be able to stand up for myself and say, 'No, that's not going to *happen* to me, I don't *care* if I'm on welfare, I don't *care* if I don't have a job. . . . I am a *person*, and I am not going to let nobody treat me different. . . . ' The first time he did it . . . I had flashbacks and everything, like day sweats and everything because I was so scared. The second time he did it . . . I left [and moved in with my mother]. Since he knew that I was serious and that I am not going to take that, he stopped the bullshit." She concludes, "He's afraid now that I am going to leave him. If it's a fear that I have to instill in him so that he doesn't put his hands on me or that he doesn't mistreat me, then that's what it's going to be. So be it. I am not going to sit there and let him think that it's alright, because it's not alright. I am dead serious. No matter how much I love you, I will leave you if you're going to hurt me."

Carmelita put up with the abuse from her baby's father for several years before she mustered the courage to stand up to him. This was partly because she was financially dependent and was afraid she would have to live with her mother and go on welfare if she left.[20] Other women are bound to an abusive relationship by fear. Corinda tells us, "My two oldest, [their] father, he used to beat me for six years. And it was like every day because he was on drugs. I mean he hit me with everything—with extension cords, with a golf [club], with a knife, with everything. I always used to be with a busted lip with black eyes. I couldn't open my mouth because he would knock me out cold in front of anybody. And nobody would help me because everyone was scared of him. I stood with him for six years even though he was in and out of jail. But I was still with him [because] I used to be real scared of him."

While mothers might not always leave to protect themselves, fear for their children's safety will often prompt them to act. Jennifer, the twenty-three-year-old Puerto Rican mother of six young children, explains, "He used to beat me up, so that's why we separated. He used to beat me up in front of the *kids*, you know, my oldest son would see him hitting me.

When he would finish hitting me, he would start screaming at them. He always used to take it out on them. I had to leave before he would do any harm to the kids." The moment of realization for Roxanne, a white mother of three—an adult, a teenager, and a ten-year-old—in her early forties, came when the father of her youngest two returned home from a bad day at work. "He came and he was in a really, really bad mood. We started fighting, he started wrecking the house. I remember I was upstairs with Allie, because she was under a year old—she was an infant. I remember him like ripping the bedroom door off the hinges—this was a solid wood door he ripped off the hinges and threw down the steps. I was running down the steps with Allie in my arms, and I remember the door almost hitting us. I remember thinking that if the door hit us it would *kill* her. And something clicked in my head. That night I just stayed awake all night next to him not moving. When he got up for work, I just packed and left."

Twenty-one-year-old Sandra, a Puerto Rican mother of two, ages five and a year and a half, says her children's father often drank heavily when he hung out with friends and then became violent with her afterward. She finally left him when the older son (from another partner) tried to intervene. "One day, he grabbed me on my neck . . . and my oldest son spit on him. He was like, 'Don't touch my mom.' And he was kind of drunk and hit my son. So I was like, 'I'm not having any more of this. . . . You *choose*, you stay with *me*, or you go ahead and party and do your *stuff* [drinking].' He was like, 'I don't *wanna* stop hanging out with my friends because of you.' I was like, 'Don't do that for me, do it for the *children*, not for me.' But he didn't care."

The threats of violence and the verbal abuse that go along with the physical violence—what many mothers call "mental" abuse—are often the most wounding. Ebony describes the incident that prompted her to leave her baby's father, who had recently hit her so hard in the face she'd bled from the wound. This eighteen-year-old African American mother of a newborn relates that shortly after this incident, "He was ironing his clothes, and we were arguing over sex. He was like, 'I could just burn your face with this iron.' I was like, 'Oh my God!' That's when I was living with him—so where could I go, you know? It's not like I could just jump up and run out. I could not believe it—I was like, 'This guy has just lost his mind!'" Twenty-five-year-old Abby, the white mother of a toddler, says her abusive partner was always "[telling me] that I'm fat, I'm ugly, I'm stupid, I'm no good. He drug me down in the dirt to where some of the dirt's not coming off. I guess it's time for once to maybe feel better about myself . . . and [find] someone to show me I'm not [nothing]."

The cause of the violence they've suffered is a mystery to most. Some believe it stems from an overload of responsibility that fathers feel. But as mothers typically take on far more of the responsibility, both financial and otherwise, for the child than the fathers do, they find it hard to accept this rationale.[21] Others see it as an outgrowth of addiction, as most violent episodes tend to occur when the men are drunk or high. Some feel the abusive behavior flows from the guilt their men feel over infidelity and other reprehensible behaviors. Still others point to the violent lifestyle the drug trade produces, and see the abuse that occurs in the home as a natural consequence of what he's been exposed to on the street. Finally, some believe it is rooted in the fathers' own childhood experiences of abuse, as is true for Ann, a white thirty-five-year-old mother of a nineteen-month-old. "[My son's] father was abused by his father, *very* badly, not just smacked, he was thrown against *walls* and everything. It's starting to come out now. . . . He held it all in [at first]." However, this dawning recognition does not make Ann willing to reunite. "He did it twice and then I left. I'm not the type of person to be hit. I feel bad for [him]. That shouldn't have happened from when he was a little boy, but you've got to grow *up* and go *past* that."

DIFFERENCES AMONG MOTHERS

Though domestic violence, infidelity, criminal behavior, incarceration, and drug and alcohol abuse are fairly common experiences among mothers of all racial and ethnic backgrounds, Philadelphia's African Americans, Puerto Ricans, and whites have distinctive histories and cultural practices, and they face different social constraints, which lead to different kinds of relationship problems.

Domestic violence, the chief culprit in most stories of relational ruin, is more common among our Puerto Ricans and whites than among the African Americans. Part of the reason may be that African American mothers are less likely to cohabit with a male partner, and the lack of common residence could serve as a protective factor.[22] Infidelity was an equal opportunity relationship wrecker.[23] The third most common problem, criminal behavior, was a more prominent feature in the breakup stories of our African American mothers. Given the restricted legal labor market for unskilled black men, this is not surprising. Similarly, incarceration figured in the accounts of more African American mothers.

Drugs seem to be the more common palliative for the male partners of the African American and Puerto Rican women, while alcohol is the preferred substance for white male partners. Of course, in most cases, drinking alcohol is legal, whereas drug use is not. While both wreak havoc within the family (and white men are certainly no strangers to marijuana, heroin, "meth," and cocaine), drugs are more likely to bring trouble with the law.

"BUT HE CAN BE SAVED."

Readers may wonder what women like Jen Burke ever see in men like Rick, or why they ever regard a relationship with men like him as a path to any kind of fulfillment. Certainly most young women would not view Rick as a promising match. Part of the answer is certainly Jen's youth and inexperience. But two-thirds of nonmarital births are now to adult women, and though Rick is more troubled than the average unmarried father these mothers describe, few of the older women we talked to seem to have made significantly better matches.[24]

The truth is that Jen Burke and others like her often have problems of their own. Jen's list of problems, like Rick's, is unusually long. She was expelled from the neighborhood middle school for fighting, had acquired a drug habit, suffered trauma when a six-year-old sibling was killed by a car, and had even been hospitalized after a suicide attempt—all by the time she was fourteen. Though a young college-bound woman raised on Philadelphia's suburban Main Line might easily have found a more promising prospect to father her child, Rick may have been about the best Jen could realistically have hoped for. Mahkiya Washington, who clearly has a lot more going for her, managed to attract a better partner, but not the doctor or lawyer she may have dreamed of. After all, she is from a family with only a tenuous grasp on the working-class respectability achieved in prior generations and hails from one of the most impoverished neighborhoods in the city.

Just as poor women lack the educational and career opportunities that their more affluent counterparts have, they also lack access to the better matches that middle-class women make. Simply put, women who are better off take the more desirable men, leaving Jen Burke and Mahkiya Washington and Antonia Rodriguez to cope with what's left. Many of these mothers realize that to find a diamond, they might have to sort through a lot of coal. Raven says of her youngest child's father, "I *saw* things in him they *didn't*. I saw he was very sensitive, and he was a very caring person underneath all this garbage. . . . Oh yeah, there's a good side to everybody, there really is. . . . You just have to weed through all the weeds." Another white mother, Angelica, who is nineteen and has a two-year-old child, is proud that her relationship with her son's father has managed to survive for three years now. The occasional cheating, she says, has stopped, and the father has now "proved back his trust to me." She admits, though, that perhaps the reason he's now stopped "is because he's with me twenty-four hours a day," as the couple now works together on the same shift at a nursing home. Still, she's seen lasting change since their baby was born, and this gives her hope. "I believe like people *do* change. [When our son was born,] it just kind of fell into place. He changed—he did a 360. Like, granted, he's still an asshole [sometimes], but he can be saved, definitely. There's something worth saving."

The pattern of negative behavior that strains or breaks the relationships between mothers and their children's fathers often crops up in the first months after the birth because young fathers find that the promises they made, perhaps at the magic moment of birth, to trade street life for family life are not ones they are truly prepared to keep. Women seem to welcome the social closure that a birth brings—the new relationship with her baby and the support of a few close female kin are often compensation enough for forgone friendships and freedoms. But for the new father, a child's arrival means that his girlfriend's attention is now divided, and he gets far less than he did before. After the birth, a young mother is often consumed by the child, quickly losing interest in the social round of activities—the partying and clubbing, and the hanging out with friends—that the couple may have enjoyed before the pregnancy. Very often, though, the father seems to catch cabin fever.

Fathers also get fewer rewards from their peers in their new status as a parent than mothers do. Staying home with the baby rather than "ripping and running" with friends brings her social recognition for behaving the way a good mother should. He, however, wins no points with his friends for staying home in the evening and on weekends, no matter how good a father he desires to be. He often chafes at being required to spend all his leisure time at home, especially when the baby wins in the competition for his girlfriend's affection. Meanwhile, there is more than ample opportunity for infidelity in a social world where the lack of clear, socially supported relational guidelines means that there are few sanctions against pursuing other relationships, and especially in a social context where the greater number of women creates a buyer's market for men who are shopping for romance and sex.[25]

The transition to parenthood means that the demands on young men dramatically increase just as the rewards of the relationship are radically reduced.[26] The story of Dominique, a thirty-four-year-old African

American mother of three (see chapter 5), supports this claim. She describes her daughter's father as "always like really jealous and possessive. . . . He just wanted me for himself. And as a matter of fact . . . he was jealous of [our daughter] because she took up my time. I was like, 'She's a *child*—she can't help that!'" Angela, twenty-two, an African American mother of a two-year-old, makes a similar claim: "Some men actually want to see you walk *away* from your child and give *them* the love. Because that's what my baby's father wanted. He wanted me to . . . just give it to him."

Many men respond to these pressures by returning to their street-corner associations in a relatively short period of time. Mothers often argue that since they don't get any time off from parenting, the fathers shouldn't expect to either. But they also recognize that his peers can be a threat to their new families. As fathers reconnect with their "associates" on the street, many resume the heavy drinking and drug use, casual drug dealing, joyriding, or other delinquent behavior, and even the sexual encounters that they may have engaged in before becoming fathers.

All couples—regardless of race, socioeconomic position, marital status, or community context—face challenges. In some ways, the forces that pull at the relationships of impoverished mothers and fathers are not so different from the conflicts that plague many affluent marriages. Couples commonly fight about money, wrangle over each other's spending habits, and feud about irritating quirks. Infidelity and abuse are not absent in middle-class marriages, though they happen less frequently than among low-income, unmarried parents.[27]

In part, the volatile relationships of these poor unwed couples may result from the fact that they've moved so quickly from courtship to child-rearing. But the social environment in which these relationships develop creates enormous pressures as well, as the same forces eating away at the fabric of the neighborhood—drugs, crime, and violence—are at work in the intimate spaces of these romantic pairings. In a social environment where young mothers are more likely to raise children without fathers than with them, where marriage is rare, good jobs are few, money is tight, and violence and lawlessness are common, the most astonishing fact may be that some of these relationships survive as long as they do.

Sometimes, however, the relationships between young, unmarried parents do endure. For couples like Antonia Rodriguez and her boyfriend Emilio, and perhaps for Mahkiya Washington and her newly reformed boyfriend Mike, the high hopes they have at the magic moment of birth may be realized. In the poorest communities within Philadelphia and its inner suburbs, there are just enough stories with happy endings to keep hope alive.

In the woman's view, the birth of a baby ought to transform the father into a family man who is as selflessly devoted to the well-being of the child as she is, just as it has transformed her. Though women often admit that they too "had their fun"—drinking excessively or experimenting with drugs—before the pregnancy, the conception motivates most to put aside these "childish ways."[28] To them, the trade-off is a no-brainer. Crime risks injury, death, or imprisonment, and drugs and alcohol drain already scarce resources that could be used for the child. Men who drink to excess or love to get high often find it difficult to show up at work on time, much less be appealing partners or responsible caregivers. Substance abuse reduces inhibitions, leading to conflict and physical abuse. A father who is drunk or strung out at home, or makes a public display of his inebriation on the corner, is a bad role model for the children she hopes will survive the destructive elements of their social environment. Infidelity breaks the trust required to keep a relationship alive, and the violence of a domestic dispute may spill over to the children.

As we suggested in chapter 1 and will show more fully in chapter 5, motherhood provides a potent sense of meaning for young women coming of age in these urban slums, as much of their self-worth is derived from the mothering role. Thus, a good mother must sometimes defend her child against the actions of the child's own father, who may become a menace to the fragile equilibrium she's trying to sustain. Dominique, whose story we tell in chapter 5, shares experiences that epitomize many of the ills we describe. She says she left her children's father because she couldn't find a way to live up to her obligations as a mother and still be with their father. "It was just a whole lot of things [the breakup] was over. I was just trying to hold on to something that really wasn't there, because it takes two to love. *I* can't love for the both of us. I [found I] can't love *him* and be a full-time *mother* at the same time—that would really wear you out."

Yet even for women who have been wounded by past relationships, the dream of a loving life partnership remains oddly powerful. Brielle, the African American thirty-two-year-old mother of four, has twice been deserted by men who have fathered her children. She was wary when an old high school flame reappeared five months into her third pregnancy. But when he began to visit the doctor with her, stayed with her during the delivery, and then showered attention on the child, another man's baby, this worn mother's heart was won. Though some women do eventually conclude that men are more trouble than they're worth, most continue to hope and pray that the men they forge relationships with will prove to be diamonds in the rough. But at the same time, most women acknowledge the insidious influences of neighborhood peers, the lack of steady, living-wage employment, the fast money available in the region's rich drug economy, and the constant lure of other women and recognize that these social forces can tempt the "love of my life" to become "my worst nightmare."

FOUR

WHAT MARRIAGE MEANS

DEENA AND PATRICK

Deena Vallas is a lively, twenty-one-year-old, third-generation resident of the South Philadelphia neighborhood of PennsPort, a modest community of compact row homes hard hit by five decades of deindustrialization. Deena's home is on the south end of a narrow thoroughfare known locally as Two Street, which runs from the affluent townhouses of Society Hill into the heart of what remains of the ethnic white stronghold of Philadelphia's southeast side. On Deena's end, Two Street is a colorful strip dotted with the private bars and practice halls of the city's marching string bands, which, for the last 150 years, have competed in the raucous "Mummers Parade," a Mardi Gras–like procession held each New Year's Day. It is spring, and Deena, like many neighborhood residents, spends much of her time on her front stoop with her two-and-a-half-year-old son, Kevin. She is outside not only to enjoy the weather. The tiny, two-bedroom row home in which she lives also houses her grandmother (who owns the place), her aunt and uncle, her son Kevin, and her live-in boyfriend. Deena's own small family shares the sleeping quarters afforded by the couch in the front room.

Deena became a single mother in the typical way of her neighborhood peers. She met her son's father, Kevin Sr., when she was fifteen and he was twenty; three years later they were living together, engaged, and she was pregnant. Deena eagerly explains her motivations for becoming a mother, exclaiming, "I *wanted* my son, I *did*. I wanted a baby. . . . I wanted somebody to take care of. . . . I *loved* it when I got pregnant with Kevin!" Initially, Deena says, Kevin Sr. was also thrilled about the baby, solicitous of her, and eager to build a stable family life. But trouble began in Deena's second month of pregnancy, when her boyfriend's father died and to "calm himself from the pain" he started "staying out all hours" and embarked on what became a seven-month drinking binge. Soon, she says, "I started hearing that he was cheating on me and he was with other people. . . . He would tell me that he wasn't [cheating on me], but he would be out all night. I didn't know where he was. I didn't know what he was doing."

Deena reached her breaking point on the night she went into premature labor. She remembers, "He was in a bar, drinking, and I had just found out [for sure] that he was cheating on me. I went up to the bar [and found him] with the girl who he cheated on me with. I told her, 'I'm gonna beat your face in. . . . ' I got real upset, like real bad. [When] we [got] home—it was like five o'clock in the morning—my water broke. I didn't know what was going on. I thought I was peeing on myself. [Then] I wound up in the hospital having my son [early]." By the time Deena was allowed to take her premature son home, she had left Kevin and moved in with her grandmother. She says, "I just got *sick* of it. I got sick of being treated like *shit*."

Deena says that Kevin Sr.'s treatment of her during her pregnancy "ruined my whole expectation of what a family was supposed to be." She recognizes that, like many young men, he could dream with her about having a child but reacted with sheer terror to the reality. Deena can now see that "he was scared, from the very beginning, when I first started getting excited about it. I would want him to touch me to feel the baby. . . . He never did that stuff."

Her new boyfriend, Patrick, is twenty-five, a PennsPort resident with a steady job at a catering firm, whom she met on her grandmother's front stoop just weeks after she brought Kevin Jr. home from the hospital. The baby she's now carrying is Patrick's, and they expect their daughter, whom they've named Magdalena, in just two months' time. Deena and Patrick have been through a lot in their two years together. For example, they are newly "clean," and though she describes her former drug habit as casual, she admits that Patrick's was serious. They both stopped using the moment the doctor confirmed her pregnancy, but the rowhouse stoop is still a popular hangout that draws friends from their "crazy" days, and the temptation to backslide is very real.

Patrick is approaching pregnancy very differently than Kevin Sr. did. She describes Patrick's reaction to the news in these words: "Oh, he *loved* it. He was all happy. He always wanted to have my kid. He always told me, 'I want to have a baby with you.'" But unlike Kevin Sr., Patrick's enthusiasm has not waned as the pregnancy has advanced. Deena says, "That's why I know I have a totally different [relationship] with my boyfriend Patrick. . . . He wants [to be] a part of everything. He *wants* to go to doctors with me."

For Deena, the most significant way that Patrick has demonstrated his love for her is through his treatment of her son, whose biological father neither visits nor supports him. Deena tells us, "[My son] knows the difference between his father and [Patrick], he knows the difference . . . he knows that he'll always be there for him, where his father's not. [Patrick] loves him." Even to the casual observer, Patrick's affection for her boy is evident. As Patrick himself explains, "If it wasn't for little Kevin, I'd either be dead or in jail. . . . He's not mine, biologically. People say, 'You're not a daddy yet.' But I've *been* a daddy for *two years!*"

In the 1950s a couple with a stable relationship, a steady income, and a child on the way would almost surely have been married, or planning to get married soon. When we ask Deena and Patrick about marriage, they say they talk about it frequently. Patrick says, "I like to do things *right* though, instead of cutting corners and doing everything half-assed. I'd rather get engaged for two years, save money, get a house, make sure . . . the baby's got a bedroom, [than get married now]." Deena adds,

"And I get a yard with grass. [And] I want a nice wedding." Patrick continues, "I'm not going nowhere. She knows I'm not going nowhere . . . so why get married [right now]?"

Patrick goes on to mention derisively an infamous north suburban Philadelphia wedding "salon," Yerkes, which, in the 1950s and 1960s, did a thriving business in shotgun weddings. The chapel still offers the services of a justice of the peace for as little as $80. Few local couples marry at Yerkes these days, but back then a Yerkes wedding was traditionally followed by case of beer shared with friends. Patrick declares, "I'm not gonna go to *Yerkes* and get a *case* . . . I want a *wedding*. If I wanted to go to Yerkes and get married, I could set it up for next week! I wanna get engaged, wait a couple of years, get a house, get stable . . . " In short, Patrick, who is the social father of one child and about to become the biological father of another, wants to do things right when it comes to marriage. Deena vehemently agrees. "[I'm going to] make sure my kids are happy. I want my kids to be stable before I do anything to alter their lives. . . . I wanna have an established environment for my kids so that my kids are happy, my kids are healthy, they're safe, they have their own house, their own toys, their own couch, their own television."

It is obvious, though, that Deena's enthusiasm for marriage has been dampened by the pain of past experience. She says, "Why get married? There's too much stuff that happens to all of those relationships. Honestly, my experience . . . I was with somebody for four years, engaged, had a kid, and then I wasn't with him. I'm not gonna do nothing, like make any promises that I'm not gonna be able to keep." Both Deena and Patrick say they worry that a premature marriage might put undue pressure on the relationship and could lead to a breakup. She says, "I don't want my son and daughter to go through see[ing] us split up. I want them to have a very good childhood."

We ask Deena what she thinks makes for a good marriage. She replies, "Somewhere where you're not getting cheated on and you're happy. If I get married, yeah, if I get married, I ain't gonna *dare* get cheated on 'cause I'll kill the guy. I got cheated on before and I don't like the way it feels." As for Patrick, Deena says she will marry him, but not yet, because she doesn't know what's going to happen. She explains, "Like I said to Patrick the other day, 'You might fall in love with somebody walking down the street and not even know it, you know what I mean? You could wanna be with that person forever. You might say that [you'll be with me forever] now because you're in love with me. But things *happen*—there's people that might alter your relationships.' I've had that happen to me plenty of times."

Avoiding marriage, at least for now, allows Deena more time to ensure the relationship is impervious to these threats before subjecting it to the higher standard a marriage requires. For the present, she feels she must guard her heart rather than get her hopes up, as she did with Kevin Sr. She says she learned an important lesson from her failed relationship with her son's father. "I keep my expectations really, really low now. I don't wanna build my family, [get married] and then all of a sudden get a phone call [with somebody telling me] 'I'm with your man.' '*Wait* a minute, I had all these . . . *expectations!* I have a happy family! We got two kids . . . this wasn't supposed to happen!' And then I'll be stuck."

Deena then reveals that though she both hopes and plans to marry Patrick, she insists on hedging her bets by having an income and some assets of her own. "I'm gonna make sure I have my *own* stability [before I marry]. I mean, because they're *my* kids. I don't care who the fathers are, they're mine. For the rest of my life they're gonna be my kids, and I'm gonna have to take care of them, with or without their fathers."

Why do Deena and Patrick view marriage as more risky than having a child together? Isn't raising children at least as difficult as being married? Why don't their decisions about whether to have a child and whether to get married seem to go together? Why, after several years of fidelity, does mistrust seem so palpable? What makes both Deena and Patrick feel that their relationship—which they both rate as strong—may prove too fragile to sustain the demands of marriage? Why does Deena keep her expectations so low when her love for Patrick and his love for her and for Kevin Jr. seem so sure? Why do they need such a long list of middle-class accoutrements, like a house, a lawn, a car, a couch, a TV, and a "nice" wedding, in order to get married? Aren't they living as a married couple, albeit on a couch in the front room, already?

Like this PennsPort couple, seven in ten new unmarried mothers believe the chances are good to certain that they'll marry their child's father, at least at the magic moment of birth.[1] However, current statistics also suggest that Deena and Patrick's chances of realizing their dreams are slim. Fewer than one in six nonmarital births will eventually lead to a marriage between the parents, though seven in ten mothers who give birth outside of marriage will marry someone one day.[2]

"WAIT TILL YOU'RE THIRTY OR FORTY TO HAVE CHILDREN? I DON'T THINK SO!"

The high rates of nonmarital childbearing in low-income neighborhoods like PennsPort have led some observers to charge that marriage has lost all meaning in impoverished communities. In fact, the meaning of marriage has changed profoundly over the last half century for *all* Americans.[3] In the 1950s childrearing was the primary function of marriage. But for many low-income mothers today, childbearing and marriage have little relation to one another.[4] Though virtually every mother we spoke with said she thought a woman should wait to marry until her schooling is complete and she has established a career—somewhere between the ages of twenty-five and forty—many believe that the ideal time for childbearing is between the late teens and mid-twenties.[5] Linnea, an African American mother of an eighteen-year-old and a newborn, who is now thirty-eight, exclaims, "Wait till you're thirty or forty [to have children]? I don't think so!"

The gap between childbearing and marriage is most evident among our African American mothers, a difference we attempt to explain in our conclusion. Nell, a thirty-five-year-old mother of three, also thinks one should be thirty or forty before marriage. She cautions her daughters: "Wait. Wait till you finish being out there in the world, exploring . . . yourself and other people." Dorothy, a thirty-six-year-old African American with two children, ages five and eleven, says, "You should finish school. If [I] had to [name an] age . . . twenty. I don't know, probably twenty-five." However, Dorothy believes that marriage should wait until one is "I'd say thirty. . . . At twenty-five, you know, you still might want to go out with your friends." She explains, "When you get married, your life stops changing."

Shante, a seventeen-year-old African American mother of a newborn, tells us, "I guess about thirty-five. Because I guess a lot of people want to go to college after they get out of high school. So that's four years. . . . And after that . . . you wanna have a nice job, get promoted, this and that, get your career going. Nice house and . . . whatever." However, her views about the ideal time for marriage also reveal that a young woman should be sure she's had her fun, for marriage is about settling down to serious business. She says, "Have fun by yourself and then just explore. . . . Especially the people who want to travel a lot [need to] do all their traveling and then come home to settle down. That's when you're like thirty, thirty-five years old. . . . You got maybe another fifty more years before you're about to die." Melissa, a white nineteen-year-old mother of one child, age three, says people should marry "when they're forty. This way you've got everything situated and you know what you're getting into by then." She then pauses, and reflects, "I guess the kids come first. I don't know, I guess that's just the way it goes."

One particularly interesting story regarding the timing of marriage comes from Natasha, a seventeen-year-old African American mother of an infant, whose own mother joins our conversation in mid-course. This forty-two-year-old grandmother warns Natasha against an early marriage because she "didn't live her life yet," but says she herself is now ready to marry because she's had all the fun there is to have. "The best time to get married is past forty. . . . If y'all wanna cheat, whatever, ya'll done all that at a younger age. Once you get past forty it ain't nothing else out there. Then you're supposed to be ready to settle, like what I'm getting ready to do. I'm forty-two and getting married in August. . . . I done did everything, you know what I'm saying? We tired. Ain't nobody looking for nothing else. Ain't nobody looking for no other man or woman. We tired now so we gonna marry each other. Don't get married right now 'cause you didn't live your life. How do you know that might be the only man or woman you wanna be with over the years?" Eighteen-year-old Elaine, however, cautions that one shouldn't wait too long for marriage. This African American mother of an eight-month-old says, "The best time to get married is before you start getting old, before you start aging. That's when I wanna get married, before I start aging. So I'll probably get married . . . near my thirties. I don't wanna get no later than thirty-five to get married. I do not wanna spend my old days by myself."

"SOMETHING TO FALL BACK ON"

Poor women are not disinterested in marriage, quite the contrary. But many, like Michelle, the thirty-one-year-old African American mother of a seven-year-old and four-year-old twins, say, "I'm not rushing into anything." Though a man with a steady low-wage job might be good boyfriend material, or even worthy of a long-term commitment, such a job doesn't usually render him "marriageable." Marriage is not so much about the bare-bones economic ability to support an independent household as it is about the capacity to sustain a respectable lifestyle. Marriage ought to be reserved for couples who've already "made it" economically, and who demonstrate their worth by acquiring the symbols of modest success: a mortgage, a house with some furniture, a car or two, and enough left over to put on a "decent" wedding. The adherence to the marriage norm, albeit on their terms, is more than mere lip service to a middle-class ideal. Today, more than 70 percent of women who give birth outside of marriage still marry by age forty, even though it is seldom to their first child's father.[6]

Michelle thinks she and her boyfriend of eight years, who has fathered all three of her children, will be married in about a year and a half. She has a year of college under her belt and a stable $16,000-a-year job at a telephone company. Within the year, her $8-per-hour wage could grow to $10. Soon, she plans to return to college part-time to finish her accounting degree, which will mean even more money. When her boyfriend gets out of prison next month, he plans to return to his managerial job at a copy store chain, where he makes a decent salary. She offers this vision of the future: "Two years from now, I see myself maybe at a higher position . . . making more money and [having] my own house— a marriage, my own car, and my family." Her dreams of marriage, a house, and a car go together.

Though women feel that having enough income to purchase the props of a respectable lifestyle is a crucial prerequisite for marriage, the money need not—and, in fact, ought not—to come solely, or even mostly, from the man. Unlike women of earlier generations, poor women today almost universally reject the idea that marriage means financial reliance on a male breadwinner. Furthermore, it is vitally important that both they and their male partners be economically set prior to marriage.[7] Champagne, a seventeen-year-old African American mother of a six-month-old, explains that she'll get married "after everything is situated the way I want it to be situated, then I'll be ready to get married. After I have a house and a car and everything, and I'm financially stable, got a job and everything and can pay [for the wedding]." Note Champagne's use of the word "I," not "we." Low-income women are waging a war of the sexes in the domestic sphere, and they believe their own earnings and assets are what buys them power. Equally important, these material things provide insurance against a marriage gone bad.[8] Most are strongly opposed to divorce and see marriage as risky and the hazard of divorce high.

Women like Deena reason that if they have a reliable income and hold title, or partial title, to assets such as a house and a car, they can control their mate's behavior with the threat—spoken or not—that they'll end the marriage and remove the children if their husband cheats, beats them, fails to stay working, or tries to make all the decisions. Twenty-two-year-old Stephanie, a Puerto Rican mother of three children under the age of six, thinks financial independence means freedom from the dominating behavior of a husband. "I think you should get married after you finish school and you have a good degree, making good money, where you can have your own place, and you don't have to have a man that's always behind you telling you what to do and how to do it." And, she adds, if they divorce, she's not "left with nothing." These women believe that getting married to a man and living off of his earnings practically ensures an imbalance of power they'll find intolerable. By waiting until both they and their male partner have "arrived" economically, they hope to establish within marriage the partnership of equals they desire.

Not only do Deena and others like her want the good job, they also expect a house and a car; in fact they might even insist on having the title to these possessions in their names. Most feel strongly that they need some insurance against a marital failure. Even when things between Jen Burke and her boyfriend Rick (see chapter 3) were especially good, Jen said she wouldn't marry him until she had a stable job and a house "in my name." She explains, "If we got a divorce, that would be my house. I bought that house. . . . He can't kick me out." Keisha, an African American mother of a one-year-old, who is about to turn twenty, says, "I wanna have a nice job, that I know if he walked out I have something to fall back on. That mortgage—everything—is in my name. That's how I wanted it to be."

Not all women insist that the assets must be solely in their name, but most still require a sense of economic independence before marriage. Seventeen-year-old Stella, an African American mother of a one-year-old, plans to marry her child's father but hedges, "We are still young. My plans are to go to college and get my career straight before . . . I make any commitments. Even though we can be together now, I want to be able to support my daughter independently [before we get married]. If things do not work out the way we want them to, I want to be able to do what I need to do for her without being stuck waiting for his help." Marie, a white thirty-five-year-old with three middle-schoolers, agrees: "I think you should have your own self established, definitely. . . . Realistically, it doesn't matter how religious [you are], the reality is, marriages end. So, yeah, you definitely should have your own life just in case."

The desire to "stay working" while married also reflects the belief that since wages for men are often low, and job tenure is uncertain, the man shouldn't be expected to provide all the money. Irene, a forty-four-year-old African American mother of three grown children and two teens, tells us, "I think both of yous should be working because two incomes is always better than one. [Women] shouldn't put the whole responsibility on the husband unless he got a real good job. Other than that, both of us should be working." Patricia agrees. This thirty-one-year-old African American mother of four, ages five to sixteen, says she wants "a nice job so I can help him. I don't believe in just sitting home. That's not fair."

"JUST A LITTLE SECURITY"

Though women spoke at great length about the need to establish their own financial stability before marriage, it almost went without saying that any prospective husband should also have achieved some measure of economic stability as well. Carol, a white forty-year-old mother of two grown children and a seven-year-old, says a marriageable man has "gotta be somebody that's got money." Dominique, whose story we tell in the next chapter, is an African American who is thirty-four and the mother of three children, seven, nine, and fourteen. She insists, "He would have to have a job. . . . You have to have a job! You don't have to take *care* of me . . . but you have to have a means for *something!*" Twenty-one-year-old Cerena, an African American mother of a four-year-old, says she wants "a [nice] home, and both [of us ought to] at least have a good job." But, she qualifies, "you ain't gotta be rich to get married though. My mom always told me [that]." Nell agrees, "It's not just the money. . . . I'm willing to struggle, you know? I'm willing to struggle if the love is there." Marie tells us that the financial security she hopes she and her baby's father can attain before marriage is also quite modest. "Not much, not much, just enough to be semi-secure."

Poor women believe that couples who wish to marry must be able to afford the things that provide this sense of security. This is what Deena Vallas's boyfriend Patrick means when he says he wants to do things right when it comes to marriage. But a young couple that wants to marry "the right way" often feel they must also save up for a "real" wedding, as both Deena and Patrick did. Nikki, an eighteen-year-old African American mother of a newborn, says she doesn't want "like nothing big or fancy or something like that. I do want it in a big church though. I want it in a big church. I just want everything [to be right]. I want the works."[9] Tina, who is white, twenty-one, and the mother of an eighteen-month-old, defends her choice to have children first and save marriage for later by saying, "I think everyone's having kids first and then getting married. A lot of people look down on it. 'Oh, well, you have a kid and you're not married!' I'm with the guy, I live with him, we're gonna get married, we talked about it, I just want a very big, nice wedding. That's how I want it."

Having the wherewithal to throw a "big" wedding is a vivid display that the couple has achieved enough financial security to do more than live from paycheck to paycheck, a stressful situation that most believe leads almost inevitably to divorce. Hosting a "proper" wedding is a sign that the couple only plans to do it once, given the obvious financial sacrifice required. Nineteen-year-old Rasheeda, an African American mother of a one-year-old, says, "He's been trying for the longest time to get his money together . . . because I want a big [wedding]. I'm only doing it once! I'm only getting married once."

Though our mothers also used terms like "elaborate" and "big" and even "the works" to describe the weddings they want, few truly envision a "show" or "storybook" wedding. Rather, they usually want a church wedding, complete with a wedding dress, perhaps a few bridesmaids and groomsmen, and a modest reception for a few family members and friends at a local hall or church basement. As these modest affairs cost just a few thousand dollars, most couples believe they can save for them. Ashley, a white mother of three school-aged children in her late twenties, says, "Right now we're getting our credit straightened out, paying off any debts. . . . Then we'll start saving money for our wedding. . . . [Not] something really big, but, you know, we want to save for it." Marie, mentioned several times earlier, whose better-off kin have hosted the South Philly "show" for their daughters, says she is far too practical to aspire to an extravagant "Tony and Tina" affair. "I guess everybody wants a nice wedding. . . . If I were to ever get married again, I would make sure I had a nice wedding. [But] as far as, like, them big extravagant, $30,000 deals, that's like half of a city house! I mean, you can buy a nice car with $30,000!"

Mothers often mock the actions of girls from better-off families who insist on having a "big show." Marilyn, a white twenty-four-year-old with two children, ages four and five, who grew up in the Italian enclave in South Philadelphia, jokes, "Tony and Tina's wedding, yeah yeah. . . . It's a prestige thing. It's a big show. You spend that $20,000, $30,000, then you get divorced." Brenda, a white twenty-six-year-old with one child, age seven, also derides young girls who demand "storybook weddings": "Some girls are, like, they want the storybook wedding, like they want the fancy dresses, the bridesmaids, like nine or ten of them, the limos and the Mercedes, and stuff like that." Even though few want a "show," getting married in a church, rather than in front of a justice of the peace, is a key way in which young couples aspire to demonstrate their seriousness with regard to the marriage vows. Thirty-three-year-old Chanel, a white mother of three, ages fifteen, nine, and three, who is divorced from her older children's father but was not married to the father of her youngest child, relates, "When I get married, I want to get married in the church and all. I never had that. My first wedding wasn't in the church or nothing [and he didn't take it seriously]." Elizabeth not only aspires to demonstrate her seriousness about marriage with a church wedding, but also by wearing white on her wedding day. This eighteen-year-old Puerto Rican mother of two children, ages two and four, is pregnant again. She has been with her children's father for over five years and is planning to marry soon. "I said to my mom, 'I'm wearing a white dress.' She says, 'Yeah, you just can't wear the . . . veil.' When you wear a veil it's because you're considered a virgin. . . . The pastor's daughter, she got married and she didn't wear a veil, she just wore like a little crown because she has a daughter already."

"HE'S GONNA SAY HE OWNS ME."

Though women like Deena Vallas seem to genuinely aspire to marriage, they fear marriage will alter the balance of power they've achieved in the relationship so far and activate more traditional sex roles their male partners tend to hold.[10] When Jen Burke was still together with Rick, she shared this concern. "He [already] tells me I can't do nothing, I can't go out. What's gonna happen when I marry him? He's gonna say he *owns* me." Dorothy, the African American mother of a kindergartener and sixth grader, offers an almost identical story. "When a man marry, I think they think they in *control* or something. . . . Like Jerome, like he tells me, 'You gotta listen to the man . . . 'cause in the Bible it says, "You obey the man,"' or whatever. Some stuff. I'm not even *married* to him, you know!" Patricia complains that husbands want someone to wait on them hand and foot. Aleena, a white seventeen-year-old mother of a two-year-old, has a similarly dim view of men's behavior after marriage. "[People don't want to be married] because the man thinks that he can rule the woman. I think it's trying to be like the Stone Age, you know, just grab them by the hair and drag them down the street. That's exactly the way they treat their women nowadays, you know. 'She's *my* woman, don't you touch [her] or I'll beat you with my night stick,' or something. That's not right."

Keisha is avoiding marriage for precisely this reason. "I never wanted to get married because I'd never wanted to be tied down with a person try to be over me, like trying to be my *boss* or something." Aleena, mentioned above, thinks women ought to be wary when it comes to marriage because "then they gonna regret it because their husband's gonna think that they own them. That's the problem with most of these guys now, because they figure that they own the girls. 'She's my wife, she ain't doing this 'cause I *said* so. . . . ' That's exactly the way he is, you know, 'She's mine, don't you touch her.' "

Azariah, forty-two, a Puerto Rican mother of ten children ages three to nineteen, believes it is difficult to predict how a man will behave within marriage just by living with him for a few months. She cautions, "Don't rush into nothing, because when you live with them, it's different than when you marry them. . . . When you live with them, you could do more things. When you get married, you have to do what they want you to do. [Now] I say, 'No! You do what you want, I do what I want!' " Some mothers are so firmly convinced that marriage corrupts men's behavior that they believe a marriage will almost inevitably ruin a relationship. Tatiana, an African American twenty-two-year-old with three children under seven, says, "I believe that [marriage] just messes [up relationships]. I mean, some men believe they own the woman after that. It's bad enough when you go through problems [when you're not married]!"

Fears about marriage activating traditional sex roles in men are especially strong for the Puerto Rican women we spoke with. Twenty-three-year-old Demi, who has a two-year-old and a six-month-old, says the men in her community seem to be consumed by sexual jealousy once girlfriends become wives. "I feel like when you get married, then it seems like, 'Oh, he *owns* you now.' That's how I grew up, seeing women, they get married, and all of a sudden, everything changes. . . . The communications stops, and the guy is more protective, starts getting jealous. She starts getting beat on. She can't go anywhere. It's like he'll tell you you can't do this or you can't do that. So it's like you have no free life anymore."

Gloria, a new mother at sixteen, is already saying, "I don't wanna get married [now] because I know a lot of stuff you gotta go through, being locked down. Like some guys, they want you in all the time. . . . That's how they are. They want you in, and you can't wear certain clothes. You gotta wear what they want you to wear. Maybe later down the line, when I meet the right person who's not bossy [I'll want to get married]." When we ask her why she thinks it's important to the men in her neighborhood to keep their wives in, she responds, "Sometimes they think that other men are gonna take [their wives] away from them."

While our Puerto Rican mothers seem especially fearful that marriage will lead to controlling behavior on the part of their husbands, mothers across all three racial and ethnic groups share the more general view that marriage changes things for the worse. Twenty-six-year-old Yolanda, a Puerto Rican mother of two preschoolers, admits, "Marriage is something that's always scary to me. That's why I've never married their dad, and I don't know if I will. . . . I mean, he's *good* enough, but I'm always scared. Because a lot of people who've [been] living common law, when they got married, the relationship changes." Similarly, Ashley tells us, "I have a lot of people, . . . they've been together for so long, it was great, and they got married. And now a year later, it's like they want to split up. It's like . . . the marriage license is *taboo* or something." A white mother of five adult children and a teenager, Elena, who is now fifty-six, married and then divorced the father of her children. When we ask her if she knew about her ex-husband's violent temper beforehand, she replies, "No, I didn't. It just came on through the marriage. . . . My mother said . . . sooner or later his true colors gonna have to come out, and boy, she was *right*."

"THE VOWS TELL YOU EVERYTHING."

Marriage means far more than a celebration of financial achievements. Poor women almost universally believe that marriage should be for life, and deride others who "get married just to get divorced." Most believe that the marriage vows are sacred and ought to be held in the highest regard. The religious and irreligious alike believe that violating these vows through divorce is a sacrilege.[11] Millie, a twenty-seven-year-old Puerto Rican mother of three featured in chapter 6, says, "I'm very religious, so yeah, I know its wrong for you to live without marriage, because that's one of the commandments. . . . Spiritually, I feel like I'm living in sin. I'm living in fornication. . . . But I'm not ready [to marry] in the fact that I wanna make sure that this [marriage] is gonna be a *lifetime*, that it's gonna be *forever*. Nothing lasts forever, so you have to be realistic. But . . . if I'm gonna get married to him, I would like for this to be my last relationship. . . . I would give this relationship more time before I would take that step further."

Few of our mothers are as religiously devout as Millie, and many aren't religious at all, yet most condemn mainstream American culture for treating marriage casually, as nothing more than "a piece of paper." Twenty-year-old Beatrice, a Puerto Rican mother of a three-month-old, has no connection to her Catholic background, yet she says, "Before I get married I gotta make sure that he's the perfect one, because I'm not gonna get married and then have to get divorced in two or three years, you understand? If I get married, I wanna be with this person for the rest of my life. I don't wanna just get married and then our relationship goes wrong, then I have to go and get a *divorce!*" Sam, twenty-one, a white, lapsed Catholic with a four-year-old son, wants a "perfect" marriage too, but is doubtful, given her own history of abuse by her son's father, now in prison for murder. (He fatally stabbed a Puerto Rican man who wandered onto their staunchly white block and then burned the man's body.) "I would *love* to have a marriage, a perfect one, like in the fairy tales. I'd love to have that. But I don't think it really happens. All the experiences I've had, never happened, so maybe that's why I feel that way."

If they can't be sure the marriage will last for a lifetime, many conclude they don't want marriage at all. Marilyn's story places these choices most clearly on the moral hierarchy that residents of poor communities have forged. She says, "I don't wanna have a big trail of divorce, you know. I'd rather say, 'Yes, I had my kids out of wedlock' than say, 'I married *this* idiot.' It's like a *pride* thing." Yet many others still dream of a lasting marriage and hold on to hope. Chelsea, a white thirty-six-year-old who has given three children up for adoption and raised three more (now nineteen, seventeen, and six), says wistfully, "You have your old-timers that have been married twenty-five to thirty years. . . . I seen a couple the other day, I was shopping at K-Mart . . . [and] I see these old people holding hands and giggling. It was a cold day and they were just the *happiest*. That brought tears to my eyes. *That's* what *I* want."[12]

Fears about making a lifetime promise they can keep resound in these women's stories. Nikki insists, "The vows tell you everything. You have to be there for that person till death do you part. To love, honor, and obey. When you get to a marriage you have to understand that it's a *big step* that you are taking and that is the person that you have chosen to be with for the rest of your *life*. If you really know the words 'the rest of your life' and you start getting that voice in the back of your head, 'Oh, that's a long time!' Maybe you shouldn't get married."

"I'M NOT RUSHING INTO ANYTHING."

Mothers contemplating marriage expect a high level of personal and relational maturity from themselves and their partners, one that may take years to attain.[13] Eunice, a white forty-two-year-old from PennsPort who has five children ranging in age from thirteen to twenty-five, the youngest by her partner of sixteen years, admonishes, "When you take your vows . . . up at that altar, I think the vows are very sacred. And if you . . . are not going to abide by them, I don't think that you should get married." Eunice thinks the ideal time to marry is "after you have been in a relationship . . . five or six years. Because then by that time you know *him* and he knows *you.*" After more than a decade and a half together, she and her partner are finally "going through the paperwork" so they can get married. She says, "It's time. Neither one of us is . . . going nowhere and we have two children together and so therefore we should be married, *legally*, as husband and wife."

A young mother who wants to show her community she's taking the moral high road ought not to even think about marriage until she has carefully mulled over the merits of the decision for years. Meanwhile, she must constantly monitor the relationship for any sign of vulnerability to trouble. Twenty-four-year-old Linda, a Puerto Rican mother of a four-year-old daughter and a son who is almost two, proudly says she is one of those people who take marriage seriously, rather than treating it as "just a piece of paper." "Look at me. I been with my boyfriend for *six years* and we have *two kids* and *I'm* not ready yet for marriage!" Sandra, a twenty-one-year-old Puerto Rican mother of a five-year-old and an eighteen-month-old, shares these high standards. "I wouldn't marry with somebody unless I know that person very good. I need like four years. Look, I lived five years with my boyfriend and never wanted to get married because . . . I thought he was going to change, but he never did. . . . *I* don't go to the church and say I wanna *marry* some guy and then later on I'm going to break *up! No!*"

Only fifteen, Jessica, a Puerto Rican mother of a two-year-old, has already internalized the belief that it takes years of careful monitoring to ensure the relationship is not vulnerable to the threats that so often topple the relationships she's seen. "Before I even get married, I'll be with the guy for a long time, see if he ever play me wrong. . . . If he treats me bad, he play me wrong, he don't do the things I need . . . abuse me, hit me, . . . cheat on me and stuff, [I can leave]. You do it *now*, wait till you get *married!*" Whatever you gonna do it worser. [He'll think,] 'Oh yeah, *I* got the *key* in the lock, you're [mine]!' " Megan, twenty-seven, a white mother of two children, four and nine, explains, "I don't wanna show him that I wanna be his wife when I don't [have him acting the way I want him to], you know what I mean—and then he gets worse or something when I'm married. . . . I wanna fix him up [now]! Maybe if he changes, *then* we'll get married."

Women often stick with their partners for years, hoping for a transformation, waiting to marry until the change comes. Pamela, a fifty-year-old white mother of seven children ranging in age from fourteen to twenty-eight, who has been with her children's father for thirteen years, says, "My fear with Karl is—I love him, I know I love him, God, do I know I love him—but . . . he's still not perfect. If I could have my way and mold him to be what I want him to be, it would be a different story." When we ask these mothers how long one needs to wait in order to ensure it is safe to marry, estimates generally start at around four or five years. Twenty-year-old Caroline, an African American mother of one child, age four, says it takes about six years. Aleena agrees, saying she would want five or six years "just to make sure things work out." Nineteen-year-old Tasha, an African American mother of a child who is three, thinks it might take as much as ten years: "It takes a long time to really know somebody. You have to get deep on they background, everything else, get their Social Security numbers, because they'll [lie to] you. . . . You have to know a person inside . . . because it's not gonna work [otherwise]."

While most poor young women believe strongly that a couple should wait for five or more years for marriage, some have wed in haste in the past, and still more know young couples who they feel have married prematurely. Nearly everyone has a morality tale to tell of two fools who rushed into marriage only to divorce. Sarah Lee, an African American twenty-two-year-old mother of a seven-year-old and a new baby, believes that some of these foolish couples are motivated by love, but feels that love is not enough to sustain a marriage. She attributes the high divorce rate to the following cause: "They [are getting divorced because] they are rushing into getting married. . . . They just figure they are in *love* and they just rush and go ahead and get married, and then get divorced!" Young women condemn such behavior as extremely irresponsible, and some even insist that it makes a mockery of a sacred institution.

The harshest condemnation is reserved for those who marry because of pregnancy. Such marriages, they believe, are almost certain to end in divorce, and thus benefit neither the couple nor the child. Brenda says, "Just because you get *pregnant*, I don't think you should just rush into getting *married* because to me if you do things like that I think you have a worse chance of breaking up." Eighteen-year-old Elaine, an African American mother of a eight-month-old, sneers, "Some people don't want their babies to be bastards, or whatever. . . . Since the girl might be pregnant, they'll get married because of that. . . . Now it's like you don't *have* to get married. Do what you wanna do!"

Readiness for marriage is partly about age, as seventeen-year-old Shante, the African American mother of a brand-new baby, tells us. "He bought me an engagement ring. . . . I was excited because I was so young." Then, she says, an older man, one who was married himself, told her, "'You're too *young* to be married . . . !' I was like, 'What [this guy says is] true.' I'm only seventeen! I shouldn't be wanting to settle down with nobody. I mean, I'm still young! I should be able to just get up and date whoever I want, and go out any time I want, and not have to worry about, 'Well, I have the baby and my *husband's* waiting for me. . . . ' I guess I'm going to have to be married [eventually] but marriage is like, it's too much. It's like a husband is always there. Like one man, just one man that you with forever and ever and ever! No! Not yet!" She exclaims, "Maybe when I'm like forty . . . because then, who wants to date a forty-year-old? You have no choice but to get married [then]. You have to find somebody to settle down with before [nobody wants you anymore]."

These young women, like their counterparts nationwide, believe the teenage and early adult years ought to be a time of experimentation, when young people should not undertake the adult roles of husband and wife. Finding one's self and having one's fun before getting on with the serious business of adulthood are the primary tasks of these years. Shawndel, age twenty-five, is an African American mother of two children, three and five years old. She says one should marry "between the ages of twenty-seven, twenty-eight to thirty, like that. Because you don't wanna get married when you are too young and you ain't finished partying and going to clubs and stuff." Nell says the right age is "thirty-five to forty. . . . Wait till you finish being out there in the world, exploring—whatever you wanna call it—with yourself, other people you know." The obvious irony in this social construction of youth is that these young women have already taken on what most Americans consider the most significant adult social role of their lifetimes, that of a parent.

For Tamika, an African American nineteen-year-old with a three-year-old child, being ready for marriage involves being willing to settle for what you've got, rather than hoping that something better will come along. "A lot of people are not ready for that commitment [of] spending the rest of their lives with that person. . . . Maybe because they want to meet somebody else that can be better than that person." Many women we spoke with believe that adolescence is an unsettled time when young people wander in and out of romantic relationships because that is simply the nature of youth. The solution to this problem for those who want to marry is just to wait this phase out. Twenty-one-year-old Celeste, a white mother of a five-month-old, says, "I guess [marriage] comes when you're ready. When you think the time is right. When you're in a relationship where you love that person and you won't wanna be with anybody else and you know that things can work out."

Young women also believe that they must be complete in their personhood before entering into marriage, rather than look to the relationship to provide that wholeness. To marry before that is to be disingenuous, because the changes that may be required to achieve wholeness could destabilize the relationship. Marilyn says, "Be set in your career. Have yourself whole. Make sure you're a whole person, and you've done what you wanna do as a single person before you bring another person into your life." Paula, forty, a Puerto Rican mother of a fifteen-year-old, says, "Get *out* there, see the *world*. *Travel*, you know. Know what you *want* out of life before you say 'I do.'" Marriage to these mothers represents not only the end of one's youth, but also the end of one's dreams for social mobility. When they get to where they are going in terms of financial success, career aspirations, and other life goals, and they feel there is no more to achieve, then it's time to get married. For young women with few skills and other resources, it is indeed true that these aspirations, even if leveled over time by experience, are unlikely to be fulfilled before middle age.

"YOU CAN'T GET A DECENT MAN
YOU CAN REALLY, REALLY TRUST."

Christine, a thirty-seven-year-old African American mother of a fifteen-year-old daughter and a two-year-old son, voices the ambivalence of many poor women toward the men in their lives in her simple statement, "Truthfully, most men . . . now are not trustworthy." Brehanna, just sixteen, an African American mother of a one-year-old, offers this assessment of the problem with marriage in her community: "Guys . . . really make me really sick. You just can't trust them anymore, you can't get a decent man you can really, really trust."[14]

Mistrust seems to permeate the very air in these neighborhoods. Some of it is born of harsh childhood circumstances. But the hard times that often come with a pregnancy and birth can transform hopeful naïveté into cynicism. Thus a young mother often feels a powerful need to guard her heart. Thirty-four-year-old Dominique, an African American mother of three (see chapter 5), can't forget the hard times she experienced with the volatile and sometimes violent father of her children, even though he seems to have reformed. When we ask her if they have talked about marriage, she responds, "Actually, he asked me and I turned him down. . . . Things I had gone through with him were always there. People say, 'Just forgive and forget.' But you can't forget those things. . . . When you go through so much with somebody [you wonder,] 'Will I be happy *forever* . . . ?' I didn't wanna take a chance with that."

Men are more likely to raise the question of marriage than women are, if mothers' accounts are accurate, and they are far more favorably disposed to the idea of marriage in general. We were surprised by the number of women who said they had turned down marriage proposals, at least for the time being.[15] Rebecca, a white twenty-three-year-old mother with three children, ages six, four, and three, has a stable eight-year relationship with her children's father, a pizza maker. He's asked her repeatedly to marry him, and she's refused him each time. "He ask me like four times. I said no. I'm not marrying. I mean, like maybe one day I'll feel comfortable and I will. I'm just not at the point yet."

Becoming comfortable with the idea of marriage is about trust—the astonishing lack of it in most couple relationships, and the profound need for it in order to sustain a marriage.[16] Young women find it difficult to trust their children's fathers in a wide variety of areas: they don't trust them to remain faithful, to stay working, to pay their share of the bills, to not beat them or abuse their children, to stay out of trouble with the law, and to stay free of addiction to alcohol and drugs. Mistrust is most often rooted in fears of infidelity. Patricia, the thirty-one-year-old African American mother of four, says, "They think they are supposed to have more than one girlfriend, making kids all over the place. It's hard to have someone be yours this day and age, just all yours. . . . Back [in the old days] you get married . . . [you] stay together until you're old and gray. You be two wrinkled prunes watching TV together at nighttime. It's not like that now." Women like Patricia therefore insist that their men demonstrate a strong track-record of sexual fidelity as a precondition for marriage. Lorelei, a thirty-nine-year-old African American mother of two children, ages one and three, agrees. "You can't really trust them, most guys now. . . . I don't want no relationship [where] the first woman he [sees] turns his head, [and] you are all packed up and leaving. . . . I'm afraid that would happen. That's the only reason why I would never get married at this point."

Though some believe a relationship can survive a one-night stand, most feel that cheating is seldom a one-time event, but rather a habitual pattern rooted in a personality trait that leads a man to repeat the behavior over time. Jen Burke has learned this lesson the hard way and now believes that any woman who marries a "cheater" is in for heartbreak, no matter how apparently sincere his subsequent change of heart. When she discovered Rick in an affair during her second pregnancy, she chose to break up with him rather than marry him, as he wanted. She explains, "You're supposed to be faithful if you're gonna get married. That's why I'm not getting married, because [of the] cheating. . . . If you get married [and he's already] cheating on you, it's not gonna be [a] faithful [marriage]. Somebody's gonna get hurt, it's gonna be you."

Though chronic infidelity is deemed unacceptable in any committed relationship, nearly everyone agrees that it's worse within marriage. After all, some remind us, the traditional wedding vows include a promise to "forsake all others." A marriage ceremony signifies that the couple has reached a point where both partners are willing to live up to their vows. The community thus holds married couples to a higher standard of behavior than their unmarried counterparts. Equally important, however, is that the pair expect more of themselves. In some sense, marriage is a form of social bragging about the quality of the couple relationship, a powerfully symbolic way of elevating one's relationship above others in the community, particularly in a community where marriage is rare. Thus, a young couple who contemplates marriage must run the risk that if the relationship is not up to the standard, they stand the chance of becoming the ultimate fools.

Sandy, seventeen and a white mother of a two-year-old, is hard-pressed to explain why she believes infidelity within marriage is so much worse: "Because that's your *husband!*" she exclaims. "You *committed!* [With] a boyfriend, you not supposed to [cheat] either. [But it's] different, because that's your husband. It's just different." The promise of fidelity is, in some ways, the very definition of marriage for these young women. Maria, a twenty-one-year-old Puerto Rican mother of a four-month-old, says, "[Being ready means] committed . . . committed to your relationship. You don't have nobody else. It's just you and her." Laura, a twenty-year-old African American mother of two children, two and nearly one, agrees. "You can't be free and be married at the *same time!* You can't *do* that, can't be with this person, then go back home to your husband or your wife. . . . I think you're supposed to stick to your vows or go see a counselor."

"NOT ANYONE FROM *THIS* NEIGHBORHOOD!"

Poor women don't usually hold their men to impossible standards. As thirty-two-year-old Lisa, a white mother of two children, ages eleven and fifteen, says, "He can't be a cheater, that's the number one. He shouldn't be the kind of guy that hangs out with his buddies four or five nights a week for three or four hours. He should be the kind of man who's ready to take care of the house and ready to work a [extra] part-time job . . . if it's needed. Basically, he has to be ready to make the family the number one priority. . . . If he's got anything else in his life that's his number one priority then he's not ready to get married." Celeste, a white twenty-one-year-old, with a five-month-old, offers a similar description of what she'd like in a husband. "[Ideally, I'd like] somebody I know that's gonna be faithful, that I don't have to worry about, that I know that'll be by my side no matter what happens, good or bad . . . [with] a good job, *going* somewhere in life." Eighteen-year-old Denise, the white mother of two-year-old twins, just wants a minimally decent man. "He would have to accept me and my kids, have a lot of respect for me, he doesn't talk to me like I'm a piece of trash, and has a good job. Not a druggie, he don't sell drugs and, like, he's not a flirt or a cheater. He's just gonna *be* there for me when I *need* him. You know, it's hard to find someone like that." She adds, "It's not that he's like, you know Arnold Schwarzenegger or whatever, but he's got to be *clean* about hisself. He has to take *care* of hisself. That's really all though, I guess, about my so-called husband." Cindi offers a similarly modest list. This white twenty-one-year-old mother of two children under four, says, "First of all, he would have to never have used drugs in his life. He would have to treat both of my kids the way I want them to be treated and not just wanna be with me, wanna be with them too. . . . I would have to meet a man that's good to me, good to my kids, and has a good job and is ready to take care of two kids that isn't his and is grown up enough to . . . [not] worry about what [his] friends say."

Of course, mothers do expect that any relationship worthy of marriage will be emotionally fulfilling as well. Kyra, an African American seventeen-year-old mother of a child nearly two, says, "I wanna be married because I feel as though then it's like [I'm on] stable ground. I know I have a partner in life that's gonna help me through things. . . . I'll always have a companion and a lover, a best friend, somebody to help me raise the kids that we have." Jerry, a thirty-five-year-old African American mother, with two children, seven and eight, also longs for the companionship she believes a good marriage can provide. "It would be nice, you know? You get lonely sometimes. You'd like to have somebody to take you out to dinner and be romantic. . . . But I don't know [if it will happen for me]. I've gone through so much." Denise also looks forward to the easy companionship a lifelong marital relationship can offer, explaining, "I want to get married though, because then you could wake up to that same person every day and, knowing that you know you can come home to that same person every day, and . . . talk about each other's days like at work or whatever."

Poor young women who put motherhood before marriage do not generally do so because they reject the institution of marriage itself, but because good, decent, trustworthy men are in short supply. Though they hope for marriage and often hold it as a central goal, most are at least somewhat skeptical that it can be achieved. Lisette, a black eighteen-year-old mother from East Camden with a three-year-old and an eighteen-month-old, says, "Truthfully, in Camden, you might not *find* one. You might have to go somewhere far away to find one, and most people are not willing to do that." Maria tells us, "I want it, yeah, but I don't think I ever will. I might not *find* the right one." Twenty-three-year-old Sonia, a Puerto Rican mother of one child, age three, who says her partner is almost maniacally controlling of her, wants "an understanding and loving man—somebody who actually *trusts* me—that's what I'm looking for. It's like a fairy tale thing now. I don't see that it's actually gonna happen but I'm looking for that man who's totally devoted to me and is understanding, [who] . . . has that undying love for me, you know. That's what *I'm* looking for. . . But I think it's a lot for me to ask for, being as though there's not much of them out there. I don't think there's such a thing as . . . Mr. Right anymore." Destiny, mentioned above, says she can't imagine a good marriage for herself. "Not with *me*. No. There's no good men. . . . There's probably some out there, but I just don't attract them, I guess, maybe because I'm [eighteen] and have two kids." When we ask twenty-three-year-old Chrissy, a white mother of a five-year-old, whether she thinks she'll find someone to marry, she exclaims, "Not anyone from *this* neighborhood!"

Despite the pervasive mistrust, women like Deena Vallas, who believe they've finally found a decent guy, still usually believe their relationship is headed for marriage. They hold marriage to a high economic standard, one requiring as much from themselves as from the men they hope to marry. Even more important are the relationship standards they hold for marriage. Though many do find men who are seemingly decent, the mistrust generated by painful past experiences means that even the most hopeful mothers approach marriage with extreme caution. Marriage, which should be for life, requires all the thought and care in the world. In the meantime, they get on with the business of creating a family.

DIVERSITY IN MARRIAGE VIEWS

Seven in ten of the mothers we spoke to clearly want to marry, though not all are confident they will find a marriageable mate. Twenty-six percent of them say they are making marriage plans now and have a relationship with a man who is seemingly in tune with these plans. An additional 40 percent are in a relationship with a man they hope to marry two, three, four, or more years into the future. The remaining third are either in no relationship at present or in a relationship with a man they fear is not "the one." This array of experiences makes up the fabric of the story we've told here.

But what about those with no such aspirations? Nearly one in five— 17 percent—adamantly tell us they do not plan to marry, and an additional 13 percent are either ambivalent or unwilling to offer an opinion one way or another. Of those opposed to the idea of marrying, more than a third (36 percent) tell stories of past abuse or infidelity, and say these traumatic experiences have made them too fearful to ever marry. Fourteen percent are too afraid of divorcing to be willing to marry. Just under a third reject marriage because they believe being single allows them to be independent rather than "tied down," or bossed around. Michelle, the thirty-one-year-old African American mother of three, says firmly, "I don't *need* a man," while forty-seven-year-old Pepper Ann, an African American mother of three, quips, "I'm having too much fun being single!" The remainder believe marriage is not worth the expense or they just don't see the point of obtaining "a piece of paper to tell us we're together."

What differentiates those who aspire to marriage from those who reject it outright? First, age is an important factor. Those under twenty-five express the desire to marry nearly 80 percent of the time, while only 60 percent of older mothers do so. This twenty-point generation gap is likely due to two other factors that differentiate these age groups. First, younger mothers are much more likely to still be in a relationship with the father of all of their children. Whereas four in ten mothers who want to marry say they are still together with the father of all of their children, only 7 percent of those who reject the notion of marriage can make that claim. Surveys also show that having children by more than one man retards marriage plans and transitions to marriage among unmarried parents.[17] Second, hardly any younger mothers have ever been married, while nearly a third of the older mothers have (appendix A shows exact figures). Twice as many of those who reject the idea of marriage have been married in the past as those who aspire to it (though, presumably, these divorcées did desire marriage at an earlier point in their lives). Surveys show too that women who have been divorced are less positive toward marriage than never-married women.[18]

There are also interesting differences in marital aspirations across our racial and ethnic groups: whereas more than two-thirds of all African American mothers say they desire marriage, fewer Puerto Rican and Caucasian mothers do.[19] Here again, there are two other noticeable differences between the groups that may explain some of these racial and ethnic group differences. First, our African American women are much more likely to be in relationships with the fathers of all their children than mothers in the other groups, and they are far less likely to have ever been married (appendix A shows the exact figures).[20] The second difference is that our Puerto Rican mothers tend to view moving in together as tantamount to a promise of lifetime commitment and eventual matrimony—a pseudo-marriage like the one Antonia Rodriguez has, where the couple "goes for" husband and wife. For this reason, one in five Puerto Rican mothers actually described themselves to us as married already, though we could find no legal basis for these unions. When we queried one such mother, she replied, "It's just something Hispanic people do when they live together."[21] This practice is by no means universal among our Puerto Rican cohabiters (about half of Puerto Rican cohabiters said they were married at first—almost always the older mothers), but it is quite common. Only a handful of African Americans or Caucasians make the same claim (see appendix A).

"I'M NOT MAKING ANY PROMISES I'M NOT GONNA BE ABLE TO KEEP."

When we ask Mahkiya Washington where she thinks her relationship with Mike will be in five years, she responds, "I don't know if we will be together [but] I hope that we will be together and married by [then]." She continues, "I hope that we are married, ... [I] went to school, graduated, . . . got a good job, . . . he went to school and graduated [too], so my daughter can have two parents as role models. . . . I don't want to have to be [in the situation where] he got another girlfriend, and I got another boyfriend. I don't want that. I don't want her to be around that 'cause I been around that. I want it to be two parents, so she will have a good role model and she knows how to bring up her family being married . . . not having different people." She concludes, "Mikey is all right, but he got a lot of maturing to do. . . . I am trying to stick in there because I want it to work."

When we discuss marriage with Antonia Rodriguez, she tells us she's "not going to get married now, but maybe in the future." Antonia has a lot she'd like to accomplish before she marries Emilio. "[First], my dream for me is to have a secure job I can count on, [with] retirement, everything else." "A lot of people are getting married [that shouldn't]," she continues. "They just love each other and they're just doing it [without thinking it through]. Just doing it for them." Antonia's strong condemnation of marrying merely for love stems from her belief that people should not marry unless they are sure they can live up to their vows.

When we interview her the first time, Jen Burke has been thinking a lot about marriage, as Rick has just proposed. She too says that both she and her boyfriend Rick have a lot of obstacles to overcome before they should embark upon marriage. Of him, she demands, "If he doesn't have a job, I want him to go get a job. . . . I think he should stay home with me and take care of [the baby], not go out and party all the time with his friends. He's gonna have to show me . . . do all that stuff before I marry him." Of herself, she demands the following: "I wanna have a real job. . . . I wanna have a nice-sized house." She clarifies, "Not a big house, just a [comfortable] one for us. I would want it to be up in the northeast [part of the city], where it's real nice at." Furthermore, as noted above, Jen wants to hold title to the house herself. She reflects, "I think about all that stuff first. I wanna have everything ready in case something goes wrong." Deena Vallas beautifully sums up these sentiments when she tells us, "I'm not gonna do nothing, like make any promises that I'm not gonna be able to keep."

While many assume that the high rate of nonmarital childbearing among residents living in high poverty areas of America's inner cities means the marriage norm is dead, our mothers say this is far from true. Despite living in a social world in which parents, siblings, and friends seldom marry, most mothers hold to the dream of marriage, and many have it as an explicit life goal. Furthermore, a substantial minority of mothers say they're now in a relationship with a man whom they think they will marry in time, though most feel that they are not ready to take that step yet. The failed past relationships of those young women living in impoverished communities, along with the pervasive distrust of men, make marriage seem risky. They mitigate this risk by holding marriage to a high standard both in economic and in relational terms—so high that many will never marry at all.

Much has been written about the retreat from marriage in recent years. Some have argued that the decline of marriage, which is most pronounced among the poor, can be traced to declining male wages. Indeed, men with a high school education or less have seen large losses in hourly wages over the last thirty years, and far fewer are able to find full-time, year-round employment. But it is clear from these stories that even if the employment and wage rates in these neighborhoods returned to their 1950s levels, in the heyday of Philadelphia's economy, the marriage rate probably wouldn't increase much. Though male wages for unskilled workers were higher in those days and jobs more plentiful, unskilled male laborers were not paid that well, and the nature of Philadelphia's system of small craft production meant that even jobholders in the 1950s still faced a highly unstable job market.

Most studies suggest that at best, declining male employment and earnings can only account for about 20 percent of the sharp downturn in marriage.[22] Our stories suggest that many of the men who would have been considered marriageable in the 1950s would not be so today, for few 1950s marriages waited on the acquisition of a home mortgage, a car, some furniture, and two solid jobs. Even fewer 1950s brides insisted on monitoring their mates' behavior over four, five, or six years' time before they believed they could trust them enough to wed.

In the 1950s, marriage equaled social personhood. Being unmarried meant being a square peg in a round hole, not able to fit into the social milieu of the community. And if marriage was deemed necessary to take one's place as a normal adult, it was even more imperative to be married in order to bear and raise children. Today, a wedding ring is no longer the passport to personhood that it once was. In a society where the middle class waits longer and longer to marry, more and more of a person's early adult years are spent single, making singleness an acceptable state. In fact, early marriage is now frowned upon as unwise in virtually all sectors of our society. Poor women clearly believe that they can be perfectly adequate adults and parents outside of marriage, though the middle class might disagree. While they recognize that marrying first and having children second is the ideal way of doing things, they don't see how they can meet that goal in their circumstances. While poor women believe strongly that a child needs two parents, they don't see why they need marriage to accomplish that goal. Couples who live together can parent as easily as those who are married. And just because a man and a woman find they can't stay together doesn't mean a man cannot still play the role of father to his child.

This does not mean that marriage has lost its significance, either for the culture as a whole or for the poor. The most fundamental truth these stories reveal is that the meaning of marriage has changed. It is no longer primarily about childbearing and childrearing. Now, marriage is primarily about adult fulfillment, it is something poor women do for themselves, and their dreams about marriage are a guilty pleasure compared to the hard tasks of raising a family. Though women living in disadvantaged social contexts often wish they could indulge in a marriage at the same time that they're raising their children, it is simply not practical for most. If a marriage is to be lasting, it must have a strong economic foundation that both partners help to build, in which the woman maintains some level of economic independence. The couple relationship must also be strong enough to overcome the problems that so frequently lead to divorce, because marriage, which most still say is sacred, involves making promises—promises to be faithful and stay together for a lifetime. And as Deena Vallas puts it, most are not willing to make promises they are not sure they can keep.

Readers may wonder why so many of these women continue to hope for marriage when the men in their lives seem to be such bad risks. As we've said earlier, these couples live in a world where the better-off men go to the better-off women. Thus, unless poor women can improve their own positions through education and work, they have no choice but to abandon the dream of marriage altogether or attempt to change the available men. For most, giving up on the possibility of marriage means abandoning the hope that their difficult economic and social situations will get better in time.

Marriage is the prize at the end of the race. Because these women live in circumstances that are often too bleak to endure without hope that someday, in some way, they can make it, they still hope for marriage. But "getting themselves together" while also trying to redeem the fathers of their children is hard work, and failure is more common than success. Yet the fact that some succeed is enough cause for hope.

FIVE

LABOR OF LOVE

DOMINIQUE WATKINS

Dominique Watkins is a quietly intense African American woman who wears her shoulder-length, straightened hair drawn away from her face in a twist. The thirty-four-year-old mother of three says she doesn't mind the long bus ride from her apartment in North Philly to her job as a teacher's aide at the Martin Luther King Jr. Middle School in the Olney neighborhood to the north and east. After all, the trip gives her precious time with her fourteen-year-old daughter, Renee, who, with her collection of stuffed-animal keychains dangling from her backpack, still has more of the air of a lighthearted child than a bored teenager. Renee—as her mother never misses a chance to tell you—is an honor student at King.

We meet on a lovely, clear day in June. Summer is fast approaching, but Dominique isn't looking forward to the break like most of the other employees at King. Her unemployment check, her only source of income in the summer months, is far less than her paycheck, and the summer is always a scramble as she tries to take classes at a local community college while piecing together adequate supervision for Renee, nine-year-old Jaclyn, and seven-year-old Elijah. Dominique worries about whether she'll be able to enroll again this summer, as she feels her kids, especially her girls, are now at the age where they need their mother, not a daycare provider or relative.

Spending time with their children is one of the most powerful tools women like Dominique feel they can use to shield their children from the dangers of their neighborhood's streets. Among her neighbors, Dominique enjoys the reputation of being a good mother, because she keeps her kids with her rather than leaving them with relatives or home alone. "When people see me and I'm by myself, they wonder where the children are, because everywhere I go, my children go," she explains. This devotion to her three children stems partly from the tragedies of her own childhood: When Dominique was nine her mother was murdered, and the culprit remains unknown. Since Dominique's parents were separated at the time, she and her five siblings went to live with a relative and shared a cramped, two-bedroom apartment with their new guardian. In the midst of the turmoil that followed their mother's death, school served as a stabilizing force for the children in the Watkins family. "We *all* went to school, everyone. You know, we was lucky. . . . Everybody finished high school, four of us went to college. My brother and sister graduated from college."

Dominique has so far managed to instill this same commitment to education in her own children and brags that they've maintained almost perfect school attendance and earn all A's and B's. She believes their success is due to her making education a family affair by enrolling in college herself. "They loved when I was going back to school," Dominique recalls. "They knew when I had to do my papers and stuff like that and they were always like, 'Did you do your work? Are you going to school tonight?' I couldn't miss a day."

Modeling a commitment to education is not the only method Dominique uses to guide her children down the right path. She says she is also vigilant about keeping open the "lines of communication" between the children and herself. "They can ask me *any* question," insists Dominique. "We talk about safety, we talk about sex, we talk about *everything*. It doesn't matter [what]." Many middle-class parents use the opposite strategy, seeking to isolate their children from the real world in a sort of cocoon where no hurtful words or harmful deeds can touch them.[1] For a child who "comes up" on the streets of North Philly, though, a childlike innocence about drugs, violence, and sexual abuse invites disaster.

Dominique believes the determination she has shown as she's struggled to care for her kids without many resources also provides her children with a strong positive model that she hopes will give them the courage and strength to make their own way in the world. "I want them to look at my life and say, 'Wow, my mom did so much and can do so much, *I* can do it too.'" In Dominique's social world, a good mother cannot assume her child's life will be untouched by adversity. But it is a mother's job to share as much of her child's burden as possible. Like many of the women we spoke to, Dominique believes a mother's resolve can become a lesson in how to endure the trials that are sure to come.

Near the end of our discussion, Dominique pauses to regain her composure. We have returned to the painful subject of her mother's death. When we ask Dominique, "How are you like your own mother?" this shy and circumspect woman bursts unexpectedly into laughter. "They say [that] I'm like my mom [because I'm] . . . always taking [my kids] places, always doing things with [them]." Her own mother had also instilled the value of education in her children, kept them with her whenever possible, was careful to keep the lines of communication open, and showed strength and determination in her struggle to raise her children alone. "Yeah," she decides after a moment, "I would say I'm like my mom."

"BEING THERE"

While fathers often drift in and out of their children's lives, Dominique Watkins and her peers believe that for a mother to do so violates the natural order of things. "A woman can't *help* but love a child," declares Carol, a forty-year-old white mother with three children, ages twenty-one, nineteen, and seven. When we ask Dominique, Carol, and other mothers—across the eight neighborhoods—to describe their views of what constitutes good parenting, almost all speak about the importance of *being there*, a philosophy that, by definition, morally condemns many of the neighborhood's fathers, who tend eventually to become absent and uninvolved.[2] For Dominique, the essence of a good mother is someone "who pays *attention* to her children, someone who's *there* for their children, supportive of them, does her best to provide for them." But, she says, in essence, good mothering is really about being there. "You don't have to be a super mom, just *be there* for them. . . . You don't have to have a fancy this or a fancy that, just togetherness with your children."[3]

Of course, poor single mothers in impoverished communities aren't the only ones who talk about the importance of being there for their children. The phrase is as widely accepted in the American family lexicon as "quality time." But what poor mothers mean by the phrase may differ radically from what middle-class mothers mean. All Americans understand that spending time with one's children is an important feature of good parenting. Yet while poor mothers see keeping a child housed, fed, clothed, and safe as noteworthy accomplishments (and the difficulty of securing these basics does make doing so noteworthy), their middle-class counterparts often feel they must earn their parenting stripes by faithfully cheering at soccer league games, chaperoning boy scout camping trips, and attending ballet recitals or martial arts competitions.[4]

What constitutes being there for mothers like Dominique takes different forms over a child's life course. For the mother of a newborn, being there means stolidly braving the sleepless nights, laying by an adequate supply of Pampers and formula, plus providing the crib, the "coach," and the outfits. For the mother of a toddler, it involves seeing the child through the developmental milestones of walking, talking, and potty training. For a mother of a school-aged child, being there means getting the child to school on time, monitoring homework, stretching the family budget to its breaking point just to include new school clothes, supplies, and field trip fees, and preaching the message about the value of education. For the mother of an emerging adolescent, being there means doing what you can to keep your children at arm's length from the tough and dangerous realities of the neighborhood, where even good kids with good mothers often fall prey to drugs, crime, school failure, and early pregnancy.

Being there begins at the moment the pregnancy is confirmed—as they make the choice to bring the pregnancy to term. Denise, an eighteen-year-old white mother, guiltily confides that she had an abortion before she gave birth to her twins, now two years old. She considered adoption when she learned she was pregnant again and believes her decision to bring her unplanned pregnancy of the twin boys to term constitutes a heroic act. Though she regrets the fact that the twins' father is not involved, she thinks her children should be grateful that she didn't have an abortion or "give them away." To her, this act alone is proof of her self-sacrifice and devotion. "I want to tell them the *good* things I did. . . . I was gonna give them up for adoption . . . and I chose to *keep* them. I want them to look at things like that."

At the dawn of the twenty-first century, a hallmark of the middle-class American family is the careful planning and painstaking preparation that generally precede childbearing, and it is poor mothers' failure to do the same that causes so much concern and public outrage.[5] Low-income mothers often have their children in conditions of scarcity and instability that middle-class women would find intolerable. The schools that are supposed to prepare these young women for the workforce are among the worst in the nation, the jobs they are suited to compete for are the least stable and poorest paying in the economy, their neighborhoods are among the most drug-infested and crime-ridden in the country, and the relationships they've forged with the men who father their children are often so fragile that only a handful survive beyond the child's preschool years.[6]

The decision to bring a child into the world under these conditions is not seen as a personal failure. Indeed, the very uncertainty and adversity involved transform the choice to bring a less-than-perfectly planned pregnancy to term into an act of valor. Irene is a forty-four-year-old

African American mother struggling to raise the two teenage children she still has at home in North Central, an especially poor Philadelphia neighborhood. She regularly reminds her children to be grateful for the choice she made to bring them into the world. "I try to explain to them, 'I don't owe y'all anything, I *paid* my debt because I brought you into the world and I didn't have to. Case closed!'"

Beatrice, a twenty-year-old Puerto Rican mother of a three-month-old, admits that raising a child with "the little bit of money that welfare provides" is a hardship, but she believes that her decision to have sex without protection creates a moral obligation to care for the life that she created. "How can mothers just have a kid and all of a sudden, just give them away? It's hard, it's hard being a parent. But if you went and did that thing [sex], you should deal with the consequences. Because I know . . . mothers that'll just give their kids away. They feel as though they can't deal with it. Because it's a struggle that you got to go through, [but] if you were able to open your *legs*, then you should be able to go *through* it."

The poor embrace the idea that motherhood requires sacrifice—especially if you have few resources and there is no man to help out—and they expect their offspring to honor the simple act of choosing to bring them into the world and raise them. They believe their children should also be grateful that they haven't abused, abandoned, or neglected them, as other mothers in similar circumstances sometimes do. Corinda, a twenty-six-year-old Puerto Rican mother of four children between the ages of three and eleven, says she regularly tells her oldest that she should "be proud of me. I tell my daughter to buy me a ring that says 'Number One Mom.'" After all, she adds, some mothers she reads about in the newspapers are "killing their kids" or "doing bad things to them, or hitting, or abusing them."

Irene says that not losing one's children to the "system" is also an accomplishment. "There are so many children being taken from these mothers because of the drug addiction; they just get the welfare check and the food stamps, and spend it up on this or that and go to their drug dealer first. They are not *being there* for their children. The children is dirty, they don't have nothing to eat—that is *my* idea of a bad mother."[7]

Being there does not necessarily mean that one has to have a lot of money. Carmelita, a young Puerto Rican mother of a toddler and a seven-month-old, who is now pregnant with her third child, describes the seemingly modest criteria that constitute being there for her: "I'm not talking just food or clothes, because like sometimes I'll get my kids name-brand things if I can, but, if not, sometimes I'll go to the second-hand shop. As long as they have love and care and food in their stomach, and they're clean and they have a bath, and I make sure they get their needles [shots] and take them to the doctors and stuff, I feel like I'm a good mother. I keep my house nice and clean. I don't teach them foul things. . . . I think I'm a very good mother for being nineteen years old."

At its core, being there for poor mothers is a childrearing philosophy born of adversity and pragmatism. Though mothers hope they will be able to give their children not just what they need, but "some of what they want too," they do not believe that doing so is a requirement for good mothering. The day-to-day hardships these mothers and children face produce modest goals. Being there is a celebration of the small victories of daily life as poor mothers do not have the luxury of taking the little things for granted. In Irene's words, "Being there for their child [means] no matter what, through thick and thin, always sticking in there with them. Don't run out on them, no matter how tough things get, just hang in there with them, do the best you can do."

"I NEVER LEAVE MY KIDS WITH NOBODY."

Having a child does not automatically confer adult status; rather, it presents a challenge that a poor young woman must meet.[8] Although motherhood is a role she usually values above all others, good mothering must be measured in small increments. Caring for her children herself is of special importance.

Corinda explains that a good mother "never leaves her kids with *nobody*. A good mother is someone who's always there with them, takes good care of them." Keeping one's children with her whenever possible shows that a young mother has embraced her parental responsibilities, earning her esteem and acknowledgment from peers. If she allows her children to "run in the street" unsupervised, or relies too much on others to care for them, she shows that she is a shirker and earns the disapproval of neighbors and kin. Aliya, an African American mother of a nine-year-old son who is now in her late twenties, relates, "The older lady on the street, she stopped by one day and she was like 'Aliya, you are such a good mother because your son don't be running up and down the street with nobody watching him. You are always with him.' And it just makes me feel so good that I am doing something *right*." Renee, a twenty-year-old Puerto Rican mother of a two-year-old, says that bad mothers "like to party and leave their kids *anywhere*. If I wanted to be like that . . . I wouldn't have *had* no kids. . . . It's okay to do it once and again," she concedes, "but not every weekend!"

The birth of a child can transform a young woman who wants to be "out partying and clubbing" or "running the streets" to one who wants little more than to be at home with her child, who puts social life aside and makes her child's needs her top priority. Keisha, a nineteen-year-old African American mother of a one-year-old, criticizes the behavior of a close friend: "Every time she came home from work, [she] took her son [out with her and went to hang out with her friends]. The baby would cry . . . you would have to *tell* her he was wet. He kept breaking out with everyone passing him around and touching him. She young, she's real young. She thought it was important to . . . spend time with her friends." Cindi, a twenty-one-year-old white mother of two toddlers, proudly describes how becoming a mother drained her of the desire to hang out with immature and childish friends. Then she says, "I know a couple of people that they just have kids and their moms take care of them or they leave them [with their moms] all the time and go out. . . . Someone that's not there for their kids the way they *need* them to be, I think that's a bad mother." Leaving the children for frivolous reasons rather than unavoidable ones, such as schooling or work, even if with one's own mother, is not justifiable by the standard most poor women hold.

"I STRUGGLE AND STRIVE."

Making ends meet on a meager budget while ensuring that their children don't feel deprived is part of what these mothers mean when they say that the crucial ingredient of good mothering is being there.[9] Irene explains how she struggles to communicate to her children that material possessions are not the most important thing. "Like I tell my daughter when she wants materialistic things [like] $50 for a pair of pants or $60 for a pair of sneaks, 'When I was coming up, we got what we could get. I remember my mother used to get our shoes at the Acme for $1.99.' It's hard now [because] children don't understand that. [But] you don't go to school for a *fashion show*, you go to school to *learn*. As long as the clothes are clean, it ain't got to be Polo or Calvin Klein, as long as it is clean."

Santana, a thirty-four-year-old white mother of an eighteen-month-old, concurs: "How she is dressed, that she is clean, I think it's important [that] even if I can't afford things, that she looks nice and clean. [So I can say,] 'She's really clean.'" When Danielle, a twenty-seven-year-old white mother of two daughters, ages nine and five, is asked to define what a bad mother is, she responds, "Someone who don't take care of their kids, they don't care if they go to school clean or dirty, with clean or dirty clothes on." "Kids are cruel," she continues. "Now, I don't want that for my kids. I work my *butt* off to give 'em clothes—and new clothes at that. That's why I always make sure that they have nice clean clothes on [with] no holes. They may not be the best clothes . . . but they look fair."

Yet when she can find a way to afford it, a good mother will try to buy her children Polo and Nike fashions because she understands how socially potent these name brands have become in the halls of her children's schools.[10] And the mothers themselves have seldom forgotten the sense of longing and social shame from their own impoverished childhoods.

Megan, a twenty-seven-year-old white mother of a third-grader and a four-year-old, says, "I buy my son what he wants, [even] expensive stuff, I wind up buying it when I get the money. I say, 'Wait 'til I get some money, I'm gonna buy it for you.' I'm trying to give [him] things *I* always wanted. Like if my friend had new sneakers, and I'd be like, 'I really wish I could wear them.'" Denise, the white mother of twins, describes her nagging guilt over not being able to provide such "extras" for her kids. "Sometimes I think they deserve better. I can't go out and buy them what I want to—they always have to wait. I always have to put something on [layaway], you know. And it bothers me because I don't want it to *be* like that."

Being there also means forgoing extras for oneself and spending that money on the children instead. Chrissy, a young white mother, says, "You feel bad when you have to say no." This twenty-three-year-old with a five-year-old son recalls a time when she broke down and bought him something he wanted rather than needed. "We went to Wal-Mart and I had $14 [to last the whole week] and I spent $13 on him for something he wanted. So I told him, 'Next time you say I'm a bad mother you know that I spent all my money for the rest of the week on *you*.'" Mahkiya Washington, whom we met in chapter 2, remembers that before the birth of her daughter, "It used to be [I'd get my] hair done every week, nails done." After the birth, she claims, all of that stopped. "I made sure my daughter had everything . . . from hats to shoes. So I basically stopped buying myself anything." In fact, mothers are harshly critical of other parents who buy these extras for themselves. Middle-class mothers can indulge in a manicure or a night out with friends without trading off their children's well-being to do so. Not so for poor mothers.

The norm of self-sacrifice is so strong that a woman risks social censure if she has nicer clothing than her children. Aleena, a white seventeen-year-old mother of a two-year-old son, says, "I can't see my son walking around with Payless sneakers on with me walking around with Nikes and Reeboks or something. My *son* is gonna have Nikes and Reeboks on. *I'll* wear the Payless shoes. My son will always come before me. There's a lot of people around my neighborhood that put their needs before their kids." Women like thirty-three-year-old Chanel, a white mother of three, hold up their dirty sneakers, worn sweats, and thread-bare coats as proof of their devotion to their children. "My girlfriend, she was [teasing me] because [I] still have the sneakers from two years ago." They are among her only pair of shoes, and so she wears them nearly every day. But, as Chanel explains, "I have to because I can't afford to buy myself [new] sneakers. I got three kids to take care of. *They* need more than *I* do." She notes bitterly, "[My friend] puts *her* needs before her *kids*, [but] then she's got a man that'll go and provide all brand-name stuff for the kids. She can't see where I can't do it."

As children age, making sure they are well dressed has an added func-tion, as it is widely believed that children whose mothers don't "do for them" will "stand out on the corner," or sell drugs, to get money for the things they want. Irene, mentioned several times above, offers her diag-nosis of the problem among the troubled youth she's observed: "They are not getting what they want at home, so they go out on the corner, and then they get locked up, get out, and that's not a life for them. That is not. But if they are not getting it at home they say they got to get it from *some-where*, and so they go on the corner, and they sell drugs, and that is bad." In Philadelphia and its poorest industrial suburbs, the drug economy is a free-for-all, where virtually anyone can stake a claim to a corner with-out having to swear allegiance to a gang. Mothers believe that a child who feels deprived is more likely to abandon the righteous path they have laid out, a path whose signposts are clear: stay in school and out of trou-ble with the law, say no to drugs, stay away from bad influences, and don't mess around with the opposite sex—at least without protection.

But in the end, these mothers affirm that material things are no sub-stitute for the crucial and long-lasting investments of time and attention. Tasheika, a twenty-year-old African American mother of three children under the age of seven, says, "I mean, you can buy your children clothes, but those things don't matter to them because they gonna put holes in those jeans. But, you know, *talking* to them and not always *screaming* at them . . . just *being* with them is [being] a good mother. Because I know a whole lot of mothers that dress their kids better than mine and don't spend an inch of *time* with them. Those kids are the miserable ones, and mine are happy, and they could have on a two-dollar shirt."

"EVERYTHING I'VE TRIED TO DO . . . IS BEING TOTALLY ERASED!"

Most middle-class youth are raised in communities with a wide array of valuable resources that are often taken for granted: good schools, plentiful opportunities for after-school and summer enrichment, and peers that graduate from high school, go to college, and establish careers before they marry and have children. Thus, for middle-class parents, the community supports and extends their efforts to parent their children well. For mothers living in impoverished, inner-city communities, however, the neighborhood is often the greatest impediment to their aspirations for their children.[11] Many women echoed the sentiments of Lisette, an African American eighteen-year-old mother of two toddlers, who worries about the challenges she knows lie ahead. "So far so good," she says, "the *real* stages didn't hit me yet of the *fives, tens,* and the *teens,* but when I get there I hope I can be there for my kids."

For children coming up in the most blighted areas of America's inner cities, a trip to school or the neighborhood store can mean navigating blocks checkered with burned-out buildings and trash-strewn vacant lots, past corners where other youth hawk nickel and dime bags to passing pedestrians and motorists, and by neighborhood ruffians looking for a fight. Ashley, a white mother of three school-aged children who is in her late twenties, says the most serious threat to her goal of "raising her children right" is the corner of her own block. "All these kids hang on the corner . . . you could see them smoking pot right out in the open. . . . And the big thing is the fighting. . . . I don't want my son involved in that." For Christine, a thirty-seven-year-old African American mother of a teenager and a toddler, the neighborhood's biggest threats are the peers that live there. "When they become teenager[s], they pick up friends that might become God to them and [they think], '*They* know more than my *mom* do!' And so that is difficult."

Elena, a fifty-six-year-old white mother of six, explains how she tried to protect her children from the negative influences of neighborhood peers. "It's tough here because it's a project, and you have to worry about who they hang out with and where they go. Most of the time, I used to say, 'If you got to go out, go out of the project.' But they'd go out and hang out on the corner. We used to have railings—like little bars that went around the property—and all the kids would go out and sit on the bars and talk or walk around the project. That was basically their night out, like on a summer night, they'd hang out up at the field or across the street at Hank's. That's where the pot smoking came in."

Some mothers also believe that the neighborhood leaves them no option but to school their children in how to be tough. In the streets of these communities, children's safety might depend on their ability to defend themselves against other youths who pose a threat.[12] Jackie, a white divorced mother of three, now faces this problem with her eight-year-old son. "On one hand I don't want him fighting. On the other hand . . . I don't wanna holler at him for it, because then he won't be looking out for [himself and his sisters] when they're out there." Jackie laments, "It seems like *everything* I've tried to do from when they were babies up to this point is being *totally erased* since the change in the neighborhood."

Mothers of teens often complain bitterly about the "attitudes" their kids begin to "cop" as they absorb their tough neighborhood peer culture. Millie, a twenty-seven-year-old Puerto Rican mother of three whom we profile in the next chapter, explains that the nearby streets, the neighboring schools, and the local children pose a triple threat to her child. "They're growing up in an area where there's [a lot of problems and] drug infestation. When they get a certain age in certain schools, their peers are so strong that sometimes, sometimes they fall off track.

And I just have to prepare myself to learn how to deal with that when it happens."

"YOU GOTTA TEACH YOUR CHILDREN."

The lessons of early childhood include the basics of walking, talking, potty training, and adapting to solid foods, and these mothers, like mothers everywhere, take great pride in helping their children to achieve these developmental milestones. Seventeen-year-old Aleena, mentioned earlier, says she loves to teach her two-year-old "everything that is expected, like the walking, the talking, showing him how to feed himself, not to be greedy and to share." Tyhera, a nineteen-year-old African American mother of one, glows with pride as she describes how she helps her three-year-old master the elemental skills of reading and math: "She got her ABCs and her 1-2-3s and she counts to four. We got [this game], like, she's talking, so we'll go over all the words she knows. I'll be like, 'Can you say this?' and she'll say it."

During these early years, most young women are filled with optimism for their children, looking intently for signs of an unusual brightness or special talent. Kyra, a seventeen-year-old African American mother of a child who is almost two, says the fact that she is "raising [her] son real good" distinguishes her from some other mothers in her neighborhood. "Like in the ghetto, they don't *teach* their kids properly." This young mother is still confident that by teaching her child well, she can ensure his success. "I sing him his ABCs, and he sing them to me—like not the whole twenty-six, but he can get up to maybe like G or E. He only *twenty months*, and he can count up to *seven!* I teach him his numbers in Spanish because I did take a little Spanish in high school. He real smart. I know when he start getting them awards and honors and stuff like that, his father gonna try to step in. I'm gonna be like, 'No. Because if you wasn't there in the *first* part of his life, you ain't gonna be there *now*. Don't try to take the credit when *mommy* did all the work.'" Lorelei, a thirty-nine-year-old African American mother with two preschool-aged children, wants them to go to college. "[I want them] to stay in school, learn as much as they can, see if they go to college for something worthwhile or you know, *be* something," but she worries that her hopes will never be realized if she remains in the neighborhood. For her children to succeed, she believes, "I would have to move."[13]

When children are young, optimism is high. This optimism begins to fade as soon as the children step through the doors of the local elementary school. While middle-class parents see schooling as an opportunity for their children to develop their talents and showcase their achievements, poor parents view school as offering just as many opportunities for failure as for success.[14] The Philadelphia and Camden public schools are among the worst in the nation, and the normal state of many classrooms is little more than mildly controlled chaos.[15] School removes children from the close parental supervision of their early years and exposes them to a peer environment mothers almost uniformly believe is negative. Thus beginning school represents the onset of a thirteen-year battle that mothers wage with these peers for the minds and hearts of their children.

Like all parents, they want to help their children to succeed in school. But these mothers must devote the time and energy they might have expended helping their children excel in the classroom to merely making sure that their children have a safe route to and from the schoolyard, seeing that they attend regularly, encouraging them to associate with the right friends, and dealing with any behavior problems that arise. But these mothers feel additionally locked out of the educational process because they are intimidated by their children's teachers and by the school itself, and they doubt that they know how to act as advocates for their children.[16]

These mothers often admit that their own difficult experiences with school make them tentative and anxious when dealing with teachers about their child's academic progress. For a mother who still struggles with reading, her seventh-grader's language arts homework may contain vocabulary words she has never heard. Likewise, a fifth-grade math curriculum may be beyond the capacity of a parent who struggled in school herself, leaving her ill-equipped to help with homework. Even many middle-class parents we know complain that they barely understand some aspects of their fifth or sixth grader's math homework. Jasmine, thirty-eight, a Puerto Rican mother of two adult children and a four-year-old, who dropped out of school in the eleventh grade, worries in particular about math. "I'm lousy with math, and that's the one thing I'm afraid of. I'm thinking, 'Am I going to be able to help him out with math?'" She says that when she was in school, "I didn't have no one to [help me]. That's why I struggled. . . . I would just sit there [in math class] terrified."

A central problem among the mothers we spoke with was how to reinforce the value of school to their children when they themselves had often not listened to their own parents in this regard. Mothers with histories of academic failure often find themselves in the awkward position of preaching the message "Do as I say and not as I do" while they threaten, bribe, and cajole their children not to "mess up," urging them to "do better than Mommy." Paula, a Puerto Rican forty-year-old who did not manage to realize her dream of completing college, tries to encourage her fifteen-year-old to take a different path by pointing to the consequences of her own missteps and failures. "I want her to be more educated. . . . I used go to school [and] clown around a lot . . . check out the boys. And I never really paid attention to reading and all the spelling." At the same time that she tells these cautionary tales, she attempts to instill the high aspirations that she believes will motivate her child to do well. "You want a *real* good job making $40,000 to $50,000 per year. You want to be a doctor? You have to know how to *read* real good, *spell* real good and know your *math* real good." "Nowadays," she reasons, "if you want a job [even] . . . flipping *burgers*, you need a high school diploma!"

Danielle has heeded the messages of public service ads that "reading is fundamental," and believes she's developed an effective strategy to get her child to read. She says her daughter "likes to read to me, and if that is gonna get her to read then I let her read to me, even if I ain't listening. As long as she thinks I am, that's fine—because she'll read." Danielle reinforces the importance of school activities in other ways as well. "When she comes home from school, [I ask], 'How was your day?' 'What did you learn?' Just to make her feel important. [Then] I tell her to teach [her younger sister] something [she's learned that day]." Danielle says these efforts far exceed the help that she received as a child. "I didn't have nobody to sit down with me and do my homework with me or, you know, tell me I did a good job."

The late 1990s saw an unprecedented number of single mothers entering the workforce full time, prompted in part by the reforms to the welfare and child support systems, by a dramatically enhanced Earned Income Tax Credit for low-wage workers, and by the largest economic expansion in recent U.S. history.[17] Full-time work and the long commutes often involved frequently mean that single parents cannot supervise homework as closely as they would like, so they come to rely on older children, kin, or, if they are lucky enough to find them, institutional resources such as after-school programs.[18] But mothers often find these strategies do not fully substitute for their own efforts. Monica, a white twenty-nine-year-old with a son in third grade and a daughter in kindergarten, has recently gone to work and tells how her work schedule makes it difficult for her to help keep her son's grades up. She admits it's hard. The demands of her job and the commute to and from work keep her away from home from 6 A.M. until 6 P.M. In the few hours before bedtime she must fix dinner, wash up, do the laundry, clean the house, pay the bills, and run the necessary errands. Because of this time crunch, she sends her child to an after-school program where she has heard homework is emphasized. This strategy, however, has not worked. "I gotta start making sure I make time for [helping him with his homework again]. [Before I had this job,] I *always* did his homework with him. Now . . . he goes to an after-school program where he's supposed to do it, and his big thing is telling them 'I don't have any.' But he has homework *every night*. . . . He don't feel like *doing* it, that's it. . . . He's at the lazy stage."

When middle-and upper-class children have trouble in school, their parents can afford to supplement what the school provides by hiring a tutor, moving to a suburb with better schools, or opting for private schooling. For low-income women raising children in poor communities, their sheer determination to see their children do well is often the only real tool they can use to respond to a child's academic challenges. Securing special educational services from the public school system is not impossible in Philadelphia or its poor inner suburbs, but it takes time and tenacity.

"I TRY TO KEEP HER OUT OF TROUBLE THAT WAY."

Middle-class mothers often register their children for a seemingly endless round of activities in order to cultivate their talents. For mothers rearing children in poor neighborhoods, such activities have the added value of offering some protection against the dangers of the street. Tracy, a twenty-five-year-old African American mother of a two-year-old son, believes that getting her son into enrichment activities will protect him from the "negativity" of the local peer environment by ensuring that he gets with "the right crowd." "I want him to be involved and experience a lot of things like going to museums and stuff like that . . . just stay involved in activities. Like he wants to take guitar lessons. I hope [that by doing that] he will get with the right crowd . . . because the stuff going on out there makes you want to keep your child in the house."

Usually, though, mothers don't have access to or can't pay for these activities, so they emphasize the importance of instilling good values—values that will carry their children through tempting or difficult situations they encounter when not under their mother's care. In the words of Tanay, "It's my job to set [their values] right, [to] see that it's going right. So far . . . they listen to me." Thirty-one-year-old Toby, a white mother of a third-grader and a one-year-old, says she has taught her older child to be strong and self-confident so she can withstand tempting or difficult situations. She coaches her to respond to these challenges by urging her to say to herself, "'I'm okay, I can do it. My mom taught me [how].'" She concludes, "I want her to be *strong* for herself, stand *up* for herself." For Yvee, a thirty-year-old African American mother of four, a deeply held religious faith reinforces these moral teachings. She says, "My hope is that I provide them with a decent upbringing where they're strong enough to be good, strong adults, where they can survive [and] also have God in their lives [to help them]."

Some do succeed in translating good parenting into positive outcomes for their children. "My oldest daughter doesn't drink, smoke, she doesn't want babies yet, and she is *twenty-two!*" boasts Susan, a forty-three-year-old Puerto Rican mother of two. "I *know* how to raise children. I can't speak for other people, but *I* raised *mine* in a good way. . . . Nobody never starved or nothing." Forty-year-old Taylor, the mother of six children between the ages of ten and twenty-four, says of her youngest, "My . . . daughter know that she always had a roof over her head, always got food for her. . . . She knows I raised her the best [I could], sacrificed. . . . [She is] knowing that I was a good mother." Carol, a forty-year-old white mother of two grown children and a seven-year-old, wants only the best for her daughter, whose teachers say shows great academic promise. She explains, "The dreams I have for her, she made them even *bigger*. I just want her to go to college. Get a high school education, go to college, pick a career that she enjoys and go for it. Once she has a career, then worry about falling in love with somebody and getting married, but don't have no kids [first]."

Even the city's poorest neighborhoods produce just enough children who succeed against the odds to keep hope alive, who somehow make it to local colleges like Temple University or the Camden branch of Rutgers, the State University of New Jersey. Susan tells us, "I give them encouragement, that's the main thing—love and encouragement and let them know they can do whatever they want to do, [like] be a lawyer, a doctor. My daughter is in training school. She wants a government job.

She's studying for that. She's gonna do it 'cause she's good at studying. She's good in science and math. She could be in the medical field if she wanted to. . . . My daughter, she does good. That's all I can say about that."

Most mothers raising children in these crime- and drug-ridden neighborhoods do not feel they are guaranteed such a favorable outcome, regardless of how hard they may try or how much they sacrifice. When we ask Jasmine what she worries about most, she answers, "My son— that's what I worry about most. That he don't grow up to be like the other kids [around here], all wild. I want to move somewhere better than this, even if it's far. . . . How [else] can I make him grow up to be a good man, always go to school, have a good job?" Like Jasmine, most mothers we spoke with believe that in the end there is only so much a good mother can do to battle their neighborhood's influence. Erica explains, "You go through so much, and you see so much, and you try to protect them so much. You *know* they're gonna fall, and you *tell* them they're gonna fall, and they don't listen, and then they come crying."

"I CAN'T EXPECT FOR THEM TO BE PERFECT AND NOT TO FALL."

One strategy mothers use to get their children to heed their advice is to unflinchingly tell the "brutal truth" about themselves, drawing on the mistakes of their own youth to craft parables that reinforce the importance of staying on track. These mothers hope that by sharing their worst and most shameful experiences, they can scare their children into staying on the straight and narrow. Cheyenne, a twenty-five-year-old white mother of two, ages eight and five, says she's been very frank with her children about her own drug addiction and the felonies that have put their grandfather in prison, in order to "make them aware" of where straying from the path can lead. "My kids are very aware now of what drugs did to mommy. They're very aware of what happened to mommy when she did drugs, and they're very aware of why pop-pop John is in jail. [I] just keep them aware and [their] eyes open."

Jasmine told the truth about herself to her youngest son in an attempt to motivate him to stay in school. "I made a lot of mistakes in life . . . not having any ambitions, not having any goals. I just wanted to fit in. I had a girlfriend who was into smoking marijuana and drinking, and I saw how she was so popular, and that's why I went ahead and followed, and made a mess out of my life. My son is going to college soon. . . . I just want him to do things *differently*." On one occasion, Jasmine says, her experience with drugs helped her to intervene quickly when her son started experimenting with marijuana. "My son used to come home high, and right away I knew. 'You're smoking *pot*. . . . You don't do that in *my* house.' . . . With my mom, there were times when I came home high smoking pot. She never really noticed."

While middle-class parents may judge their parenting skills by their children's success in college admissions or choice of professions, in the context of urban neighborhoods where drugs, violence, and poverty seem to destroy lives with alarming regularity, mothers often believe that they must hope for the best but prepare for the worst. As children reach adolescence, "being there" demands that a parent maintain open lines of communication and provide support for children who seem to have lost their way. Twenty-three-year-old Demi, a Puerto Rican mother whose two children are still in diapers, has a well-developed philosophy about how mothers ought to be there for their children as they enter their teen years. "Letting [the kids] know that whatever the problems they have, they can come to me or their father, and tell us *anything*. No matter what they do, I'm *there* for them. If they do something wrong, I will support them. [I tell them,] 'I let you know that you did something wrong,' [that] I'm not *proud* of them, but I will still *support* them."

But even diligent use of these strategies does not guarantee success. Corinda, the Puerto Rican mother of four introduced above, fears that it is already too late for her eleven-year-old daughter. "All I can do is talk to her and give her advice and tell her, you know, that I don't want her to be in the same conditions that I was in. I always be telling her to [finish school]. She says she wants to be a lawyer. I tell her, 'Finish school. Then you gotta go to college for a couple of years, and don't think about no boyfriends, so that [you] won't come out pregnant.' But to tell you the truth, I see her having kids when she be young." Marie, a white thirty-five-year-old mother of three children between the ages of eleven and fourteen, laughs bitterly when she remembers how naive she was about raising a family in her tough PennsPort neighborhood. "Oh, I thought I'd be the perfect mother, you know—no mistakes, perfect kids, never get in trouble. It doesn't work that way. . . . Oh, the *reality* [is] getting called to the school because your son set a fire in the bathroom. Having to ride in the *police* car. *That's* the reality! He goes through stages when he gets in trouble, then he does real good. He's just one of those kids."

Brielle, a thirty-two-year-old African American mother of four, has concluded that it is dangerous to be too optimistic about the fate of her children.[19] "I try not to be too hopeful . . . because they're girls, and it's like [I have] that fear that they might end up pregnant or whatever. Mainly get[ing] pregnant. That's my biggest concern. But I would like them to go further in school than I did . . . like college and work. And [I'd like them to] have better relationships than I did so they can find that one person—even if they're not married—just that one committed person instead of breaking up and get with somebody else, have kids [with different people]. I don't want them to continue the way *I* [did]." As their children age, few mothers in Brielle's situation can deny the obvious—that the odds are stacked against their children.

It is not surprising, then, that the women we interviewed believe the true mark of good mothering is the ability to "hold on," to continue to support their children in the face of missteps and adversity. Stella, a seventeen-year-old African American mother of a one-year-old, sees her grandmother as the model of a good mother because she "has been there" for three generations of her children's and grandchildren's travails. "*Being* there for your child, loving your child *no matter what*," makes a mother a good mother, she says. "My grandmother, she's been there for her *kids*, her *grandkids*, and *our* children." Lisette also admires her grandmother for similar reasons. "My grandmother . . . is the most courageous person in the world. She's been through so much, and still she stands by her [own] two feet and says, 'I'm here and I'm going to *make* it.' My grandmother has had a heart attack, a stroke, she has raised her kids, her kids' kids, her kids' kids' kids, and she is raising kids to this day. My grandmother is fifty-four years old this year. She has been through so much. I mean so much. She is a very good example. I hope I turn out just like her. She is just *too good*."

The women we came to know tend to compare their children to those of families even lower on the class ladder, not to those of the middle class. Bearing up when a child does wrong is all that a good mother can expect to do. Because going astray is so easy in the troubled sections of Philadelphia and its impoverished inner suburbs, where the social boundaries separating "decent" residents from the "street" are so permeable, the ability of mothers to simply hold on in the face of setbacks commands a very high social value.[20] No one, they believe, is entirely safe from the negative social forces that have made their communities a minefield. Dorothy, a thirty-six-year-old African American mother of two and pregnant with a third, who deeply desires her children to do better than she has, also believes that troubles will inevitably come their way. For this reason, the strength she has gained in the face of hardship is the most important legacy she can pass on to her children. "I just pray to God they get some kind of *knowledge*," she says. "I want them to know how to *survive*. I tell Jessie, 'You got to take the bitter with the sweet. You got to learn to struggle like *I* did.'" Although these mothers generally hope for "the world" for their children when they are young, as children grow into middle childhood and early adolescence, mothers begin to envision the worst-case scenario as well, and steel themselves for the hard times, praying they have the strength to endure the troubles that may lie ahead.

Millie, the Puerto Rican mother we feature in the next chapter, says, "I want for them to go to school, graduate. I want them to go to college if possible." But Millie's hopes are tempered by the realization that even the best mother cannot always overcome the destructive social forces that devastate the lives of people around her. "I hope that they stay out of trouble. I wish the best for them, but I'm realistic. I know the environment they are growing up in. I know I might go through a lot with them, and they're gonna have their mistakes, and I hope they don't have to go to the Youth Study Center like my mom did with my brother, but she went through all that. But I'm realistic enough that I might have to . . . I might have to go through it with one of them." Millie says she prays for the resolve to be there for her children when travails come. "I don't know how I'm gonna deal with it, but I have to prepare. I know I can't take it like it's the end of the world. . . . I just hope that what I'm instilling in them right now will be much stronger than out there, but I can't expect for them to be perfect and not to fall. They're gonna make their mistakes and I just have to be strong enough to deal with it."

Looking back on the pain and disappointments she's endured in raising her older children, now adults themselves, Elena, a white mother we introduced before, tells us, "I've [thought back] through my life and thought, if only I could have done better, if only I could have had a better house, a better neighborhood, a better husband—a Christian husband— if only if I could have done better. I used to fantasize on that, but fantasizing doesn't get you through life. I had to bring myself back to earth and say, 'This is what I have, this is what I have to work with, and I'm gonna make the best of it. I really tried. I know I tried.' [My son Ron, who is in prison], says 'Mom, I don't blame you. I feel bad for hurting you.' He goes, 'I brought this on myself.' [My son Mark, also in prison], says the same thing. I thought, if I raised them differently, they wouldn't be [in prison]. They said, 'No, Mom, there's nothing you could have done.'"

GOOD MOMS AND BAD MOMS

Nearly everyone we interviewed can tell stories of "bad moms" in their neighborhoods who put their own needs ahead of their children's, and a small but significant minority admit they have been, at one time or another, what they'd call a bad mom. Even though most of our mothers insist on distinguishing themselves from the disreputable mothers on the local street corner or on the nightly TV news, our years in these communities did put us in touch with a number of mothers who had clearly, at least for a time, failed in the mothering role. On one warm summer weekend, Edin interviewed three mothers in a row who had lost all of their children to state custody. Two shared a public housing unit stripped clean of furniture—everything sold to finance their habit. After a nearly incomprehensible two-hour conversation with the second mother, Edin paid her the promised twenty dollars, and within minutes, the woman had run out the back door, returned, and was shooting up in the upstairs bedroom.[21]

Few mothers we met say they've knowingly abused or abandoned their children (though if their misdeeds were serious enough for them to lose custody of their children, they would not be included in our study), though some admit to having neglected them in an addict's determined pursuit of a high. Others confess that they failed to protect their children from an abusive boyfriend or male relative. In some cases, these situations have been public enough to prompt a neighbor or relative to call social services, and chronic enough to warrant the removal of one or more of their children from their custody, at least for a time.[22] The media often portray such mothers as inhuman monsters who have no maternal feeling for the innocents in their care. Yet even those who admit to these failings say their actions do not negate the love they feel for their children or their commitment to find ways to be there for them in the end.

Cheyenne, introduced above, has now been off hard drugs for more than a year, though she sheepishly admits that she still smokes marijuana and drinks beer from time to time. Her mother is the legal guardian of her oldest daughter, but she sees the girl regularly because the two families share a house. Cheyenne has struggled to beat her addiction for nearly a decade, so the fear that she could use again and lose her fragile hold on her newfound sobriety looms over the family. When eighteen-year-old Destiny, a white mother of two toddlers, was arrested for dealing crack out of her grandmother's Kensington home, the judge told her she had to go back to school and sever her ties to her criminal associates or risk losing her younger daughter to foster care. To break free of old habits, Destiny had to move out of Kensington and find new housing, then submit to routine drug testing, counseling sessions, and monthly visits from a state caseworker.

For Cheyenne, Destiny, and thirty-six-year-old Chelsea, redeeming lost ties to children can serve as a guiding force. Chelsea, a former prostitute and recovering addict who is HIV positive, retains custody of her youngest child, seven-year-old Robbie, but the older five, ranging in age from eight to nineteen, have been adopted, are in foster care, or are on their own. The fact that she was a mother, she says, is what "kept me alive." Chelsea has been in and out—mostly out—of her children's lives for nearly two decades, but she's just celebrated her twentieth month of being clean. Robbie is the only child she's managed to maintain consistent contact with, and although her mother has mostly raised him, Chelsea recalls that prior to rehab "I would just leave my son with my mother and disappear, running between Olney and Kensington. I'd get a place, and my son would come live with me. My mom would come visit and see things weren't too kosher . . . so she'd kind of like bail my son out before [things got too bad]." "I was like a walking zombie," Chelsea admits, but insists that if she hadn't been a mother, "I think I'd be dead. Because all through my drug abuse, it was just having those children that gave me a moment of sanity, that made me a little fearful of taking that next bag or the next joint. They somehow get me grounded spiritually, if you can understand that."

Denial is a hard habit to break for a recovering addict, but Chelsea seems to comprehend how profoundly she's failed her children, and she knows there is no way to make up for the lost years. Instead, she's focusing on the future and on what she can do to redeem herself in the here and now. For her oldest, a nineteen-year-old daughter with a baby of her own, Chelsea hopes to be able to offer some kind of practical support. For the other older kids, her goal is to regain some sort of regular contact and take on some minimal role in their lives. Robbie is the only one she believes she can still be a good mother to, and she hopes to have the strength to claim "the honor" of being there for him the way a mother should.

WHAT MOTHERS DO FOR KIDS

Delaying childbearing until one's thirties and even forties has become so common among middle- and upper-class couples that Oprah Winfrey recently aired a segment entitled "When Should I Have a Baby?" The program featured a thirty-nine-year-old realtor and former flight attendant who had spent her twenties traveling the world and her early thirties establishing a career in real estate and finding a mate. Though she married at thirty-five, she did not immediately have children because the newlyweds wanted to "enjoy each other as a couple" first. The pair then purchased a five-bedroom home in a Miami suburb known for its fine public schools. When she'd completed the extensive redecorating she believed the house required, she announced to family, friends, and coworkers she would take a break from her career. "My husband and I planned to fill the house with children," the woman tearfully tells the audience, but biology would not cooperate with these carefully laid plans. After three miscarriages and thousands of dollars spent on fertility treatments, the couple now fear that they have missed the chance to have the family they had dreamed of.

In an overheated classroom on a college campus on the western border of Philadelphia, not far from some of the neighborhoods where our mothers live, a group of African American and white students have just viewed a videotape of this segment of *The Oprah Winfrey Show*. These adults returning to college start a discussion of the question the show has raised: When is the best time to have children? Most of the students—ranging from twenty-three to fifty-three years old—hail from the city's working-class and poorer areas, though a few middle-class students are also enrolled. For some, this classroom is a way-station on the route from welfare or low-wage employment to better-paying work. Others aim for a promotion from the shop floor to a supervisory position.

Tonight, the women do most of the talking. A twenty-six-year-old student who does secretarial work to support herself and her eight-year-old son, shifts uncomfortably in her chair as one of her classmates explains how she sees having children as a choice and professes ambivalence about whether children are something she desires. Finally, her hand shoots up in the air, and she exclaims, "I can't understand that. A woman's body is meant to have *children!* Your breasts, your ovaries were given to you by God to bear *children*, not just to give a man sexual *pleasure.* It is *selfish* and *wrong* to be childless!"

The single mothers in the poorest neighborhoods of Philadelphia and its industrial suburbs more often echoed this mother's sentiments than those of her ambivalent counterpart. The women we spoke to saw children as a blessing, and childbearing and rearing as natural parts of young adulthood. Parenting is the most important role these women expect to play, and they want very much to play it well. The high value poor women place on children, childbearing, and motherhood seems at odds with their willingness to have them while they are still young, uneducated, and in economically precarious positions, as does their willingness to bear children by men whose current circumstances and future prospects are equally grim. The middle-class model of motherhood requires that women complete their education, establish a career, enter into a marital relationship, and then decide if they are ready for parenthood. For the middle class, which has adopted the norm of intensive mothering, children ought to be planned and prepared for years in advance.[23]

Young women raised in inner-city neighborhoods of the Philadelphia metropolitan area believe that marriage, not children, is what requires the years of careful planning and preparation and that childbearing is something that happens along the way. When dreams of children turn from fantasy to fact, young women focus their energies on what they *can* do for their children, rather than what concerned middle-class observers fear they cannot do. Poor young women facing the choice of whether to get pregnant or bring a pregnancy to term are not completely naive about the hard realities that lie ahead. They know that many of the men in their neighborhood who seem eager to become parents may not be able to meet the demands of fatherhood. They know that raising the children, possibly alone, on the meager earnings their education and skills can command will be extraordinarily difficult. And they understand that their dreams for their children can get tattered and lost in the gritty reality of everyday life. But these mothers hope that love will prove to be enough to overcome the difficulties of their environment.

Social class plays a significant role in how these mothers measure success.[24] Middle-class parents assume that they will be able to keep their children fed and clothed and safe from the dangers of inner-city streets. Poor mothers cannot assume these things and therefore take great pride in providing their children with the basic necessities and safeguards in the face of economic hardship. While more privileged women may fulfill the role of good mother by using their resources to cultivate their children's talents in science, gymnastics, soccer, or dance, poor mothers by definition have few resources. Thus, they adopt an approach to child-rearing that values survival, not achievement. While their early aspirations for their children are indeed high, what these women hope for and what they expect and prepare for are often quite different. In general, they make tentative and modest plans for their children. After the dangers of the neighborhood—the drugs, violence, misguided peers, and underperforming schools—take their toll, mothers recognize that even love and commitment cannot produce miracles.

Therefore, the poor women we spoke to celebrate the self-denial and determination it takes to keep putting food on the table day after day, to keep their children adequately clothed, to ensure that they attend school, and to stick with them through thick and thin. They recognize that bringing a pregnancy to term in the face of difficult circumstances is a tough row to hoe, and they believe that choosing to do so is heroic. Good mothers love their children, draw on their own experiences to help teach them right from wrong, and try to protect them from neighborhood and peers. But above all, they know they must somehow find the grit and determination to "be there," no matter what heartaches the future might bring. Though virtually every mother worries that her daughter might "come out" pregnant or her son might get "sent away" for dealing drugs, a mother whose child ends up in these sad circumstances has not necessarily failed. For it is foolish for them to believe that the viciousness of the streets will not touch them and their families. Everyone knows, they tell us, that kids in their neighborhoods may easily take a wrong turn. Mothers feel that they can succeed by just doing their best and sticking with it, fighting for their kids no matter how tough things get. For them, there is no more important job and no greater accomplishment.

SIX

HOW MOTHERHOOD
CHANGED MY LIFE

MILLIE AND CARLOS

Millie Acevedo is a diminutive, twenty-seven-year-old Puerto Rican mother of three who "came up" on Eighth and Indiana, one of the roughest corners in the West Kensington section of Philadelphia. She greets us at the door of her rowhouse with a well-scrubbed look—in a crisp white T-shirt with a face free of makeup and her hair pulled neatly back in a bun. A block and a half away, a bulldozer grinds noisily at the remains of another abandoned neighborhood factory. But Millie's block is relatively well-maintained and peaceful. The telephone poles up and down the street are plastered with advertisements for neighborhood events and give some indication that a community still exists here.

At fourteen, Millie believed she had found her future in Carlos, an older boy of nineteen whose best friend lived on her block. Carlos had a job and an apartment of his own. They had been together for a month when Millie moved in with him, and the couple began describing themselves as husband and wife, though they had no legally binding tie. Millie and Carlos were eager to have children but agreed to wait so that she could stay in school. Despite being on birth control and "taking my pills every day," she became a mother before her sixteenth birthday. Though the conception was not planned, the prospect of becoming parents delighted them both. The pair shared old-fashioned, Puerto Rican family values, and she willingly dropped out of school to care for their child full time. A year later, they conceived a second son, this one planned, reasoning that as long as they had started a family, they might as well finish the job.

Millie and Carlos enjoyed a fairly stable relationship until she became pregnant a third time, a "total accident" in Millie's words, three months after the second child was born. When she told Carlos about the pregnancy, he "totally flipped." Though he'd been ecstatic about the first child and had been the one to push hard for a second, he immediately threatened to leave if she didn't end the third pregnancy. Millie relates the story this way, "He couldn't deal with [having another child], and he left. And he was with a couple of other girls out there. Then, after [I went through] the whole pregnancy by myself, he came back after the baby was born. He wanted to be with me again. . . . We tried to stay together for like a whole year after the baby was born."

But during this year, which Millie recalls as the worst in her life, Carlos "had so many jobs it wasn't even funny." His frequent conflicts with supervisors led to violent confrontations at home. "And when it got to that point, I was like, 'This is no good for my kids, this is no good for me, either he's gonna hurt me, I'm gonna hurt him, one of us is gonna be *dead*, one of us is gonna be in *jail*, and what's gonna happen with my kids *then?*' That's when I put an end to it," she says. "I got a restraining order on him, I got him out of the house, and that was the *end* of it. I never took him back." She told him, " 'That's just it. I'm not taking abuse.' "

Millie is matter-of-fact when describing her failed relationship with Carlos, but visibly lights up when she talks about being a mother. As Millie imagines what life would be like had she not had children, she tells us her dream was to finish high school and enroll in college. Yet, like so many other mothers we met, Millie believes that her children have proved far more of a help than a hindrance. "My kids, they've matured me a lot. If I hadn't had them and had gone to college, I probably would have gotten introduced to the wrong crowd, and would have gotten lost because of the drugs and stuff." She believes having children was providence's way of saving her from this fate. "Maybe I needed my kids [to keep me safe]. They come first. I've always stayed off of drugs for them, and they helped me grow up. . . . I can't picture myself without them."

Millie's story shares many themes with other stories we heard. She believes that having children is a normal part of life, though she feels she and Carlos got started a year or two too early. Millie and Carlos's first and third pregnancies were both accidents, but poor women are often more favorably oriented toward having a child than not. Once pregnant, poor mothers pursue parenthood with few of the reservations that middle-class observers assume they must (and should) have about raising children when they are young, poor, and single.

Mothers raising children in the toughest sections of Philadelphia almost always hope and plan for their children's fathers to be part of their children's lives, just as Millie did. When a man and a woman cannot survive as a couple, though, it is an immense disappointment but not the end of the world. As Millie puts it, "[I've] got a good home for [my kids]. They have everything they need and I give them a lot of love and attention." When we ask about Carlos's ongoing role, she replies, "They don't *need* anything from him—you know what I'm saying—so I don't *ask* for nothing."

MOTHERHOOD AS A TURNING POINT

In an America that is profoundly unequal, the poor and rich alike are supposed to wait to bear children until they can complete their schooling, find stable employment, and marry a man who has done the same. Yet poor women realize they may never have children if they hold to this standard.[1] Middle-class taxpayers see the children born to a young, poor, and unmarried mother as barriers to her future achievement, short-circuiting her chances for what might have been a better life, while the mother herself sees children as the best of what life offers. Though some do express regret that an untimely birth robbed them of chances to improve their lot in life, most do not. Instead, they credit their children for virtually all that they see as positive in their lives.[2] Even those who say they might have achieved more if they hadn't become parents when and how they did almost always believe the benefits of children far exceed the costs. As Celeste, a twenty-one-year-old white mother of a five-month-old, explains, "I'd have no direction [if I hadn't had a child]. I could sit here and say, 'Oh, I would have . . . gone to a four-year college,' [but] I probably wouldn't have." Like Celeste, many unmarried teens bear children that are conceived only after they've already experienced academic difficulties or dropped out of school.[3]

Despite the ascent of feminism and the rapid entry of women into jobs formerly reserved for men, motherhood still offers a powerful source of meaning for American women. This is particularly true for low-income women living in the poorest sections of the Philadelphia area, who have little access to the academic degrees, high-status marriages, and rewarding professions that provide many middle- and upper-class women with gratifying social identities.

Poor youth are driven by a logic that is profoundly counterintuitive to their middle-class critics, who sometimes assume that poor women have children in a twisted competition with their peers to gain status, because they have an insufficient knowledge of—or access to—birth control, or so they can "milk" the welfare system. Yet our mothers almost never refer to these motivations. Rather, it is the perceived low costs of early childbearing and the high value that poor women place on children—and motherhood—that motivate their seemingly inexplicable inability to avoid pregnancy.[4]

These poor young women are not unusually altruistic, though parenthood certainly requires self-sacrifice. What outsiders do not understand is that early childbearing does not actually have much effect on a low-skilled young woman's future prospects in the labor market. In fact, her life chances are so limited already that a child or two makes little difference, as we document in the next chapter. What is even less understood, though, are the rewards that poor women garner from becoming mothers. These women rely on their children to bring validation, purpose, companionship, and order to their often chaotic lives—things they find hard to come by in other ways. The absolute centrality of children in the lives of low-income mothers is the reason that so many poor women place motherhood before marriage, even in the face of harsh economic and personal circumstances. For women like Millie, marriage is a longed-for luxury; children are a necessity.

A REASON TO GET UP IN THE MORNING

Children provide motivation and purpose in a life stalled by uncertainty and failure. As Adlyn, a pregnant nineteen-year-old Puerto Rican mother of a three-year-old and an eight-month-old, exclaims, "It's what gets [me] going. . . . It's like a *burst* of *energy*." Seventeen-year-old African American Kyra says her son, nearly two, gives her "something to look forward to. Like when I don't even have enough energy to get out of bed in the morning . . . I know I have to. When I turn over and look at him, it's like I'm trying to give him a better life, so I gotta get up and I gotta *do*."

Motherhood offers young women with limited options a valid role and a meaningful set of challenges. Zeyora, a white fifteen-year-old with a six-month-old, recalls, "I wanted a baby to take challenges into my *own hands*." Allison, twenty-eight and white, was a heroin addict who joined a methadone program when she learned she was pregnant. She says her life was going nowhere before her daughter, now nine months old, was born. "There was nothing to live for other than the next day getting high. [My life had] no *point*, there was no *joy*. I had lost all my friends—my friends were totally disgusted with me—I was about to lose my job, [and] I ended up dropping out of another college. . . . Now I feel like, 'I have a beautiful little girl!' I'm *excited* when I get up in the morning!"

Amanda, a twenty-year-old Puerto Rican mother of a three-year-old, says the birth of her son ignited her ambition and drive. She recalls, "When I had him was when I started thinking, '*Damn*, you know, I have to *change!*' When you have a kid, you really need—I think you should have an education so that [your kids] can look forward. You can look forward to telling him, 'Look, mommy works here.' He can go to school and tell his friends, 'Look my mom is *this!*' not 'Oh my mom works in a factory,' or 'We get food stamps every month.'" Destiny, an eighteen-year-old white mother of two girls, ages two and three, hopes her daughters "will grow up to *be* something and not depend on anybody. No man, no welfare, no nothing." She's doing her part by "making [the] kids smart and taking care of them, making them feel good." Thirty-year-old TJ, an African American mother of three, ages four, two, and four months, says that motherhood has completely reoriented her life. "I'm complete, and I've done what I am supposed to." She adds, "I don't see myself as being an individual anymore, really. Everything I do is mostly centered around my children, to make *their* lives better."

Jen Burke remembers feeling as if she just wanted to disappear into the background before she had her son. "I think about [my life] before I became a mom, what my life was like back then. I [saw] these pictures of me, and I would hide in every picture." But the birth of her son set a new goal for her to "look up to." "Before, I didn't have nothing to go home for. Now I have my son to take care of, I have him to go home for. I don't have to go buy weed or drugs with my money, I could buy my *son* stuff with my money. I have something to look up to now." Aliya, a twenty-seven-year-old African American with a nine-year-old boy, says this about being a mother to her son: "It is wonderful feeling because this is my child and he can come to me . . . his future is in my hands." "Your children have to come first," declares forty-year-old Carol, a white mother of two teens and a seven-year-old. "You gotta put your children before your [man], even though he was first in your life. They didn't ask to be brought into this world, and it's up to you to take care of them and you gotta see to their needs."

Part of the reason that motherhood breeds such a strong sense of purpose is the high cost of failure. Mothers repeatedly offer horrific examples of neglectful and abusive mothers from well-publicized child abuse cases as haunting counterpoints to their own mothering. Jennifer, a twenty-three-year-old Puerto Rican mother of six children under age seven, told us, "At least I don't throw my children in the *trash* or drown them in the *bathtub*." Danielle, a twenty-seven-year-old white mother of two children in elementary school, distinguishes herself from mothers "who be killing their kids, or doing bad things to their kids, or hittin' them or abusing them, you know." Lena, a fifteen-year-old white mother of a thirteen-month-old, draws a damning portrait of the bad mothers she sometimes observes in her Kensington neighborhood, and in doing so marks a clear moral boundary between herself and these failures. "There are people who just leave their kids laying on the floor with *roaches* crawling all over the baby, screaming at their kids, shoving bottles in their mouth with no *milk*, bringing them around with no *socks* and *shoes*, leaving them all night so they can just go have fun and party." "They don't bathe their kids and leave 'em covered in dirt. My daughter is bathed *every* day."

"MY SON GIVES ME ALL THE LOVE I NEED."

Many Americans believe that though the poor don't have much in the way of economic resources, they compensate by forming unusually rich social and emotional ties. But in the neighborhoods we studied, nothing could have been further from the truth. Indeed, many mothers tell us they cannot name one person they would consider a friend, and the turmoil of adolescence often breeds a sense of alienation from family as well.[5] Thus, mothers often speak poignantly about the strong sense of relational poverty they felt in the period before childbearing and believe they have forged those missing attachments through procreation, a self-made community of care. Brielle, a thirty-two-year-old African American mother of four children between the ages of three and eleven, says that few outsiders understand how central this motivation is for single mothers like herself. "A lot of people . . . say [young girls have babies] for money from welfare. It's not for that. . . . It's not even to keep the *guy*. It's just to have somebody . . . to take *care* of, or somebody to *love* or whatever." Nineteen-year-old Keisha, an African American mother of a one-year-old, paints the following picture of her bleak social landscape: "I don't have *nobody* that I can talk to. I don't have no friends, only got my baby. I can't even talk to my mom. I don't have nobody but my child." Sonia, a twenty-three-year-old Puerto Rican mother of a three-year-old, says, "No, no I didn't use no birth control, because I wanted a baby. I guess I needed something to fill up that hole." Aliya offers the following before-and-after portraits of her life. "The way I was raised, [with] so much violence and confusion going on around me, I just wanted to love somebody. And . . . then [my child] just filled me up with a lot of stuff that was needed."

For many, not even a relationship with a man can fill the relational void. "When I didn't have kids," remembers Yolanda, a twenty-six-year-old Puerto Rican mother of two, ages three and four, "me and [my son's father] were together but something was missing. . . . It was like we *needed* something. And then there were babies, you know, to fill the void we were feeling." We ask her, "Is that the most important thing?" She replies, "Kids, I think so. In my life, yes." Beatrice, a twenty-year-old Puerto Rican mother of a three-month-old, simply states, "My son gives me all the love I need."

Children cure relational blues like no other medicine their mothers have known. Jennifer says of her oldest, "What I like best about being a mother is that my son always keeps me company. I could be in a real bad mood and be real cranky, he'll just look at me and start playing or laughing at me, and he'll just crack me up." Twenty-three-year-old Amber, a legally blind white mother of a four-year-old and a six-month-old, exclaims of her oldest, "I never *imagined* that there was any kind of love like that *out* there, never imagined it! My son . . . knows I have bad eyes, and he always say, 'Mommy, I'm your eyes. I'll help you do it.' It's the love your children can give you. Because nobody in the world can give you the love your children can give you. There's no way." She concludes, "I don't know what I would do without the kids. I don't know where I would be right now if I didn't have them."

The relationship between a mother and her child offers a haven from the often harsh world of adult relationships, especially those with men. Jen Burke remembers how her son was there for her after a particularly ugly fight with her boyfriend Rick. "After a fight with my boyfriend, I was crying, I was mad. And my son is sixteen months, and he came in and he was hugging me with his little arms, so I got happy!" "That's the one good thing about being a mother," she finishes. "Your baby is always there for you." Abby, a white twenty-five-year-old, says her three-year-old daughter offers her refuge from a painful relationship with a man. "I can only take so much. I don't need a man who abuses or cheats all the time. I have a beautiful daughter now! Because I was on the verge of killing myself; I thought I was worth nothing. My daughter is the only thing that keeps me alive. If I didn't have no kids, I wouldn't be here. I know that for a fact because I'm *not* that *strong*."

Children provide the one relationship poor women believe they can count on to last. Men may disappoint them. Friends may betray them. Even kin may withdraw from them. But they staunchly believe that little can destroy the bond between a mother and child. Champagne, a seventeen-year-old African American mother of an six-month-old, exclaims, "The best part [is] I got somebody that I can say that's *mine*. I know he gonna be there *with* me and *for* me. I know that he got love for *me*, and I got love for *him*. We can do things *together*. We have that type of bond."

In motherhood, young women who live in the city's hardscrabble core can find a powerful source of validation, for they believe that childrearing is something they can be good at, a meaningful and valued identity they can successfully realize. Pepper Ann, a forty-seven-year-old African American mother of two grown children and a twelve-year-old, recalls how as a child she "always wanted a baby." She says she thought "babies were the most precious thing on this earth," and she "wouldn't know what to do without [her daughter]. . . . She is my little heart."

The birth of a baby also tends to mobilize others on the child's behalf. And while the baby takes center stage, the mother enjoys some of the limelight. Rosita, a twenty-three-year-old Puerto Rican mother of a two-year old, tells how becoming a mother made her feel "special." "Well, when I first became a mom, I got more attention, like everybody was closer to me. After I had her, I was coming out of the room, the hallway was packed with all my friends and family, and everybody was there, and I just felt real special, and everybody used to come every day to see the baby. Then when I went home, they was always around me and the baby all the time."

"BEING A MOM IS SOMETHING I KNEW I COULD DO."

But simply having a baby is not enough to earn social rewards; rather, a young mother must demonstrate that she has risen to the challenge of her new role. By presenting a clean, healthy, well-behaved child to the world, a young woman whose life may seem otherwise insignificant can prove her worth. Aliya, mentioned earlier, says that neighbors and kin see her differently now that she has a child and is managing to raise it on her own. "I guess they respect me more. I am taking care of my son myself."

There is no greater proof of a young woman's merit than the spontaneous praise of her mothering from a stranger on the street. The well-dressed child transforms the shabbily dressed mother. A child swathed in layers of warm clothing, even in a spring thaw, is testimony that an aimless teen is now a caring, competent, and responsible adult. The almost obsessive concern she has with her newborn's cleanliness, however, exposes the fragility of her new claim to respectability. According to Keisha, "It's *hard* when you don't have money to take care of your baby. People talk about you when—like if your child is dirty and stuff. So that's why I try to keep my child clean and buy . . . for Cheresa before I buy for myself. I don't have no clothes, she has everything."

Young women whose lives revolve around their children know that others are judging their failure or success at motherhood by these outside appearances. Santana, a thirty-four-year-old white mother of an eighteen-month-old girl, says, "When I go out with her, I think [about] the way she . . . will reflect on me. I feel that people look at her and then look at me. . . . Before, I went out alone, and I didn't think people were observing me. . . . Now I feel like they do. Like if she starts crying on the bus, and they look at me. They're thinking, 'Can't you make her *quiet?*' And so how *she* is is about *me.*"

This is why, though most mothers try to deemphasize material possessions, many still occasionally bypass the K-Mart on Broad Street for the designer discount chain across the street where Hilfiger and Polo abound, or even the Gap down on South Street. Having at least one "name brand" outfit for the baby is important to a young mother's quest for validation. "[It's] because of the status thing—to show people that you can afford to take care of your family," says Marilyn, a twenty-four-year-old white mother of two, ages four and five. Sonia, a twenty-three-year-old Puerto Rican mother with a child of three, confides, "Even though I was on welfare—I ain't gonna lie—I always like my baby to wear name-brand things you know? So they could never say that they ever seen my son dirty, in bad clothes or shit, that I wasn't taking care of him."

A well-cared-for child is the tangible evidence of a young mother's importance. *She* is the one raising the happy, healthy, carefully dressed child. *She* is the one who is teacher and guide. *She* is the one who is helping the child reach each developmental milestone: the first step, the first word, a dawning awareness of right and wrong. Her identity is secure as she basks in the glow of the child's accomplishments. Marilyn speaks passionately about the importance of a mother in her child's life. "When you have a baby, people don't realize you're raising not only the body, but the *mind*—the psychology, the mentality, the emotions, you're raising *all* that. You're actually teaching another person how to speak *English*, speak the *language*. I mean, to know that I brought this person into the world and they didn't know anything, and now I'm teaching and they're learning—that was a great feeling."

Mothers take enormous satisfaction from their child's accomplishments. Cheyenne, a twenty-five-year-old white mother of two, ages five and eight, starts out each school year by reserving a place on the wall of the front room for her eight-year-old daughter's school artwork and awards. "I like the rewards [from being a mother], the stuff they make for me to have. I'm so proud. Well, yeah, this is gonna be this year's wall [pointing to a blank space on the wall]. If I had the money, *every one* [of her pictures and awards] would be in a frame." Carmelita, a nineteen-year-old Puerto Rican mother of a four-year-old boy and a seven-month-old girl, says, "I'm proud of myself, [I know my son is] extremely smart. . . . I'm proud of that because *I* made my son what he is."

These mothers see themselves in their offspring—often so much so that children become a reconstituted, yet more positive, image of themselves. The family resemblance between the two makes the child's accomplishments the mother's own. Carol brags about how her seven-year-old daughter Tabitha, the youngest, "is my prodigy child." Tabitha, she says, was "walking at nine months, talking at ten months. She's smart," Carol beams. "The kids fight over who gets to sit with her at school. I love it. First grade, and she was the most popular kid in the classroom! And she looks like me!" Kyra, talking about her one-year-old, says, "It's like I got this little *me* to take care of because he looks just *like* me."

Women near the bottom of the American class ladder hope their children will give them a vicarious second chance at the social mobility that has slipped out of their grasp. Even though a woman's own prospects might be limited, a new baby's life is a clean slate. As she "struggles and strives," to give them a better life, she heals the regret of having "messed up" her own. "I have so many aspirations for my daughter," proclaims Jerri, a thirty-five-year-old African American mother of two children just a year apart. She tells her older child, now eight, "'Look for something that you want to be, but be good at it and be useful to somebody.' A lot of times I've felt I was useless to people. I didn't matter."

"TO BE SOMETHING BETTER"

In these decaying, inner-city neighborhoods, motherhood is the primary vocation for young women, and those who strive to do it well are often transformed by the process. Nineteen-year-old Shonta, an African American with one child who became a mother at only fourteen, says she knows motherhood "has its ups and downs, [but] I never felt my daughter held me back from anything. If anything she taught me how to be responsible and mature." Nineteen-year-old Adlyn declares that if she were childless, "I would be on the street . . . because I used to be out on the streets getting high. And look at me *now!* I'm going to school, doing what I got to do. I'm telling everyone, *watch* me when I'm *done!*"

Middle-class observers often believe that the lives of poor youth could be salvaged if not for the birth of a child—but this is seldom the case. Our mothers' stories show that young women raised in poor neighborhoods can suffer far worse fates than having to drop out of school to care for a baby. The poor women we came to know often describe their lives prior to motherhood as spinning out of control. They recall an existence blemished by more than mere economic insecurity. For most, the "rippin' and runnin'" days before children were marked by depression, school failure, drug and alcohol use, and promiscuous sexual activity. Along with this self-made chaos were their sometimes troubled and abusive home lives and the danger, violence, and oppression of the neighborhood.[6]

Over and over again, mothers tell us their children tamed or calmed their wild behavior, got them off of the street, and helped put their lives back together. Children can banish depression, calm a violent temper, or serve as do-it-yourself rehab from alcohol and drugs. Children—and the minute-by-minute demands they make on their mothers' time, energy, and emotions—bring order out of chaos. "I would still be wild and stuff, hanging in the streets, hanging on the corners and stuff," testifies fifteen-year-old Jessica, a Puerto Rican mother of a two-year-old. "[But] I didn't want to get in trouble and then DHS come and take her away from me. I used to be *bad*, go around break windows and stuff. Now I don't do *nothing*. I be with *her* all day. I come to school, go home, be with her." Cheyenne, introduced above, is a recovering drug addict who says, "With [my daughter], it was instant love. That kid was my whole world. She was such a happy baby and a good baby. It was easy giving her love." Now, she says, "I like the stability [being a mom] gives me, it's very routine."

Fifteen-year-old Zeyora says her six-month-old was clearly a blessing from God. "You know, maybe God gave [a baby] to you so you could calm down, you know? God *chose* you to have a baby so you could let yourself calm down, to stop being what you *are*, to be something *better*. I felt that God led me to be with [my child] to *change*, to get back to school, to calm down so I wouldn't be hurt. That's what I feel." Madeline, an eighteen-year-old Puerto Rican mother of a four-month-old, shares a similar story. "Before I was pregnant with him, I was doing *real* bad in school. I'm a real smart person, but I was messing up in school . . . smoking marijuana, drinking beer. . . . Sometimes I didn't come home for four or five days, didn't even see my mom or nothing. Then I got *him*, and my life just changed. God's *given* me something—I didn't really *want* him yet but He's *given* me something. It's for a *reason*."

Denise, an eighteen-year-old white mother of twin two-year-olds, says the conception of her sons gave her enough self-respect to leave drugs and alcohol behind. "Before I got pregnant, I was like smoking a lot of weed. And like drinking and taking pills. And I realized it was getting me nowhere, because I was losing my friends, and I was like losing my self-esteem. . . . [Now] I try to stay focused on what I want in life and for my kids. . . . It was like hard for me to tell myself, 'I can stop smoking weed,' and, 'I can stop taking pills,' and, 'I can stop drinking,' and, 'I can stop getting with all those guys and having sex with them to feel good.' . . . I look at my kids, I keep them in my head, like they're telling me, 'Don't smoke, Mommy,' or 'Don't run away and have sex with him.' That's what I tell myself."

Champagne even believes that her son has helped her heal from the sexual abuse she suffered at the hands of a cousin and from her painful experiences as a "dancer" in a tawdry North Philadelphia bar. "I tried to kill myself before. There's a lot of stuff going on in my life. I hadn't seen my father since I was ten . . . my cousin raped me, and it was hard because my mom didn't believe me." With the birth of her son, this young woman has come "to see myself different . . . I feel *different* about myself. [Being a mother] makes me feel like a *whole another person*." In fact, a recent decision to return to school was inspired by her son. "If I wasn't gonna do it for *me*, it was for the sake of my *child*. . . . That's why I stopped dancing. I stopped doing a whole lot of stuff I was doing because, like, I feel I'm a *mother* now. I got a child, and I can't raise him around that stuff. I have to do *better*."

Fifty-year-old Pamela remembers a terrible night she spent homeless on the Delaware riverfront with her children. This white mother of seven, the youngest now in middle school, had fled from their father, who had threatened to shoot her and her yet unborn baby earlier that day. "I told the kids we were going camping. There was a whole bunch of big boxes from refrigerators and washers and dryers . . . so we took them up over the other side where we were going to stay, and we built this campfire. . . . I had food stamps, so I got cookies and cakes, and we got hot dogs and beans. I put the kids in the boxes [but] the river was right there, and I spent the whole night chasing away these sewer rats so they wouldn't get into the boxes with my babies. That night we stayed at Penn's Landing I was going to commit suicide. [But then] I thought to myself, if I did, who was going to take care of my babies?"

WHAT MOTHERHOOD DOES FOR MOMS

Some readers may be deeply troubled by the idea that poor, unmarried women reap so many benefits from the children they bear. The idea of a woman viewing her offspring as a resource violates powerful social norms about how a mother should behave. Altruism, not need, ought to govern her relationship to her children. Yet, as we've shown, altruism is also common and strong among poor mothers who are raising children alone. In reality, the motivation to mother among women of all social classes is a mix of self-sacrifice and expected reward.

One of the many advantages of membership in the privileged classes is greater access to a range of satisfying social roles. All parents presumably derive some additional degree of validation, some greater sense of purpose, some new sense of connection, and at least some level of reorientation because of their children. Yet few middle-class women approach mothering with such a great sense of need, and few see their children as very nearly their sole source of fulfillment.

When we've told these mothers' stories to audiences around the country, many of our listeners are surprised to learn that, for young women on the economic edge, having a child can bring order to a life with no point or purpose. One woman, a new mother herself, conceded that having a child had improved her life, but found our claim that children bring order to the lives of poor mothers difficult to swallow. Her once-regimented, childless, middle-class lifestyle was more out of control since the birth of her child than she had ever dreamed possible. "How out of control must their lives *be?*" she asked, unable to conceive of how a child could *reduce* rather than *multiply* a mother's day-to-day level of chaos.

On another occasion, a listener told us she simply couldn't accept our contention that poor women express so little regret over having had children when and how they did. She demanded to know more about the "ambivalence" women must feel toward their children and toward motherhood. "There *has* to be some tension or sense of regret!" she exclaimed. But as the question-and-answer period ended and the crowd dispersed, a pregnant woman who had not spoken up earlier turned to her companion and asked, "Why is it so hard for people here to believe that the women would *want* their children?"

After spending six years talking about these issues with poor unwed mothers, the worldviews they hold no longer seem strange to us. But we must admit that at first, we were as astonished by their viewpoints as many of our listeners have been. Looking back over our own experiences on the street corners and stoops, the coffee shops and fast-food restaurants, and the front rooms and kitchens of these mothers, we can now identify the one question we asked that proved most revealing: "What would your life be like without children?" We assumed this question would prompt stories of regret over opportunities lost and ambitions foiled, and some did indeed say what we had expected to hear. But there were startlingly few "if only" tales of how "coming up pregnant" wrecked dreams of education, career, marriage, or material success. Instead, mothers repeatedly offered refrains like these: "I'd be dead or in jail," "I'd be in the streets," "I wouldn't care about anything," "My child saved me," and "It's only because of my children that I'm where I am today." For all but a few, becoming a mother was a profound turning point that "saved" or "rescued" them from a life either leading nowhere or going very wrong. Rather than derailing their lives, they believed their children were what finally set them on the right track.[7]

Aside from a few notable exceptions, some of which we discuss in chapter 5, the mothers we met seemed, in our judgment, to be adequate parents. Our central point here is not that these mothers were exceptionally good, but that they use motherhood as a way to make meaning in a void. Their life stories are testimonials to motherhood's transforming influence, leading them to abandon their "drinking and drugging," to trade a wild life for one spent at home, to return to school, pursue employment, reconnect with family, and to find a new sense of hope and purpose.[8] This does not mean we accept at face value that these mothers are right when they say they are better off having had their children when they did. Some could probably have benefited from waiting. What we are saying is that these mothers perceive these things to be true, and it is this *perception*, rather than reality, that guides their actions. Before we dismiss their claims about the redemptive value of children, however, we should contrast their lives to those of their male counterparts, who do not usually bear the primary responsibility for their children. By any measure, the behaviors of men who populate these neighborhoods are considerably worse than those of the women. We simply do not know what these mothers' lives would be like without the responsibility for children, and the sense of identity, purpose, connection, or demand for order that it brings.

Yet motherhood's influence may be fleeting for some. We're not claiming that every poor, young woman will stop "using," get her high school diploma, find a career, or never again have an abusive relationship with a man when she becomes a mother. What motherhood offers is the possibility—not the promise—of validation, purpose, connection, and order. More important, children allow mothers to transcend, at least psychologically and symbolically, the limitations of economic and social disadvantage. These women put motherhood before marriage not primarily out of welfare opportunism, a lack of discipline, or sheer resignation. Rather, the choice to mother in the context of personal difficulty is an affirmation of their strength, determination, and desire to offer care for another. In the end, establishing the primordial bonds of love and connection is the ultimate goal of their mothering.[9]

CONCLUSION: MAKING SENSE OF SINGLE MOTHERHOOD

In September 2003 we reconnect with Mahkiya Washington, introduced in chapter 2, who still lives in the same Strawberry Mansion neighborhood but now in an apartment of her own. We meet her at her grandmother's place, a tiny row home on one of the narrow, cramped side streets tucked between the avenues lined with grander dwellings. It has been three years since we've talked, and Mahkiya's daughter Ebony, now a kindergartener at a small neighborhood charter school, bounces around the room proudly showing off her new school uniform.

Mahkiya, her hair neatly coiffed in a bob, has a new air of confidence about her. She's come a long way since we last saw her, completing a two-year degree in the culinary arts while holding down a full-time job. Her plan now is to transfer to a local four-year college and get a BA in business. Then she hopes to pursue an MBA and open a catering company. But during the last three years, her demanding schedule has kept her away from home from 6:00 A.M. to 9:00 P.M. Though her grandmother has taken good care of Ebony, Mahkiya resents missing out on so much. Right now, she is taking time off from school to make up for the lost time with her daughter, but she's promised herself she'll go back next year. Meanwhile, she's secured a lucrative management job in large food service company.

Ebony's father Mike left Mahkiya during the pregnancy. But the couple reunited just before Ebony's first birthday—shortly after he'd finally managed to secure a full-time, relatively well-paid janitorial job. Initially, they moved in with her sister and were saving to get an apartment of their own. But almost as soon as they met that goal, Mike lost the job. After that setback, he couldn't seem to stick to subsequent jobs for one reason or other—didn't like the work, didn't like the hours—it was always something. And the friends who had brought him down during the pregnancy were back. So as Mahkiya kept up her breakneck fourteen-hour schedule of work and school, and her ambition soared, his seemed to deflate and then collapse altogether. She kicked him out once and for all about three years ago. "I couldn't do both," Mahkiya explains. "He just was not supportive of me [when I was both working and] going back to school." Rather than help out with Ebony, she complains, "He still wanted to party and spend time with his friends."

When we ask Mahkiya where Mike is now, she holds her hands out in front of her, pantomiming wrists in a pair of handcuffs. Mike, once the honor student, has had repeated run-ins with the law. Mike and his mother take Ebony every weekend, but Mahkiya has moved on. She is undeterred in her ambition to marry someday—her parents were married, and she sees marriage as part of the successful lifestyle she aspires to. She has just begun dating Andre, a man who might well fit the bill. Andre and Mahkiya grew up together, so they already knew each other well. The two attributes that most clearly distinguish Andre from Mike are his maturity and work ethic. Andre is very involved with his son, a boy about Ebony's age. At twenty-three, he's already started his own drywall installation business.

Right now, though, Mahkiya's main focus is on working toward her goals—the new job, the college degree, and the catering business she hopes to start. So she's not ready to think about marriage yet. The hard times with Mike have made her cautious. She insists she does not want to create a "revolving door" of men in her daughter's life. Mahkiya likes the fact that Andre already knew Ebony before the two of them started dating. She now realizes, though, that love and romance are not enough to sustain a couple over the long haul. "I didn't know the *rules* of being together. You need someone who will *support* you." She adds, "I'm on a journey right now with my family and school, but it's still not finished." For Mahkiya, marriage is at the end of that journey.

- - - -

We catch up with Deena Vallas, from chapter 4, on a warm fall day in 2003, nearly four years after we last saw her. Kevin Jr., a kindergartner now, clowns around to the squeals of his younger sister Magdalena, now three, who is a beauty like her mother. And there is another child too, six-month-old Cameron, a mellow baby content to watch his half-siblings play. A few minutes into the conversation, we are startled to learn that Patrick is now out of the picture. Deena seems a bit stunned herself. The faithful Patrick seemed like such a big improvement over Kevin, the womanizer who'd cheated on her while she was pregnant with his son. Deena believed that Patrick's eagerness to take on the father role with Kevin Jr. proved he was ready to be a family man.

But things began to fall apart with Patrick almost as soon as she had Magdalena. Playing the role of social father was one thing, it seems, but having a child of his own to support was another. Before Magdalena came along, Deena regarded every dollar Patrick put toward Kevin Jr.'s support as a gift, as he had no legal or moral duty to provide for the child. But Magdalena represented an obligation, and the pressure Patrick felt was apparently too much. By the time their baby was just a few months old, he had returned to the habits he'd left behind when they learned Deena was carrying his child, "smoking crack, cocaine, pills, anything he could get his hands on."

Deena tried to intervene by moving the family to her mother's home in the New Jersey suburbs—as far away from the negative neighborhood "element" as she thought she could get. There, she landed the first good job she had ever had—as a manager of a hair salon—and Patrick found steady work too. But her effort to curb Patrick's rapidly escalating drug habit failed. "I figured if I took him to Jersey, he would stop doing drugs. Well, he never stopped."

As Patrick's cocaine use became steady, things got ugly between the two, especially after Patrick left his job to pursue his addiction. This act, added to the growing tension between Deena and her mother, prompted Deena to move back to her grandmother's PennsPort home, while Patrick returned to his mother's house. She describes the months in New Jersey as "a long struggle with him with drugs. I mean, if *I* can't help him, who *can?* If you love me so much, *why*, like why would you do this to your *family?*"

Back in PennsPort, Deena landed on her feet. She found work as a waitress at a busy Greek diner in downtown Philadelphia, and used a hefty tax return to make a down payment on a three-bedroom condominium next door to her grandmother. "I [was] really excited. I bought my own place. I did all these things for myself. I bought all these things for it. Everything going good. I was working at a restaurant, like a diner. I loved it." And during this period, when she and Patrick were neither together nor officially broken up, Deena rekindled a relationship with Sean, a childhood sweetheart.

When she learned she was pregnant a third time, she knew Sean, not Patrick, had to be the father. She was afraid, though, that Sean was not ready to be "serious," so she let Patrick move in to help pay the bills while she took time off to have the baby. She also allowed him to believe the child was his. On Father's Day, when baby Cameron was two months old, it all came apart. Returning home, Deena discovered that her CD player, CDs, television and VCR, the beds, the couch—virtually everything she'd purchased for the home—had disappeared, sold for the meager proceeds such second-hand items command. "I made a *home!*" she exclaims, remembering her reaction to the desolate scene. "He made it feel like it was this horrible *crack* house. And it was a beautiful house. My house was clean, it was nice, the kids had their own rooms, and the beds were always made, and I had my clothes washed, and it was perfect. It was a beautiful home, and he turned it into this horrible place." In her rage, she told Patrick that Cameron, whom he had named and legally claimed, was not his. He moved out almost immediately, and, as she had no income at the time, she could not keep up with the mortgage.

Deena is now living with her grandmother again and works six days a week at the diner while grandma watches the kids. She is with Cameron's father, Sean, now, who has responded positively to her ultimatum to "either be with me or don't be with me." "With kids you can't keep coming in and out of their lives either, because not only are you just with *me*, you're with me *and* my kids. You take the *whole package*." Deena is delighted by how things have turned out, though she admits that the discovery of her third pregnancy made her feel that her life "was over." "I love my boyfriend now, and I'm happy with him, and he makes me happy. I haven't been this happy in a very, very long time." She describes her love for Sean as "an extreme love, the craziest love I've ever had in my whole life." "I don't even think I loved Patrick," she now reflects. "I settled for Patrick because I couldn't have what I wanted. And I was pregnant with Magdalena, so what could I do?" She still feels some guilt that she couldn't work things out with Patrick. "We tried, we tried our best. He let it go to the extreme. Rock bottom—he was there. I don't want to live that way. I don't want to be scared now. I didn't want to [spend my life just] wonder[ing] what it would be like to be with a normal guy, one who didn't do drugs."

On the surface, Sean seems like an excellent bet for a long-term relationship. He is apprenticing with a local plumbers' union, has no other kids, and is willing to play daddy to all three children. He has no prison record, and though he gets high occasionally, he is not a drug addict. These attributes qualify him as a PennsPort version of a Rhodes scholar. Deena says marriage is "definitely" where her relationship with Sean is headed. But the couple has much to accomplish first, for she still insists on having the "white picket fence" before she'll marry.

- - - -

We meet up with Dominique Watkins, from chapter 5, at a music school in North Central Philadelphia, where her children, now ages sixteen, eleven, and nine, take classes after school. She now owns a home there, which she inherited when her father passed away two years ago. Dominique still works as a teacher's aide, but her goal is to become a head teacher. To that end, she is pursuing an associate's degree. She has class after work two nights a week, leaving the other evenings free for her busy family life. Dominique is taking "Introduction to Psychology" this term, a course with weekly quizzes. When she returns home after class, her middle child, Jaclyn, queries, "What'd you get on the quiz today?" If it's not an A grade, the daughter chides, "That's not good enough! You have to *study*, Mom!"

Dominique's children remain on the honor roll. Renee earns straight A's, loves to sing, and seems quite musically talented. Dominique says she is an independent girl who doesn't "follow the crowd," though the middle daughter is vivacious and "likes the crowd," which worries her a little. Yet eleven-year-old Jaclyn excels at school too, and her teachers have identified a particular gift for writing. Elijah is in fourth grade and is also at the head of his class. When we ask her how she's kept them so focused on schoolwork, she replies, "Talking to them, being around them a lot, . . . encouraging them whatever they want to do, . . . show up for everything, staying involved with them."

While we chat with Dominique, Elijah is deeply engrossed in the task of composing music on a computer. As we watch Dominique help him, we can see he is clearly the light of his mother's life. "My son . . . he's my protector. . . . He says, 'Mom, you seem sad.' He worries about me a little bit." It's been over three years since we saw Dominique last, and we're surprised to learn that she's back together with Ron, the children's father. They'd broken up over his failure to work steadily, with increasingly explosive encounters when both parents were at home. That is part of why Elijah, a witness to some of these traumatic events, is so protective of her.

Dominique explains that about a year after her breakup with Ron, the father of all three of her children, he showed up at her door penniless with no place to stay. "I'm like, 'Okay, I'll let him stay.' Because I couldn't see somebody staying out on the street or whatever. I think that was his way of gradually working his way back in." For the next year, the couple was "living together, but not *together*, you know." During that period, "he was [working] steady, things like that, and he spent time with the kids more, he [was] contributing and stuff like that. So, I decided, I'd said, 'Okay, I'd give him another chance.'" She chuckles as she says, "But he *knows* that he messed up!"

When we ask Dominique why she thinks Ron finally changed, she replies, "I think he felt that he was really losing me, and that I wasn't paying him any mind, so he knew he *had* to get himself together before he truly, truly lost me. So that's what I really think. He finally grew up [at] thirty-eight. . . . I think he realized 'She really doesn't need me, it doesn't matter one way or the other.' And I really think he got himself together because of that. I really do." The financial independence that her job provided seemed to provide the key to Ron's reform.

We then ask Dominique what she is thinking now about "the 'M' word." She replies, "We've talked about it; he's recently actually *asked* me . . . and actually, I've thought about it, and [I'm] like, 'All this time? I don't know. . . . No matter how much I love you, I don't know.'" For Dominique, the turnaround in Ron's behavior is too new, and perhaps the mistrust spawned by the past too deep, to think about marriage yet. "Maybe one day I would get married, but I don't think about it right now. I wanna do what I need to do for *me*. . . . Get my associate's [degree]!" she exclaims.

- - - -

Four years ago, at age seventeen, Jen Burke, from chapter 3, says her life hit rock bottom. The man who had just asked her to marry him, with whom she already shared one child and had just conceived another, had gotten another girl pregnant, and she had decided to leave him and then lost the baby. She swore to us then that she was done with Rick for good, but she now admits that she found herself "back with him" just weeks later. As we explain, however, Rick isn't exactly available for a relationship these days.

Right now, Jen—once the aimless high school dropout with the depressed air—is not exactly on the top of the world, but she is close. Monday through Thursday she enters data at a warehouse distribution center, earning an astonishing $10.25 an hour. She has held the job for three years now, and has shown high aptitude for the task and a strong work ethic. No one is more surprised by this happy turn of events than Jen, and she delights in ticking off on four proud fingers the job's many perks—the two weeks of paid vacation, the four personal days, the sixty hours of sick time, and the all-important medical benefits.

Since her son has started school, she's been faithfully attending a high school completion program offering evening and weekend classes, and a single test—in her least favorite subject—is all that stands between her and a diploma. She confides, "My plan is to start college in January. [This month] I take my math test . . . so I can get my diploma."

Ambition is now Jen's middle name, but the passion to succeed—to make a better life for herself and her son—only began after Rick's dramatic exit from the scene about three and half years ago on the night of his twenty-second birthday. "You know that bar [down the street]? It happened in that bar. I was at my dad's. I was supposed to meet [Rick and his friends] there [to celebrate], but I was sick. . . . They were in the bar, and this guy was like bad-mouthing [Rick's friend] Mikey, talking stuff to him or whatever. So Rick had to go get involved in it and start with this guy. . . . Then he goes outside and fights the guy, [and] the guy dies of head trauma. . . . They were all on drugs, they were all drinking, and things just got out of control, and that's what happened. He got fourteen to thirty years."

While Rick was in jail awaiting trial, Jen embarked on a radically different future. "That's when I really started [to get better], because I didn't have to worry about what *he* was doing, didn't have to worry about him *cheating* on me, all this stuff. [It was] then I realized that I had to do what I had to do to take care of my son. . . . When he was there, I think that my whole *life* revolved around him, you know, so I always messed up somehow because I was so busy worrying about what *he* was doing. Like

I would leave the programs I was in just [to] go home and see what he was doing. My mind was never concentrating."

Now things are far different for Jen, and her transformation is evident to many. "A lot of people in my family look up to me now, because all my sisters are dropped out from school—you know—nobody went back to school. *I* went back to school, you know? . . . So that makes me happy . . . because five years ago *nobody* looked up to me." Yet the journey has been far from easy. "Being a young mom, being fifteen [when I had him], it's hard, hard, hard, you know." When we ask how hard it is, she says, "I have no life. . . . I work from 6:30 in the morning until 5:00 at night. I leave here at 5:30 in the morning, I don't get home until about 6:00 at night. So my stepmom, she takes him to school, she picks him up afterwards. Then when I get home I have my own homework to do, I have to do Colin's homework with him, and I'm tired, you know." Yet despite the hardship involved, and perhaps even because of it, Jen is fiercely proud of what she's been able to accomplish—especially since she's done it largely on her own. "I don't depend on *nobody*. I might *live* with my dad and them, but I don't *depend* on them, you know. Everything Colin has, I bought. Everything he needs, *I* bought, you know?" "There [used to] be days when I be so stressed out, like, 'I can't do this!' And I would just cry and cry and cry. . . . Then I look at Colin, and he'll be sleeping, and I'll just look at him and think I don't have no [reason to feel sorry for myself]. The cards I have I've dealt myself, so I have to deal with it now. I'm older. I can't change anything. He's *my* responsibility . . . so I have to deal with that. . . . I know I could have waited [to have a child], but in a way I think Colin's the best thing that could have happened to me. Because when I had my son, I changed. . . . I think Colin changed my life, he *saved* my life, really. I had a really big problem, like I had my stomach pumped for popping pills, I almost died from popping pills, so I think if it wasn't for Colin I probably wouldn't be here because he—Colin—is the only person out there that I . . . . stopped everything for. I stopped on pills, you know? My whole life revolves around Colin!"

Becoming a mother has transformed Jen's point of view on just about everything. For example, she says, "I thought hanging on the corner, drinking, getting high—I thought that was a good life, and I thought I could live that way for eternity, like sitting out with my friends. But it's not as fun once you have your own kid. . . . I think it changes [you]. I think, 'Would I want Colin to do that? Would I want my son to be like that?' It was fun to me, but it's not fun anymore. Half the people I hung with are either—some have died from drug overdoses, some are in jail, and some people are just out there living the same life that they always lived, and they don't look really good, they look really bad." But Jen does wonder about how Colin will fare growing up without a father. "By the time Rick comes home, Colin will be [at least] eighteen. He's not coming home any time soon. That's the only thing that bothers me now, is that he don't have his dad. When I got pregnant, I didn't *plan* to raise him by myself. I had no *choice*. . . . I would never want Colin to do the things I did in life. When I was younger, I stopped going to school. . . . I was doing drugs, I was drinking. . . . I would *never* want him to do stuff I did. I want to keep his mind occupied on things . . . so he doesn't have to get in the street. I always say, 'Colin . . . do you want to be a leader or a follower?' I was like, 'People look up to leaders, and followers are just people [hanging] with people thinking they're cool when it's really not, you know.' I said, 'If you be a leader, people look up to you.' Colin wants to be a policeman or a fireman. I was like, 'Well, you have to go to school for that and stuff', and I was like, 'You can be anything you wanna be as long as you do the right things to *get* there.'"

- - - -

In the previous chapters we have used the experiences of the single mothers living in neighborhoods like Kensington and West Kensington, North Central and Strawberry Mansion, PennsPort and the Camden neighborhoods across the Delaware River to redraw the portrait of nonmarital childbearing and the forces behind it. In doing so, we give a voice to people who are seldom heard in Beltway debates. We gathered our data in the kitchens and front rooms, the sidewalks and front stoops of those declining neighborhoods where the growth in single motherhood has been most pronounced. What we learned—and the stories we tell—challenge what most Americans believe about unwed motherhood and its causes. This on-the-ground approach creates a portrait of poor single mothers that goes beyond the statistics that are so often used to describe them.[1]

Mahkiya, Deena, Dominique, and Jen all face unfavorable odds in their search for a lasting relationship with a man.[2] In the poor black and Puerto Rican neighborhoods of Philadelphia and Camden, the sex ratios are badly out of balance.[3] Both Mahkiya's new love interest and Dominique's long-term partner—who, despite his past problems, has a trade that pays well, stays away from drugs, and has no children by other women—are both lucky finds. Even in the white neighborhoods of Kensington and PennsPort, there is not an overabundance of sober, stably employed men, so Deena feels fortunate as well. Jen has not been so lucky.

WHAT CAUSED THE RETREAT
FROM MARRIAGE?

Over the past three decades, scholars have offered a number of intuitively appealing theories to explain the huge changes in family formation that are so vividly illustrated in the lives of Mahkiya, Deena, Dominique, Jen, and the other 158 women we spoke with. The leading explanations are the increasing economic independence of women, the growing generosity of welfare, and the declining pool of marriageable men in America's inner cities.[4] These ideas have generated a large volume of research. Yet two or more decades of empirical work have told us as much about what doesn't explain these changes as what does.

In the early 1980s Nobel Prize–winning economist Gary Becker advanced a compelling explanation for the retreat from marriage in his *Treatise on the Family*.[5] Using market logic, Becker argued that the gains to marriage for both husband and wife depended on the degree of specialization within the relationship. Maximum efficiency resulted when one spouse was mostly dedicated to homemaking and childrearing while the other specialized in market work. Becker argued that women's entry into the labor market and the rise in their incomes relative to men's made marriage less attractive—and less profitable—to both parties. A variant of the same general idea holds that as women began to work more and earn more, they married less because they could afford to stay single.[6] According to this version of the argument, often called the "women's economic independence theory," women who fail to find satisfactory male partners no longer have to marry for economic survival.

A second idea—what we call the welfare-state hypothesis—gained prominence in the mid 1980s, when conservative commentator Charles Murray published his best-selling book *Losing Ground*.[7] Murray noted that during the 1970s, both nonmarital childbearing and the value of a welfare check grew dramatically. He argued that the rise in nonmarital births was a direct result, and a rational response, to this increased state support for poor single mothers. This, he charged, had the unintended effect of penalizing poor couples who had children within marriage. Once the poor realized they could even live together and share resources without having to forgo welfare benefits, he claimed, the marriage rate plummeted, and nonmarital childbearing soared.

Shortly after Murray made his controversial claims, a leading liberal social scientist from the University of Chicago, William Julius Wilson, offered an alternative hypothesis. In his groundbreaking book, *The Truly Disadvantaged*, Wilson argued that it was the declining number of marriageable men in inner-city neighborhoods—neighborhoods just like those we studied—that created an impossible dilemma for young women who wanted to start families.[8] As deindustrialization drained manufacturing jobs from inner-city neighborhoods, there were fewer and fewer "marriageable"—that is, stably employed—men to go around. The result, said Wilson, was a decline in marriage and a sharp upturn in nonmarital childbearing. This theory has been dubbed the "male marriageable pool hypothesis."

These theories have motivated scientific study for more than a decade, yet the empirical support for each has been amazingly slim. Let's begin with the women's economic independence thesis. Contrary to Becker's theory, most studies find that women who earn higher wages—both in general and relative to men—do not marry less.[9] In fact, among disadvantaged populations, women with higher earnings are *more*, not less, likely to marry.[10] The welfare-state explanation also largely fails the empirical test. The expansion of the welfare state could not have been responsible for the growth in nonmarital childbearing during the 1980s and 1990s for the simple reason that in the mid 1970s all states but California stopped adjusting their cash welfare benefits for inflation. By the early 1990s a welfare check's real value had fallen nearly 30 percent.[11] Meanwhile, marriage rates continued to decline while the rate of unmarried childbearing showed persistent growth.[12]

Wilson's male marriageable pool hypothesis does the best job of the three explanations, as declines in inner-city men's employment, as well as their higher incarceration and death rates, do seem to explain a statistically significant—albeit modest—part of the decline. The problem is that the changes in family life have been so gigantic that they have dwarfed the effects of even these seemingly powerful economic forces.[13] But another, more fundamental flaw in Wilson's argument is his assumption that employment, even at a menial job, pays enough to make a man marriageable. In the 1950s all but the most marginally employed men found women who were willing to marry them. Now, however, even men who are stably employed at relatively good jobs at the time of their child's birth—men like Mike, Patrick, Ron, and Rick—aren't automatically deemed marriageable by the women in their lives. Nor are Mahkiya or Deena even close to feeling ready to set a date with Andre and Sean, their stably employed new partners.

MARRIAGE REDEFINED

The stories our mothers tell suggest that the reasons for the major shift in family formation are not fully captured by any of the three explanations advanced so far. They suggest that the poor are responding to a redefinition of marriage that has been evolving over the last century but has changed most dramatically since the 1950s.[14] Though economic forces—especially the low number of so-called marriageable men at the bottom of the income distribution—have certainly played a role, the criteria poor women have for marriage have changed far more than the economic circumstances of the men in their lives. Thus, many of the men these women would have been willing to marry *then*, in the 1950s and 1960s, would not meet the standards they hold for marriage *now*, even if unskilled men's employment hadn't declined at all.

Any explanation of the decline in marriage and the growth of nonmarital childbearing among the poor must take into account not just economics but the profound cultural changes America has undergone over the last thirty years. Americans' views about virtually all aspects of family life have shifted dramatically to the left since 1960—shifts which now mean that having sex, establishing a common household, and having children have all become decoupled from marriage. In the 1960s two-thirds of Americans thought premarital sex was morally wrong. By the 1980s only one-third opposed it.[15] In the 1970s only one-third of American women agreed that living together outside of marriage was a good idea, but that figure had grown to just under 60 percent by the late 1990s. Opposition to nonmarital childbearing also declined dramatically, and only one in five Americans now believe that couples who don't get along should stay together for the sake of the children, though fully half believed so in the early 1960s.[16] What is crucial to note is that *now there are few differences between the poor and the affluent in attitudes and values toward marriage.*[17]

For the poor and affluent alike, marriage is now much less about sex, coresidence, and raising children than it used to be. In a cultural context where everyone had to marry to achieve a minimal level of social acceptance—as well as to have sex, live openly together, and bear children—women's and men's expectations for marriage had to be limited to the actual pool of those partners available to them. The sexual revolution, the widespread availability of birth control, the dramatic increase in the social acceptability of cohabitation, and the growing rejection of the idea that a couple should get or stay married just because there is a child on the way, have all weakened the once nearly absolute cultural imperative to marry.

At the same time, the feminist movement has succeeded in making marriage far less necessary for social personhood among American women: in the late 1950s eight in ten Americans believed a woman who remained unmarried was "sick, neurotic, or immoral," while only a quarter still held that view in 1978.[18] When people may have sex, live together, and even have children outside of marriage, and when unmarried women are no longer treated like social pariahs, marriage loses much of its day-to-day significance. But at the same time, the culture can afford to make marriage more special, more rarified, and more significant in its meaning. Therefore, we argue, along with noted family scholar Andrew Cherlin, that while the *practical* significance of marriage has diminished, its *symbolic* significance has grown.[19]

Conservative social commentators often charge that the poor hold to a deviant set of subcultural values that denigrate marriage, but these claims miss the point entirely. The truth is that the poor have embraced a set of surprisingly mainstream norms about marriage and the circumstances in which it should occur.

WHAT ABOUT ECONOMIC FACTORS?

Though we believe that a culture-wide redefinition of marriage is the primary reason for changes in marriage rates over time, we assert that the role the economy has played, and continues to play, is still profound. Inequalities in income and wealth, which have increased dramatically over the last thirty years, have bifurcated the life chances of the affluent and the poor.[20] Although the growth in inequality slowed during the 1990s, we still live in an America that is deeply unequal.[21] We argue that the growing divide in the material circumstances of the poor and the affluent has led these groups to make radically different family adaptations to the new cultural norm about marriage. Consider first how most members of the middle class have adjusted to the new standard. They are waiting much longer to marry—often entering into lower-commitment, "trial marriages" first in order to be "sure"—and they frequently divorce when their relationships fall short of the high expectations they hold. Meanwhile, the poor have been delaying marriage and divorcing more too, but they have also been marrying less overall. We believe that the primary reason for the rather striking class difference in marriage rates that has emerged since the 1950s and 1960s is quite simple: though the poor and the middle class now have a similarly high standard for marriage, the poor are far less likely to reach their "white picket fence dream."

"I WANT THAT WHITE PICKET FENCE DREAM."

For women in Deena's generation, the bar for marriage is high. Whereas most couples—middle class, working class, and poor—used to view marriage as a starting point in their quest to achieve a series of life goals, today the poor insist on meeting these goals before marriage. Those at the bottom of the class ladder today believe that a wedding ought to be the icing on the cake of a working-class respectability already achieved. For the middle class too, marriage no longer comes right after college graduation, but only after both partners have embarked upon careers.[22]

Yet though few poor women can imagine marrying without some level of economic security, it is equally true that few can imagine "making it" *without* marriage. Mothers like Mahkiya Washington show their adherence to middle-class marital norms when they insist that the "perfect picture" of the lifestyle they aspire to includes a man and a woman with wedding rings. In the worldview of the poor, marriage and class respectability still usually go hand in hand. Thus, for a poor single mother to say she's abandoned the goal of marriage is the equivalent of admitting she's given up on her dreams for a better future. Both marriage and upward mobility are as central to the American dream as apple pie.

Poor single mothers like Deena understand that in their neighborhoods a marriage can either confer respectability or deny it, and "poor but happily married" does not make the cut. Deena Vallas knows that no "respectable woman" agrees to marry when living paycheck to paycheck—even if there is a baby on the way and she's living with the father. Marital relationships ought to be free from the severe economic stress that wrecks so many lesser unions. For the poor, divorce is the ultimate loss of face; the couple must bear the reproach of neighbors and kin for daring to think they were ready for marriage in the first place.

"I'M GONNA MAKE SURE I HAVE MY OWN EVERYTHING BEFORE I GET MARRIED."

But who is supposed to pay for the white picket fence lifestyle? Unlike women a generation or two ago, mothers like Dominique Watkins do not anticipate reaching their economic goals by relying on a man; rather, they want to reach them on their own. For them, marriage is about more than collecting the right material props. Rather, it is about ensuring a certain level of quality in their relationship. Perhaps even more important, it is about guaranteeing her survival in the face of a marital disaster.

The threats to relationships that most worry mothers like Mahkiya, Deena, Dominique, and Jen are infidelity, domestic violence, substance abuse, and criminal activity. In their view, and that of most Americans across the class divide, these behaviors should not be tolerated, especially in marriage. At the same time, the poor also want their marriages to be the same "partnership of equals" that middle-class women now usually demand. Surveys show that since the sexual revolution there has been a sea change in the attitudes toward gender roles among most American women and men.[23] Unskilled men have been a notable exception: The difference in attitudes between women and men on the bottom rungs of the economic ladder is abysmally large.[24] Among poor couples, therefore, domestic battles for control over decisions about the household and the children are especially bitter. Poor women who insist on being "set" financially before marriage are, in part, equipping themselves with the weapons that will ensure that they will have more say within the marriage. Dominique Watkins's relationship with her children's father, Ron, is a vivid demonstration of this principle: A woman with income and assets of her own—one who does not *need* her man—can insist that he conform to her expectations. If he refuses, she can follow through on her threat to leave him without being "left with nothing."[25]

"MY BABY IS MY HEART."

If the poor shared both the middle class's marriage standards and their childbearing behaviors, few Americans would question their behavior. What troubles most middle-class citizens is why women like Mahkiya, Deena, Dominique, and Jen don't wait until they are married to have children. Though marriage ideals are widely shared, the differences between America's classes are as profound as their similarities, and the rise in nonmarital childbearing can only be understood by looking at both.

The most important difference is that the poor ascribe a higher value to children than members of the middle class do. One 1986 survey asked more than ten thousand Americans whether it was better for a person to have a child rather than to go through life childless. Those lower on the class ladder were nearly *twice* as likely to agree to this statement as those in the middle (57 percent of high school dropouts versus 30 percent of college graduates). In a 2001 survey, poorly educated women were also much more likely than the more highly educated to agree that motherhood is one of life's most fulfilling roles.[26]

The poor view childlessness as one of the greatest tragedies in life. Surveys show that the differences between the social classes are striking: female high school dropouts are more than *five times* as likely and male high school dropouts more than *four times* as likely as their college-educated counterparts to say they think childless people lead empty lives. This statistic even takes into account other distinguishing differences such as their race and age, and their parental and marital status.[27] For most women living in impoverished, inner-city communities, remaining childless is inconceivable.

We believe the high social value the poor give to children has two sources: fewer forgone opportunities and stronger absolute preferences. First, a growing body of evidence shows that the opportunities the poor forgo when they have children early are fewer and less significant than for middle-class women.[28] So the incentives and disincentives for childbearing are very different for women at different class levels. We are not saying that early childbearing costs nothing—in fact, it demands a large share of these mothers' meager resources. But the *out-of-pocket costs* of kids—the diapers and formula, the clothing and shoes, the stroller and the crib, the childcare, the larger apartment or home—are incurred regardless of the age or marital status of the parent. However, the lost future earnings—what economists call an *opportunity cost*—that women at different class levels face when they have children early are quite different.

The public often assumes that early childbearing is the main reason why so many girls from poor inner-city areas fail to complete high school, go on to college, gain valuable work skills, or earn decent wages, but there is virtually no evidence to support this idea. Ironically, however, any childbearing at all, and especially early childbearing, has huge opportunity costs for middle-class women.[29] Disadvantaged girls who bear children have about the same long-term earnings trajectories as similarly disadvantaged youth who wait until their mid or late twenties to have a child.[30] Nor do they seem to suffer significantly in other domains.[31] Current research suggests that the initial disadvantage is what drives both the early childbearing and the other negative outcomes that one observes over time. In other words, early childbearing is highly selective of girls whose other characteristics—family background, cognitive ability, school performance, mental health status, and so on—have already diminished their life chances so much that an early birth does little to reduce them much further.

Second, the survey evidence on class differences in family attitudes noted above also suggests that the poor may have stronger preferences or, in economists' terms, a greater "taste," for children. Not that middle-class parents don't love their children or fail to invest in them. Indeed, family demographer Sara McLanahan argues that never before in American history have middle-class parents invested more heavily in their progeny.[32] However, survey data show that far fewer middle-class women believe their lives would be empty if they did not have children. The stronger preference for children among the poor, especially at an early age, is not, we believe, evidence for deviant subcultural values. The stereotyped image that many have of poor single mothers—one which assumes four, five, or even six children—is rare: the total lifetime fertility of women with a high school diploma or less is now just over two children.[33] While this is still higher than for college-educated women, few Americans would call the desire for two or three children pathological or deviant.[34] Furthermore, the rate of teenage childbearing has dropped sharply in recent years—so much so that today, the typical first nonmarital birth occurs to a woman at age twenty-one—the age at which middle-class childbearing began only two generations ago.

Finally, we believe that the stronger preference for children among the poor can be seen in the propensity of the women we interviewed to put children, rather than marriage, education, or career, at the center of their meaning-making activity. Presumably, people of all social classes share a deep psychological need to make meaning. Over the last half-century, new opportunities to gain esteem and validation have opened for American women. But these new alternatives—the rewarding careers and professional identities—aren't equally available. While middle-class women are now reaching new heights of self-actualization, poor women are relegated to unstable, poorly paid, often mind-stultifying jobs with little room for advancement. Thus, for the poor, childbearing often rises to the top of the list of potential meaning-making activities from mere lack of competition.

But more than the lack of viable alternatives drives the desire to make meaning through children, often at such a young age. The daily stresses of an impoverished adolescence lived out in the environs of East Camden or West Kensington breed a deep sense of need for something positive to "look to." The strong sense of anomie, the loneliness, rootlessness, the lack of direction, the sense that one's life has little meaning or has spun out of control—the very feelings Jen Burke and Deena Vallas describe in the period preceding pregnancy—create a profound drive to make life more meaningful.

"I'M NOT GOING TO MAKE ANY PROMISES I CAN'T KEEP."

To fully understand the set of social dynamics behind the retreat from marriage among the poor, and the rise in the rate of nonmarital childbearing, we need to understand clearly how their moral hierarchy has adapted to the new marriage standard. Most poor women we spoke with say that it is better to have children outside of marriage than to marry foolishly and risk divorce, for divorce desecrates the institution of marriage. Recall from chapter 4 what Marilyn, the twenty-four-year-old white mother of two, says: "I don't wanna have a big trail of divorce, you know. I'd rather say, 'Yes, I had my kids out of wedlock' than say, 'I married *this* idiot.' It's like a *pride* thing." The poor avoid marriage not because they think too little of it, but because they revere it.[35] They object to divorce because they believe it strips marriage of its meaning, rendering it little more than "a piece of paper." And their prerequisites for marriage reflect the high standards they've adopted. As Deena vows emphatically, "I'm not going to make any promises I can't keep."[36]

We did not talk with middle-class women, so cannot know for certain how their moral hierarchy has evolved, but we can find clues in their behavior. Middle-class women rarely give birth outside of a marital union. Though nearly four in ten births to high school dropouts are now nonmarital, this is true for only three of every hundred births to college-educated women.[37] Middle-class Manhattanite Rachel, the star of the popular sitcom *Friends*, who had a baby outside of marriage, is still little more than a myth even in today's seemingly permissive society. Rather than follow in her footsteps, unmarried middle-class women are logging onto Match.com in droves, many in hopes of making a marital match.[38] Perhaps the culture still dictates that for women of their social standing, the husband ought to come before the baby. Perhaps raising a child alone requires too many sacrifices for the affluent, middle-class career woman who has so much to lose economically.[39]

Meanwhile, the poor view middle-class women who, in their view, privilege career above children, as reprehensible. Early on in our field-work in Camden, Edin struck up a friendship with Angela, an unmarried twenty-two-year-old African American cosmetology student with a two-year-old son. About a year after Edin and Angela first met, she conceived a second child—by the same man, who had gotten another woman pregnant and then abandoned Angela for the new paramour while Angela was still carrying their first child. Once again abandoned and on welfare, she was clearly embarrassed to relate her news. Midway into the conversation, she joked, "Someday I'm going to *plan* my pregnancies like . . . *white* [middle-class] women do. You know, like Murphy Brown! You have your fancy car, . . . your fancy house, your career all set, and *then* maybe you'll have a baby!" Edin got the point—that in Angela's view, middle-class women who delay having children just so they can get ahead in life, as the 1980s sitcom character Murphy Brown did, are selfish and unnatural. For Edin, who'd waited to become a mother until she was thirty and had a PhD and a university teaching job, the message was clear.

This is not to say that the poor believe having children outside of marriage is the right way, or even the best way, to go about things—more than eight in ten tell survey researchers they believe that people who want children should get married first.[40] They are also even more likely than those in the middle class to say they believe that a child raised by two parents is better off than a child reared by one. Their responses show that poor mothers also believe that children born and raised within marital unions generally do better than those who are not.

However, these abstractions are largely irrelevant to their lives. Poor women must calculate the potential risks and rewards of the actual partnerships available to them and, given their uncertain future prospects, take a "wait and see" attitude toward the relationships with the men who father their children. From their point of view, this approach makes enormous sense, as the men in the neighborhood partner pool—the only men they can reasonably attract, given their own disadvantaged place in the marriage market—are of fairly uniformly low quality. How does a poor woman like Deena sort the losers from the winners except by relying on the test of time? How else can she know which one her new boyfriend Sean will prove to be?

In the meantime, there is no doubt that a pregnancy tests the man's mettle. If the pair can come through this trial intact and work toward a future together, they are likely to marry eventually. If not, poor women take it as a sign that the relationship was never meant to be. While middle-class couples jealously guard their romantic relationships against the stresses of childrearing—now waiting several years after marriage to have children, poor women seem to welcome the challenge that pregnancy presents.[41] For them, a romantic relationship should not be protected but tested. Better to gauge a man's worth early on than waste years investing in a lost cause.

Among the middle class, the couple relationship is at the heart of family life, with the children as desirable complements. Middle-class couples place great value on enjoying each other first before having children, perhaps because they anticipate what statistics clearly show, that marital satisfaction declines precipitously after a couple has children.[42] But among poor women, the mother-child relationship is central, with the father as a useful complement.

Middle-class women delay marriage until they've completed schooling and established their careers by entering into trial marriages (e.g., cohabitation), and they delay children further still, waiting to have them until well after the wedding date. Women in the middle class now typically order life events as follows: get established economically, get married, get even more established economically, and then have children. However, this strategy risks running out the biological clock.

Poor women instead treat the search for the ideal marital partner as a lifelong quest and the bearing and raising of children as tasks they will accomplish along the way. They see little point in waiting to have children, since they do not believe that having children early will have much effect on their economic prospects later on.[43] They also do not think that their age or their resources have much to do with good mothering. Anyone can be a good mother, they say, if they are willing to "be there" for their children. For the poor, then, the most *sensible* (though not the ideal) way to order life events is: have the children, get established economically, and then get married. At the outset, poor women hope to accomplish these goals with a single partner and work cooperatively toward these goals. But despite an often promising start, few of the men they partner with prove able or willing to stay the course.

In sum, we show that poor women consider marriage a luxury—one they desire and hope someday to attain, but can live without if they must. Children, on the other hand, are a necessity.[44] Thus, even if a woman finds herself in a match she fears might not be ideal, she is often willing to bring a child into that relationship. On the one hand, she hopes the match will improve with the birth of a child. On the other, she figures she might not have a better chance to have a child or complete the task of building a family.[45]

WHAT MAKES FOR GOOD MOTHERING?

Though the poor hold a middle-class standard for marriage, they do not, by and large, adopt middle-class childrearing norms. This constitutes the second crucial difference between the classes. Middle-class women hold to a set of childrearing norms that measure their success as mothers by their children's achievements. The middle-class child is a hothouse plant whose soil is concertedly cultivated and fertilized by a wide variety of meaningful activities. Ask a middle-class woman if she's a good mother, and she'll likely reply, "Ask me in twenty years," for then she will know her daughter's score on the SAT, the list of college acceptances she has garnered, and where her career trajectory has led. A poor child lives in a field—not a hothouse—where he is expected to grow naturally. His mother's job is to ensure that his environment provides the essential elements that allow for natural growth—the roof over his head, the food in his stomach, the clean and pressed clothing, the rudimentary knowledge of "numbers" and "letters"—but the rest is up to the child.[46] Ask a poor woman whether she's a good mother, and she'll likely point to how clean and well-fed her children are, or how she stands by them through whatever problems come their way.

Despite these rather modest notions of what makes for good mothering, children come to mean, quite literally, *everything* to women like Mahkiya Washington, Deena Vallas, Dominique Watkins, and Jen Burke, for they are the only truly safe emotional harbor. Poor women realize that marriage is fragile, and so they make their primary emotional investments in their relationships with their children, which are not subject to the threats that so often destroy relationships between men and women. Sonia, a twenty-three-year-old Puerto Rican mother of a four-year-old son, puts it this way: "[My son is] my heart. [When I have hard times] I always tell myself I wanted him. Even if I get that rock on my finger, that white picket fence, and that deed that says the house is mine, [I'll still have my son] just in case anything goes sour. I'll say to my husband, 'You leave! This boy is *mine.*'"

THE SIGNIFICANCE OF RACE

Nationally representative surveys show large racial and ethnic differences in a number of family-related behaviors. For example, though large numbers of unmarried African Americans, Hispanics, and whites cohabit around the time of their child's birth, surveys show that African Americans are less likely than the other groups to do so. African American women are also less likely to marry than Hispanics, who are, in turn, less likely to marry than whites, even when income and other demographic characteristics are taken into account.[47] And African American divorce rates are also higher than those for whites or Hispanics.[48]

Despite these important differences in family-related *behavior*, our data show few differences across racial and ethnic groups in the *attitudes* and *worldviews* that are the subject of this book. By and large, the themes in these chapters ring as true in white PennsPort as in Puerto Rican West Kensington, or in the African American neighborhood of Strawberry Mansion. This similarity in views regarding marriage and children suggests that what drives the large behavioral differences is not that these racial and ethnic groups differ in their adherence to mainstream norms, but that they see real differences in their chances of finding a mate for a marriage that meets the high standard for marriage they share.

There are some exceptions to this rule (see appendix A). First, as we show in chapter 1, some differences exist across the groups in the extent to which children are conceived according to an explicit plan. Yet the most important story the data reveal is that, across all three racial and ethnic groups, the majority of children were the result of *neither* explicit planning *nor* contraceptive failure. Most conceptions were described in terms that place them between these two ends of the continuum—between planned and accidental.

Second, as we show in chapter 3, the problems that women in the various racial and ethnic groups encounter in their relationships with their children's fathers also vary. White women's relationships suffer most from the ravages of domestic violence and alcohol abuse. Puerto Rican women seem to experience even higher rates of domestic violence, and drug addiction is also a common cause of failed relationships. For African Americans, criminal behavior, incarceration, and drug abuse are the most common relational problems. Infidelity, however, is a common corrosive factor for women in all groups.

Third, in chapter 4, we show that African Americans are more likely to aspire to marriage than whites or Puerto Ricans, while whites are the most likely to reject the notion of marriage outright. Given the large differences by race in the U. S. population with regard to marital behavior, this finding is somewhat surprising. However, as we noted in chapter 4, those opposed to marriage had usually been married in the past, and our

African American mothers were far less likely than our whites (though not our Puerto Ricans) to have been married.[49]

Fourth, we also show in chapter 4 that for African Americans, the ideal age for marriage comes later in life than for the other groups and is higher than the age at which they believe childbearing should ideally occur.[50] This difference may simply reflect real differences in the average timing of marriage across groups, as African Americans often marry much later.[51] It is also possible that African Americans have a higher standard for marriage than whites, an idea suggested by several studies showing that men's earnings and employment are more important for predicting marriage among African American women than among whites and Hispanics.[52]

In sum, though the 162 women we spoke with varied along an numerous dimensions, their individual stories reflect many of the themes we have elaborated here. Though the eight impoverished neighborhoods in which they live are in some ways distinct social worlds, the differences in the worldviews of the single mothers that live in them are usually quite subtle, while their commonalities are striking.

LESSONS FOR MARRIAGE POLICY

American children suffer from more family disruption than children anywhere else in the industrialized world. Though some European countries have similarly high rates of nonmarital childbearing, unmarried European parents usually cohabit and tend to stay together for decades, whereas their U.S. counterparts typically break up within a couple of years. U.S. divorce rates among couples with children, while lower than for couples without, are also much higher than those of other Western industrialized countries. The fragility of both marriage and cohabitation means that by age fifteen, only half of American children live with both biological parents, whereas roughly two-thirds of Swedish, Austrian, German, and French children do so, as do nearly nine in ten children in Spain and Italy.[53] These sharp differences in the rate of family disruption are undeniably part of the reason that the United States has the highest child poverty rate of any Western industrialized country.[54]

At the dawn of the new century, American lawmakers and taxpayers alike have noted the high correlation between poverty, poor child outcomes, and the rise of single motherhood, and some have concluded that marriage is the missing ingredient in America's policy recipe. The new conventional wisdom is that the lack of *marriage*, rather than the lack of *skills* or living-wage *jobs*, is at the root of the disadvantages faced by so many American children.

"Can government be the solution for everything that ails the American family?" asked Bush's White House marriage czar Wade Horn. "Of course not. But I do think that we have moved beyond the question of *whether* government ought to be involved in some way on the issue of marriage to the question of *how*." How indeed? It's not education or job training or a low-interest mortgage, but something called "relationship-skills training." The idea is to provide unwed parents with the relational skills that can bring their dreams of a lifelong marriage to fruition.[55]

At the heart of the relationship-skills training they plan to provide are the "speaker-listener" techniques that have helped couples in premarital counseling resolve their day-to-day conflicts in more constructive, less emotionally charged ways. Couples who learn these techniques before marriage, generally in the context of premarital counseling, do tend to have more satisfying and long-lasting relationships.[56] It is easy to see how such techniques would be helpful with such conflicts as how to squeeze a tube of toothpaste, whether the toilet seat should remain up, how often the in-laws can visit, or when to have sex. It's harder to see how these tools will be of as much use when the quarrels result from chronic infidelity, physical abuse, alcoholism and drug addiction, criminal activity, and incarceration. Indeed, it is hard to envision any type of social program that would, or even should, motivate couples to wed in the light of such serious problems.[57]

Yet despite the emphasis on promoting marriage, no one will be coerced to wed. Nor does the government intend to promote marriage at all costs. The last thing most conservatives want is to increase the divorce rate. Rather, the goal is to give unwed couples who are hoping to marry the skills that will lead to healthy, lifelong, marital relationships. They recognize that these are the kinds of marriages in which children do best, and the marriage initiatives are supposed to improve the well-being of children. The focus on a healthy marriage, not marriage at any cost, recognizes that half of all children living in single-parent households are in that situation because their parents divorced, not because they failed to marry. And research shows that children who live with single parents because of divorce fare no better on average than those whose parents never marry at all.[58] *The point is that living apart from either biological parent at any point during childhood is what seems to hurt children.* And it is important to note that remarriage, the typical middle-class response to divorce, solves nothing for the typical child, as those with a stepfather typically achieve less and suffer more than those living with a single mother.[59]

Despite the sharp critiques of the institution of marriage from the left, the overwhelming majority of both male and female Americans still want to get married, expect their marriages to last a lifetime, and plan to raise their children within marital unions.[60] Yet there have been significant declines in the proportion of poor Americans who will marry over their lifetimes, and half of all recent marriages end in divorce.[61] Even among married couples with children, the divorce rate is quite high: up to 30 percent of children born to marital unions can now expect to see their parents part before they reach adulthood.[62]

American society as a whole seems to be struggling with the institution of marriage, what it means, and how to make it work better, particularly for women, who are the "leavers" in marital breakups two-thirds of the time.[63] To single out the poor and their marriage attitudes and behaviors ignores the fact that rich and poor alike now hold to a similar marriage standard. What the poor demand from marriage is no more than what everybody wants.

Marriage will probably never regain its status as a nearly universal cultural characteristic. People do, and will continue to, raise children in a wide variety of ways, and social policymakers concerned with the next generation must seek to enhance their well-being in whatever family form they find them. There is no question that the diversity of the American family is here to stay, so the policy response must be equally diverse.

Yet the acute vulnerability of relationships between poor parents demands a targeted policy response, because although having children early may not affect a young mother's life chances much, it may diminish the life chances of her children.[64] These costs are not evident to mothers, though, as their folk wisdom supports the notion that even very young mothers can be good mothers.

Some of our readers may conclude that the poor should lower their standards for marriage, but remember that they are often reluctant to marry because of the dangerously low quality of the relationships they are in. Given the alternatives they have to choose from, their reluctance to marry might be quite reasonable. If this is so, then the only course for those who want to promote marriage is to try improving the quality of the male partners in the pool. Teaching poor women to have better taste in men is hardly a solution, since their choices are made in a partner market where the better-quality men go to better-off women, especially given the unbalanced sex ratios in many poor communities.

Following Wilson, liberals have generally advocated a renewed focus on job training or employment among unskilled men. Given the alarming declines in employment among unskilled men, particularly young African American men, such an approach is in order. But we believe it is not enough to focus solely on male employment. Nor do we advocate the punitive approaches to single motherhood that conservatives often promote; researchers have found that no matter how stingy welfare becomes, that tactic has failed to get many more poor couples to wed.[65] We believe that though Wilson's explanation for the decline of marriage in the inner city was not completely correct in its particulars, his general approach is exactly right—the problem is one of marriageability.

No modern marriage can, or even should, survive the ravages of domestic abuse, chronic infidelity, alcoholism or drug addiction, repeated incarceration, or a living made from crime. Given the prevalence of these problems in the low-income population, promoting marriage will do more harm than good unless policymakers figure out a way to make low-skilled men safer prospects for long-term relationships with women and children. If we wait until the "magic moment" of a child's birth to intervene in the lives of these men, it will likely prove too late for most, for their problems are already too numerous and too entrenched. The best course is undoubtedly to intervene at a much earlier age, before these troubles have had a chance to take root. In addition, it is well-established that by the time men reach their late twenties, they tend to "age out" of crime and other delinquent behaviors. If we could find ways to convince poor men to postpone fatherhood until their late twenties, their behavior will likely prove far less toxic to family life.[66]

Of course, convincing men to wait means getting their female partners to wait as well, and, as noted above, waiting would probably improve their children's lives too. Well-crafted social programs aimed specifically at reducing pregnancy among at-risk teens show promise. Several have been experimentally evaluated, and the results show that a well-organized program that engages poor teens in meaningful after-school activities over a significant period of time can decrease the teen pregnancy rate substantially. These programs range in cost from $1,000 to $4,000 per teen per year, but since experts estimate that the typical nonmarital birth costs taxpayers roughly $3,750 annually over eighteen years, these programs might eventually save, not cost, money.[67] Research also shows that programs which engage these at-risk youth in service learning are especially effective, though the experts aren't sure why. Dominique Watkins would probably quickly explain that having the opportunity to give of oneself, and the chance to feel useful to others, is, in many ways, what having children young is all about. Social programs that feed this need are on the right track.

Finally, we must recognize that young people growing up in poor communities have few positive models of marriage. Poor young women and men need some sense of what constitutes a healthy couple relationship to understand what it can reasonably withstand and what it cannot, and to learn what helps couples who want to stay together and even someday marry. So some form of relationship-skills training is needed, though it must impart far more than mere speaker-listener techniques.

Shoring up these fragile families will also require concrete methods of increasing access to the economic security that helps to make relationships strong. Poor women say they'll marry when they and their partners reach a certain standard of living, providing men also meet their behavioral standards.[68] This living standard is not lavish; it is a scaled-down version of the classic American dream. A modest home, a car, and some savings show that a couple is not merely living paycheck to paycheck but has some surplus, and has used that surplus to work cooperatively toward a common economic goal. These financial accomplishments represent a deeper form of security than mere money income can buy. Policy that ignores these strongly held moral views and aspirations is wrongheaded and will not move the marriage rate much, if at all. One way or another, the wider culture has arrived at these high standards for marriage, and they are unlikely to change now. American society cannot now hold out one set of values for the middle class and expect the poor to abide by another lower standard. Conservatives are acting on the premise that not being married is what makes so many women and children poor. But poor women insist that their poverty is part of what makes marriage so difficult to sustain. Their keen observations of middle-class behavior tell them that given all the expectations Americans now place on it, modern-day marriage is hard enough without the added burden of financial worries. How, they ask, can an economically strained marriage hope to survive?

The government is already experimenting with asset-creation strategies on a modest scale, matching the savings of the poor with public dollars and limiting expenditures to down-payments on homes or investments in education. However, policymakers must keep in mind that to acquire assets, one must have surplus income—something neither welfare nor low-wage employment typically provides.[69] The evidence is clear that men who work more and earn more also marry more, and that, at the bottom of the income distribution, women's employment and earnings also tend to positively predict marriage.[70] Providing more access to stable, living-wage employment for both men *and* women should therefore be a key policy objective.

Putting the economy back into the policy equation is probably even more crucial for early childbearing than for marriage. As long as they have so few other ways to establish a sense of self-worth and meaning, early childbearing among young women in precarious economic conditions is likely to continue. If they believe they have a reason to wait, more may take steps to prevent early pregnancy. During the late 1990s, when America saw several years of unprecedented economic growth and very low unemployment, many of those on the bottom were swept up into the economic mainstream. Most people who wanted a job could suddenly get one, the tight job market moved wages for unskilled workers sharply upward, and for the first time in modern memory, the rate of nonmarital childbearing stopped increasing—it even declined somewhat.[71] What this suggests is that disadvantaged people don't entirely ignore new opportunities in the labor market. When they see new reasons to hope for meaning in a variety of life paths, some may choose to forgo early childbearing because of it.

However, it is irresponsible to make marriage promotion or teen pregnancy prevention the only social policy games in town while more than half of those mothers who have recently left welfare remain poor and, at any given time, nearly six out of ten have no job. In 2002 one in seven reported no visible means of support at all.[72] Meanwhile, one-fifth of all American children, and more than half of those living only with their mothers, remain poor.[73] As the unemployment rate rises for the population as a whole, it lifts doubly for the most disadvantaged segments of the American population.[74] With the federal safety net for these poor women and children in shreds and state budgets in crisis, we must identify the new needs of poor families and find new ways to meet them.

ACKNOWLEDGMENTS

We've written this book to appeal to a wide range of interested readers, in and outside of the academy. Lisa Adams, our agent, and Naomi Schneider, our editor, helped us learn how to transform academic prose into a more lively narrative that we hope will appeal to policymakers and the educated public as well as to scholars and students.

During the five years we were doing the fieldwork and collecting the interview data for this book, we had the good fortune to work with a very talented group of graduate student interviewers and ethnographers, including Susan Clampet-Lundquist (interviewer, West Kensington, Strawberry Mansion), Rebecca Kissane (ethnographer and interviewer, Kensington), Tasheika Hinson-Coleman (interviewer and ethnographer, Strawberry Mansion and North Central), Jeff Gingrich (ethnographer, North Central), and Shelley Shannon (interviewer and project manager, Camden).

Shelley Shannon introduced us to the City of Camden and even rented us the ground-floor flat in her Camden home. Sam Apple taught us much about the history of Camden after the civil rights era. Mary Ann Merion helped us draw up a preliminary list of community leaders and introduced us around town. Camden's Westminster Presbyterian Church provided a spiritual home. In Philadelphia we were introduced to the broad array of neighborhoods we studied by colleagues and graduate students at the University of Pennsylvania, where Edin was a faculty member and Kefalas a postdoctoral fellow. In the field, Joanne Weill-Greenberg, Emily Rice-Townsend, and Joanne Lombard proved especially helpful, as well as the staff at Philadelphia Head Start, the St. Francis Inn, the Lighthouse, and the Lutheran Settlement House. Keisha Moore and Tasheika Hinson-Coleman shared their knowledge of the North Central and Strawberry Mansion communities.

Coders included Verity Decker, Renee Dinges, Anna Gold, Alena Herklotz, Bethany Nicholson, and Julia Sorisho. Mary Bowman assisted with fact-checking. The amazing Renee Dinges took a year off from college to help with the analysis, tirelessly (and even passionately) plowing through the roughly nine thousand single-spaced pages of transcribed data for the various analysis tasks. Her keen insights are reflected throughout the manuscript. Donna Tozer performed the invaluable service of hiring and supervising the activities of a team of part-time transcribers.

Gretchen Wright edited the manuscript time and again and offered critical feedback and practical support along the way. Patricia Reese used her marvelous editing skills to pare down a very lengthy conclusion. Last-minute assistance with references came from Andrew Cherlin, Greg Duncan, Paula England, Irv Garfinkel, Richard Gelles, and Phil Morgan. Patrick Carr and Timothy Nelson, our spouses, read and commented on multiple versions of every chapter. Timothy Nelson also formatted the manuscript. In the early days of the project, he also proved willing, and even eager, to join in the adventure of living in Camden with two young children.

This project was nurtured in the intellectual community of the William T. Grant Faculty Scholar's Program, which brought Edin together with two dozen other young scholars each summer for five years and proved flexible and imaginative enough to cover Edin's Camden rent, pay Kefalas's salary, and fund all the other project costs. A supplementary grant from the William T. Grant Foundation paid for the data analysis, and a third allotment covered the cost of a trip from Ireland to

Philadelphia for photographer Michael Smyth and his supplies. The University of Pennsylvania, Saint Joseph's University, and Northwestern University offered crucial financial support to us while writing the book, and released us from some of our teaching duties. Our children, Kaitlin, Marissa, Camille, and PJ, showed extraordinary patience as we struggled to finish the book.

Many of the theoretical ideas in the conclusion were sparked and honed in the quarterly meetings of the MacArthur Network on the Family and the Economy, whose members, Jeanne Brooks-Gunn, Lindsay Chase-Lansdale, Cecilia Conrad, Paula England, Nancy Folbre, Irv Garfinkel, Sara McLanahan, Ron Mincy, Robert Pollack, Tim Smeeding, and Robert Willis, offered invaluable feedback. Joanne Spitz, the network facilitator, also offered intriguing responses.

We would like to especially thank those who offered comments on earlier drafts of the manuscript, including Nicola Beisel, Andrew Cherlin, Paula England, Sharon Hays, Mark Jacobs, Annette Lareau, Jim Quane, and William Julius Wilson. In early presentations of these ideas, we benefited from the advice of Camille Charles, David Ellwood, Frank Furstenberg, Jerry Jacobs, Robert Merton, and Eric Wanner. One of the largest debts of gratitude we incurred was to Ness Sandoval, Edin's colleague at Northwestern, who spent far more time than he should have helping us prepare the census tables for this book. Likewise, Susan Clampet-Lundquist was kind enough to generate the census maps that appear in appendix A.

Of course, our greatest debt is to the women who opened their homes and lives to us. We owe them our heartfelt gratitude.

CITY, NEIGHBORHOOD, AND FAMILY CHARACTERISTICS AND RESEARCH METHODS

CITY CHARACTERISTICS

The setting for our study, the Philadelphia metropolitan area, is poorer than most, though it is quite similar to other very large cities and other cities in the region. The center-city poverty rate for America's one hundred largest cities averaged 18.2 percent in 2000, but the rate for the Philadelphia PMSA's (Partial Metropolitan Statistical Area's) central-city populace (which includes Camden) was significantly higher: 22.9 percent. And while central-city poverty declined slightly in the nation's hundred largest cities between 1990 and 2000, Philadelphia's grew by nearly 3 percent. Yet, it is quite similar to that of the central cities of the Los Angeles/Long Beach PMSA (22.2 percent) and the New York PMSA (21.2 percent), and a little higher than the central cities of the Washington DC (20.2 percent), Chicago (19.6 percent), or Houston PMSAs (19.2 percent).[1]

PHILADELPHIA   Table 1 presents poverty figures for Philadelphia City. It shows that 18 percent of Philadelphia families lived below the poverty line in 2000. Nearly a quarter of black residents were in poverty as compared to less than one in ten white residents. Hispanic residents, however, were the city's most economically disadvantaged group: nearly

TABLE 1: INCOME AND FAMILY CHARACTERISTICS FOR PHILADELPHIA, BY PERCENTAGE

	All Philadelphia	Black	Hispanic	White
Families below poverty line	18	24	39	9
Population in 20+ poverty neighborhood	51	74	75	23
Population in 40+ poverty neighborhood	13	16	45	4
Children under 18 in 20+ poverty neighborhood	59	76	79	22
Children under 18 in 40+ poverty neighborhood	17	18	49	3
Adults over 25 without high school degree	29	32	51	23
Male unemployment	11	16	17	7
Males earning less than $10,000 last year	20	23	20	17
Female unemployment	11	14	18	7
Females earning less than $10,000 last year	27	26	36	26
Children under 18 in female-headed, single-parent households	31	37	52	14

Note: The female/male ratios for adults 21–34 are as follows: all Philadelphia, 1.03; black, 1.29; Hispanic, 1.07; white, 1.03.

four in ten city residents who claimed Hispanic or Latino heritage were poor in 2000. More than two-thirds of these residents are Puerto Rican.

Philadelphia is also a city where the poverty population is quite geographically concentrated. More than half of all Philadelphians live in neighborhoods of concentrated poverty (20+ percent),[2] with blacks and Hispanics roughly three times more likely to do so than whites. Thirteen percent of Philadelphians live in neighborhoods with an extreme poverty concentration (40+ percent). The percent of African Americans living in such neighborhoods is four times that for whites, and the rate for Hispanics is nearly three times higher than for blacks.

Nearly three in ten Philadelphians over the age of twenty-five lacked a high school degree in 2000. The rate is 32 percent for blacks and 23 percent for whites, but half of all Hispanic adults have less than a high school education. The U.S. Census reports that male unemployment in 2000 was at 11 percent (nearly twice the national average). Rates are more than twice as high for ethnic and racial minorities as for whites. And a sizeable minority (roughly one in five) who did work reported very low earnings. The same patterns are evident among Philadelphia's females, except that female workers (particularly Hispanics) were more likely to report very low earnings than their male counterparts.

Finally, 43 percent of Philadelphia's children live in households with a single female parent, as do nearly two-thirds of black children, over half of all Hispanic youth, and just over one in five whites.

CAMDEN   We do not present comparable figures for Camden City, because all of the Camden neighborhoods, divided into three larger geographic groupings, are represented in our more detailed neighborhood breakdowns that follow (see table 2). Yet Camden is much poorer and more disadvantaged than its sister city across the Delaware. In Camden, the poverty rate is 33 percent, and only 49 percent of adults over twenty-five had a high school degree in 2000. In that year, unemployment averaged 15.9 percent across the city. Camden is also a more heavily minority city. Just over four in ten Philadelphians are black, and a little more than four in ten are white, with 8.5 percent claiming Hispanic or Latino/Latina heritage. In contrast, about half of Camden residents are black, four in ten are Hispanic, and only 7 percent are white.

NEIGHBORHOOD CHARACTERISTICS

We wanted to study the role of children and marriage among residents of the neighborhoods with the greatest increases in nonmarital child-

TABLE 2: INCOME AND FAMILY CHARACTERISTICS FOR EIGHT PHILADELPHIA/CAMDEN NEIGHBORHOODS, BY PERCENTAGE

	All	Black Neighborhoods		Mostly Black Neighborhoods with Some Hispanics			Mostly Hispanic Neighborhood	Mostly White Neighborhoods	
		Strawberry Mansion	North Central	North Camden	South Camden	East Camden	West Kensington	Kensington	PennsPort
Families below poverty line	18	36	38	36	31	32	41	22	22
Population in 20+ poverty neighborhood	51	100	100	98	100	100	100	67	58
Population in 40+ poverty neighborhood	13	45	66	64	27	28	62	25	0
Children under 18 in 20+ poverty neighborhood	59	100	100	100	100	100	100	77	60
Children under 18 in 40+ poverty neighborhood	17	47	72	68	29	32	68	29	0
Adults over 25 without high school degree	29	43	43	53	50	43	53	43	43
Male unemployment	11	26	20	21	16	15	19	15	9
Males earning less than $10,000 last year	20	30	30	38	21	24	24	15	19

Female unemployment	11	17	18	16	14	17	16	12	13
Females earning less than $10,000 last year	27	34	35	40	34	29	35	28	20
All family households with own children under 18 in single-parent households	20	34	33	37	30	40	29	21	16
All family households with own children under 18 in married-couple households	23	10	11	16	23	15	20	26	25
All children under 18 in female-headed, single-parent households	43	71	73	66	51	63	56	42	35

Note: The female/male ratios for adults 21–34 are as follows: all Philadelphia, 1.03; Strawberry Mansion, 1.35; North Central, 1.25; North Camden, 1.44; South Camden, 0.67; East Camden, 1.20; West Kensington, 1.24; Kensington, 0.94; PennsPort, 1.05.

bearing: neighborhoods of concentrated poverty. Philadelphia and Camden offered many such neighborhoods. We wanted to interview neighborhood residents and make independent observations of their social environments. Because the fieldwork we had planned for each neighborhood proved to be quite time-consuming, we limited our focus to eight neighborhoods: three in Camden and five in Philadelphia.

These geographic areas are not strictly "neighborhoods," since they have somewhat arbitrary geographic boundaries. In Camden we grouped the twenty-two officially designated neighborhoods into three larger clusters, which our fieldwork revealed were commonly recognized by neighborhood residents as the main "sections" of the city. We made this decision because Camden is so small geographically.

The eight "neighborhoods" met three criteria: at least 20 percent of the population lived below the official poverty threshold in 1990; each had a significant concentration of single-parent households (at least 20 percent of all family households), and each contained sufficient numbers of either black, white, or Hispanic residents. Table 2 shows that most of these neighborhoods also met the poverty and single-parent household criteria in 2000 as well.[3]

We chose Strawberry Mansion and North Central because North Philadelphia, the larger section of the city in which they are located, has the highest concentration of African Americans in the city. All three sections of Camden were selected because they contained large numbers of both blacks and Puerto Ricans. West Kensington was included because it includes such a large portion of the city's Puerto Rican population. We chose Kensington and Port Richmond because they were the only white neighborhoods that fit all three of our criteria.[4] Both had tracts with a combined poverty rate of more than 20 percent in 1990 and in 2000 as well. Table 2 presents data for each of the neighborhoods for 2000. In the five mostly African American neighborhoods, the poverty rates ranged from 31 to 38 percent, whereas poverty in the predominantly white neighborhoods was at 22 percent. However, the largely Puerto Rican neighborhood of West Kensington met the designation of a very high poverty neighborhood, with 41 percent of its residents in poverty.

As each of our neighborhoods is made up of many individual census tracts, we also present figures for the level of poverty concentration among neighborhood residents. The tracts in the predominantly African American neighborhoods and in West Kensington virtually all reached the designation of moderate poverty concentration (20+ percent). In the largely white neighborhoods of Kensington and PennsPort, some tracts met this criterion and others did not.

The story with regard to the proportion of each neighborhood's population living in very highly concentrated poverty (40+ percent) is more mixed, with predominantly black neighborhoods showing considerable heterogeneity.[5] However, 62 percent of West Kensington's primarily Hispanic population lives in very highly concentrated poverty. One of the mostly white neighborhoods, Kensington, has three in ten residents living in high poverty concentration, but no one in PennsPort lives in those conditions.

While our neighborhoods vary in terms of their poverty rates and the levels of poverty concentration, we found smaller differences in the percentages of adults without a high school degree. Male unemployment in the predominantly African American and Puerto Rican neighborhoods, however, was extraordinarily high (with East and South Camden males reporting more employment than males in other neighborhoods). Male employment was much lower in the largely white neighborhoods. In fact, PennsPort's male unemployment rate was below the city average.

The same general pattern of minority disadvantage is evident when we look at the proportion of male workers who were earning very low wages (less than $10,000 per year). Male workers in the predominantly African American and Puerto Rican neighborhoods were quite likely to report very low earnings. However, the number of very low earners was surprisingly high in the mostly white neighborhoods as well. Females show the same general pattern in unemployment and very low earnings.[6]

The percentage of family households that were single-parent households with children under eighteen ranged from 30 to 40 percent in the African American and Puerto Rican neighborhoods, but was lower in the white neighborhoods. Single-parent households with children vastly outnumbered married-couple households with children in all of the predominantly African American and Puerto Rican neighborhoods (with largely Puerto Rican West Kensington showing a less dramatic difference than the rest). In the largely white neighborhoods of Kensington and PennsPort, however, married-couple households outnumbered single-parent households, though not by a very large margin. The percentage of children in female-headed households ranged from about half to three-quarters in the predominantly African American neighborhoods, just over half in West Kensington, and just over a third in the largely white neighborhoods.

Finally, table 2 shows the ratio of females in the prime family-building years (ages twenty-one to thirty-four) to men in the same age range. In 2000, the sex ratio was grossly out of balance in all of the minority neighborhoods, whereas the white neighborhoods showed no such imbalance. The exception to this pattern is North Camden, which recorded far more men than women. Two features of the community can explain these unusual figures. First, the neighborhood is home to the Camden County Jail. At the beginning of January 2004, the number of prisoners in the jail stood at just under 1,700 (about 300 over capacity), presumably most of them male.[7] The total male population for the neighborhood in 2000 was just under 3,400 (the neighborhood had 2,085 female residents). Second, during the 1990s a growing number of Central and South American residents moved into North Camden, a disproportionate number of them male.[8]

FAMILY CHARACTERISTICS

Table 3 shows demographic and social characteristics by race and ethnicity for our sample of 162 low-income single mothers. The racial and

TABLE 3: SELECTED DEMOGRAPHIC CHARACTERISTICS OF OUR SAMPLE, BY RACE AND ETHNICITY

	All (n = 162)	Black (n = 63)	White (n = 52)	Hispanic (n = 47)
Age				
Mean	25.8	25.9	26.2	25.3
Median	24	22	24	24
Range	15–56	15–47	15–56	15–43
Age at first birth				
Mean	18.3	18.3	18.1	18.4
Median	17	17	17	17
Range	13–36	13–36	14–33	14–28
Teenage birth (%)	72.8	76.2	75.0	66.0
14–15 (%)	19.8	23.8	19.2	14.9
16–17 (%)	29.6	25.4	28.8	36.2
18–19 (%)	23.5	27.0	26.9	14.9
Number of children	2.2	2.2	2.1	2.3
Age < 25 (n = 93)	1.6	1.3	1.5	1.9
Age 25 and over (n = 69)	3.1	3.3	3.0	2.9
AFDC within 2 years of interview (%)	48.8	39.7	53.8	55.3
Age < 25	49.3	37.1	56.7	53.6
Age 25 and over	48.4	42.9	50.0	57.9
Education: Age > 25 (n = 69)				
Some college (%)	31.9	32.1	27.3	36.8
High school only (%)	8.7	10.7	13.6	0
GED (%)	14.5	17.9	9.1	15.8
Less than high school (%)	44.9	39.3	50.0	47.4
Work status: Age > 18 (n = 130)				
Not working or in school (%)	47.7	49.0	41.5	52.5
Working part time (%)	20.8	20.4	26.8	15.0
Working full time (%)	19.2	16.3	26.8	15.0

ethnic groups do not differ appreciably in age or age at first birth. Yet though roughly three-quarters of the white and black mothers had their first children as teens, only two-thirds of the Puerto Rican mothers did so. For the sample as a whole, 73 percent had a first birth as a teen, a much higher rate than for the entire population of mothers who ever have a nonmarital birth (as cited earlier, about four in ten first births among those who ever have an unwed birth are to teens).

Mothers in all groups averaged between 2.1 and 2.3 children, with older mothers reporting nearly twice as many children as mothers under twenty-five. Thus, the total lifetime fertility of the mothers in our sample is considerably higher than the average for U.S. women who have never gone to college (which, as we pointed out earlier, is between 2.1 and 2.3).[9]

We screened our sample to ensure that their average income over the last twelve months would place them below the poverty line for a family of four, but we did not collect detailed wage rates or calculate their total annual incomes. Yet the very high number who report receiving cash welfare at some point during the two years prior to our first interview attests to the fact that most were officially poor (welfare benefit levels in both Pennsylvania and New Jersey offer incomes far below the official poverty threshold). Nearly half of our respondents said they'd received cash welfare benefits in the prior two years, though the rate was lower among African Americans than among Puerto Ricans or whites. These rates of welfare receipt are much higher than the neighborhood rates in 2000. Only about 8 percent of Philadelphia households reported public assistance income in 2000, but in our eight neighborhoods, the range was from 10 to 25 percent. However, it is important to note that the city's welfare receipt rate fell by 50 percent during the last half of the 1990s.[10]

Table 3 also shows that about six in ten adult mothers (those over twenty-five) in our sample lacked a high school diploma, more than twice the percentage for adults in the city as a whole but only somewhat higher than for the neighborhoods from which they were drawn. African Americans were the most likely to have completed high school, and Puerto Ricans the least likely. Comparing these figures to neighborhood census data (table 2), we see that our African American mothers were somewhat more likely to have high school diplomas than other adults in their neighborhoods, whereas our Puerto Rican and white mothers' rates of high school completion were quite similar to those for their neighborhoods.

The bottom section of table 3 shows that nearly 40 percent of our sample was working at a formal-sector job at the time of the first interview—half part time and half full time. However, labor force participation rates were lower for Hispanic women than for whites, while work rates for blacks were in between those of the other groups. Just under half of our sample was neither working nor in school. This rate is much higher than the female unemployment rates across the eight neighborhoods, but these figures are not comparable, because those counted as unemployed by the census must be actively looking for work.

Table 4 summarizes the living arrangements of the mothers. When we first interviewed them, nearly three in ten mothers were living alone, more than one in five were living with a boyfriend, another 7 percent were living with a boyfriend and another friend or relative, and four in ten were living only with relatives or friends.

Whites were the least likely to live alone, whereas blacks were the least likely to live with a boyfriend, either alone or with other relatives. Hispanics were the most likely to live with a boyfriend in a household of their own and the least likely to be doubled up with relatives or friends. Younger mothers were the least likely to be living alone and the most likely to be doubled up with a friend or relative. Older mothers usually lived alone, but were also quite likely to live with a boyfriend in an independent household.

Table 5 shows the degree to which each woman's last birth was planned, accidental, or "in between." These results are discussed in chapter 1. The second section of table 5 reports our findings with regard to past marital status, relationship status, and marriage views. We discuss these results in chapter 4.

TABLE 4: RESIDENTIAL STATUS OF OUR SAMPLE, IN PERCENTAGES BY RACE AND ETHNICITY AND BY AGE

Residential Status	All (n = 162)	Black (n = 63)	White (n = 52)	Hispanic (n = 47)
Living alone (n = 47)	29.0	34.9	17.3	34.0
Age < 19	3.1	0	0	14.3
Age = 19–25	25.5	23.8	13.3	30.0
Age > 25)	47.8	60.7	31.8	47.4
Living with boyfriend (n = 36)	22.2	11.1	23.1	36.2
Age < 19	6.3	0	9.0	14.3
Age = 19–25	22.4	14.3	46.7	30.0
Age > 25	24.6	14.3	18.2	47.4
Living with boyfriend and other (n = 12)	7.4	4.8	11.5	6.4
Age < 19	9.4	0	27.3	0
Age = 19–25	10.6	9.5	6.7	15.0
Age > 25	2.9	3.6	4.5	0
Living with other only (n = 68)	41.4	49.2	48.1	23.4
Age < 19	81.3	100.0	63.6	71.4
Age = 19–25	31.9	52.4	33.3	25.0
Age > 25	24.6	21.4	45.5	5.3

PRELIMINARY FIELDWORK AND SAMPLE SELECTION

Though we made use of several highly trained graduate student interviewers, we conducted nearly half of the interviews ourselves and personally conducted the intensive fieldwork in five of the eight neighborhoods. As outlined in the introduction, fieldwork activities in each of the eight neighborhoods included informal interviews with a variety of local experts, from public officials, teachers, and public health nurses to clergy and nonprofit social service organizations, local employers

TABLE 5: MOST RECENT PREGNANCY, CURRENT RELATIONSHIP, AND MARRIAGE ASPIRATIONS IN OUR SAMPLE, IN PERCENTAGES BY RACE AND ETHNICITY

	All (n = 162)	Black (n = 63)	White (n = 52)	Hispanic (n = 47)
Intentionality (most recent pregnancy)				
Planned birth	17.2	20.6	9.6	21.3
Unplanned birth	37.7	33.3	36.5	44.7
In between	45.7	46.0	55.8	34.0
Current relationship status and marriage aspirations				
Ever married	14	10	23	11
In relationship currently	65	63	65	68
In relationship with father of at least one of her children	47	48	38	53
In relationship with father of all her children	32	39	25	32
Aspires to marriage	70	77	65	64
Neutral/no opinion	6	6	4	9
Ambivalent toward marriage, but mostly negative	6	5	6	6
Does not want to marry	17	10	25	19

and business owners, and heads of local public housing residents' councils.[11]

Forging ties with these intermediaries served two purposes. First we gained valuable insight into the neighborhood and its residents, which were crucial to formulating the questions we asked respondents (see appendix B). Second, these intermediaries referred us to respondents and vouched for our trustworthiness. To make our sample as heterogeneous as possible, we took no more than five referrals from a single source. Typically, though, sources generated only one or two referrals. To avoid interviewing only mothers who had strong ties to the community, we also asked successfully interviewed respondents to refer us to people they believed would not be known to our intermediaries. In addition, we posted fliers on public phone booths and made cold contacts with mothers on neighborhood streets in the course of our field observations. About half of the sample was generated in these ways.

We stratified our sample in two ways. First, we attempted to sample even numbers of African Americans, whites, and Puerto Ricans. As the tables show, we sampled slightly more blacks than we had intended to (our goal was fifty per group), and somewhat fewer Puerto Ricans. Furthermore, within each racial and ethnic group, we wanted roughly equal numbers of older mothers (twenty-five and over) and younger mothers. In the end, however, we sampled somewhat larger numbers of younger mothers. The resulting sample is not random or representative, but is quite heterogeneous.

INTERVIEWS

To enhance rapport, we talked at least twice with each of the 162 mothers in the study. Sometimes respondents shared openly the first time we met with them, but often the first interview was just a warm-up for a second, where the mother was willing to share her experiences and views more freely. We sometimes interviewed mothers who were especially shy or recalcitrant a third time. We paid each of them $20 per interview.

We tried to keep each interaction as natural and non-intimidating as possible. When entering a respondent's home, we usually made positive comments on the furnishings, décor, a school picture, or a family portrait. We dressed casually and brought treats for small children. In addition, we tried not to intrude too much on the household routine, sometimes lending a hand with a child's homework, playing "itsy-bitsy spider" with an alert infant, chatting with an elderly grandmother, or helping to prepare a snack or change a diaper before the "sit-down" conversation began. All mothers agreed to the interviews being audiotaped.

Though we were asking about areas of women's lives that were often painful or potentially embarrassing, the large majority of the mothers we spoke to quickly warmed to the experience of being interviewed. After the first conversation, most were quite eager to schedule a second, and even a third. Some mothers kept in contact even after our interviews with them were completed, and were anxious to update us on the events in their lives.

Such experiences led us to realize how socially isolated many of these mothers were. They often told us outright how few opportunities they had to talk with a sympathetic listener about their associations with men or their relationships with their children. These were subjects they cared deeply about and enjoyed reflecting upon, even if the recounting sometimes provoked deep emotion. After sharing their experiences and views with us, most willingly introduced us to friends or acquaintances who were in similar straits. One such chain of referrals led to a hastily organized pizza party at one Puerto Rican mother's South Camden home. Soon, the five mothers were tearfully relating their common experiences of violence and abuse.

A rough approximation of the questions we asked each mother appears in appendix B. Yet though we did ask for the same types of information from each respondent, we almost always changed the order and wording of questions, and probed for details of specific examples, statements, and evaluations offered by respondents. Thus, each interview was unique in some ways. This interviewing process retained the advantage of being highly systematic yet allowed for unanticipated constructs to emerge in the give-and-take of the interview.

CODING

We coded each verbatim transcript in its entirety. A team of trained coders sorted transcribed text into predetermined or emergent topics, or "fields." For example, we constructed topical fields for "father's reaction to the pregnancy" (called "pregreact") or "description of the breakup with child's father" (called "breakup"). Coders were instructed to draw material from any portion of the transcript that was relevant to the field's topic, even if given in answers to questions not related to that field. Data that were appropriate to more than one field were entered into as many fields as were applicable. As coders sorted chunks of text (which ranged in length from a single sentence to several pages) into fields, they closely monitored each others' practices and met regularly to ensure that their judgments and practices were appropriate and consistent.

The result of this labor-intensive coding was a dataset saved and manipulated electronically. The file is organized much like quantitative survey datasets, in a case-by-variable (or "field") format. However, where a survey dataset would have a single number or alphanumeric code in a case-by-variable cell, most of our fields have relevant chunks of text from the transcript. Our in-depth interviews also collected data that are inherently quantitative on topics such as education, history of welfare use in the past two years, housing situation, and so on. In addition, coders created a large number of dichotomous variables indicating the presence or absence of some situation (e.g., the presence of a formal child-support order) and other categorical variables drawn from narrative fields.[12]

INTERVIEW GUIDE

INTRODUCTION

I am writing a book about how mothers and fathers cope with pregnancy and with parenting during their children's first few years of life, and the support systems they are able to draw on for help. If you don't mind, I am going to tape this conversation. This is so I can listen to you, rather than take notes. First, let's make up a name for you, so that your privacy will be protected. You are the expert here. I am the learner. I'll ask a few general questions, but you can talk about anything you feel is important, even if I don't ask about it. And, if you don't like my questions, you don't have to answer them. One more thing—if you want to answer off the record, we can turn the tape recorder off, and then turn it on again later. In fact, why don't you hold the tape recorder? That way you can turn it on and off yourself. Are you ready to get started?

1. Let's start with you telling me a little bit about yourself. (Probe for parents' occupation, education, whether they grew up in Philadelphia, where their parents and grandparents grew up.)

    –How old are you?
    –Where did you grow up?
    –Tell me about your parents, grandparents, brothers and sisters?
    –Where did you go to school? (Probe for last year completed.)
    –How have you spent your time since you left school?

2. Tell me a little bit about your own family. How many children do you have? (Get names and ages.)

3. What do you like best about being a mother?

   –What do you like least?
   –How did your expectations about becoming a parent compare with the reality?

4. Now that you have the baby to take care of, what is a typical day in your life like?

   –What was a typical day like before you had this baby?

5. Now I am going to ask you to think back to the moment you thought you might be pregnant with this child.

   –What was the first thing that went through your mind?
   –What happened after that?

6. Was this an expected pregnancy?

   –[IF NOT]
   –Did you think about the possibility that you might get pregnant (i.e., were you afraid of it, open to it)?
   –Had you and the father discussed having children?

7. When you thought about whether or not to have this baby, what went through your mind?

   –Did you consider not keeping or not having the baby? Giving the child to a family member, a friend, to raise? Placing the child in an adoptive home?

8. How did your baby's father, your family, his family, and others find out?

–What did they say? How did they feel?

–What kind of advice did they give you?

9. Was this your first pregnancy? If not, tell me a bit about the others.

   –How did this pregnancy compare with the others?

   –Was this the child's father's first experience as a father? If not, tell me about his other children.

10. What about when the child was born?

    –How did your baby's father, your family, his family, and others respond?

    –Did you nurse or use formula? Why or why not?

11. What would your life be like now if you had never had any of your children?

12. Do you think others think of you differently now that you have kids? Do they treat you any differently?

    –Did you feel different about yourself?

    –Did people treat you differently?

13. Tell me about your relationship with your [youngest] child's father.

    –How did you meet?

    –What was your relationship like before you found out about the pregnancy?

    –How about during the pregnancy?

    –How about after the birth?

    –How about now?

14. Let's talk more about your child's father.

    –Tell me about him.
    –Is he a good father?
    –What have you told your child about his/her father?
    –(Probe for age, level of emotional support, level of in-kind and
    cash support, sources of cash support, education, occupation,
    plans for future.)

15. In a typical week, how many hours does your child's father spend
    with your child?

    –What exactly do they do together?
    –Who else spends time with your child during a typical week?
    –How much time for each with different people?

16. What do you think his situation will be like in one year, five years,
    ten years, when your child enters adulthood?

17. So far, what role have your child's father, your family, his family,
    and others had in helping you to care for your child? (Does father
    help financially?)

18. What role do you think your child's father, your family, his fam-
    ily, and others will have in helping you to raise this child in the
    future?

19. What about your child's future? Ideally, what kind of a future
    would you like for your child to have?

    –What can a parent do to help a child have this kind of a future?
    –Do you do things that will help your child do better in school?
    –How might you protect your kids from things like drugs, violence,
    crime, economic difficulty, "getting in trouble"?
    –How does a parent's job change as the child ages?

–Do you think your dreams for this child will be fulfilled? (probe for why or why not).

20. How about your own parents? What kind of a future did they plan for you?

    –Did it turn out the way they had planned? (probe for why or why not).

21. Now let's talk about your future.

    –How did you see your future before you found out you were pregnant with this child?
    –How do you see your future now?

22. What about work?

    –What kind of work situation would you like to pursue?
    –What would be your minimum criteria?
    –What about your ideal work situation?

Now I'm going to ask you some general questions about parenting.

23. What makes for a good mother?

    –Ideally, what kind of a mother would you like to be for this child?
    –Do you know any mothers like this?
    –What about your own mother?
    –How do you want to be a mother like your own mom? How not?
    –How do you want to raise your child that is different/same compared to how you were raised?
    –Describe a bad mother you know. Describe a specific person.

24. What is an ideal time to become a mother?

25. When did your mother and sister(s) first become mothers? (probe for whether these kin were married).

26. What makes for a good father?

   –Ideally, what kind of a father would you like for this child?
   –Do you know any fathers like this?
   –What about your own father?
   –What is a bad father? Describe a person you know who is a bad father.

27. What is an ideal time to become a father?

28. When did your father and brother(s) first become fathers? (probe for whether they were married).

Now I am going to ask you some general questions about relationships and marriage.

29. Ideally, what should a marriage be like?

   –Do you know any marriages that are like this?
   –What is a bad marriage?
   –Describe the marriages that you know.

30. What is the ideal time to get married?

31. When did father/mother, grandparents, uncles/aunts, etc., get married?

32. Do you see marriage in your future?

   –What about marriage to the father of your child?
   –What kind of a man WOULD you consider marrying—like what would be your minimum criteria?
   –How about your ideal man?

33. Today, fewer and fewer people are getting married. What do you think keeps people from getting married these days?

–What about people you know?

34. In your view, what makes for a good wife? Bad wife?

35. A good husband? Bad husband?

36. Can you list the first names of all your close friends for me? Tell me about each of them.

–Do you have other people that you associate with but are not really friends? Tell me about each of them.

37. When did your friends first become mothers/fathers? (probe for whether any of these were married).

38. What are your plans for the future regarding work, education, marriage?

–Do you want to have more children?
–Where do you see yourself in two, five, or ten years?
–What do you worry about for the future?
–If you won a $1,000 per month for the rest of your life, how would your life change?
–What are the most important things you use your money for when it comes to your children?
–What would you like most to get your children that they do not have now?

NOTES

INTRODUCTION

1. Nancy Gibbs, "Making Time for a Baby," *Time*, April 15, 2002, 48–58.

2. Only two in ten high school dropouts reach age twenty-five without having borne a child, almost always outside of marriage, and few are childless by age forty. Meanwhile, nearly 25 percent of middle-class women reach forty without having any children (Ellwood and Jencks 2001).

3. *National Vital Statistics Reports* 51, no. 11 (June 25, 2003): 3, table A.

4. Ellwood and Jencks use education, not income, as a measure of socioeconomic status. The comparison referred to here as between the "poor" and "affluent" is between the least educated third and the most educated third of the educational distribution. See Ellwood and Jencks (2001).

5. Unpublished figures from the Fragile Families and Child Wellbeing Study (McLanahan et al. 2003), calculated by Marcia Carlson. These figures are for all unmarried mothers in the survey sample (not just those with first births) who reported annual incomes below the federal poverty threshold, and their male partners.

6. Wu, Bumpass, and Musick (2001).

7. Unpublished figures from the Fragile Families and Child Wellbeing Study, calculated by Marcia Carlson. These figures are for all unmarried mothers in the survey sample (not just those with first births) who reported annual incomes below the federal poverty threshold, and their male partners.

8. McLanahan and Sandefur (1994).

9. Parke (2003).

10. Child Trends (2002).

11. The Fragile Families and Child Wellbeing Study (McLanahan et al. 2003) is a longitudinal survey of roughly five thousand couples who had just had a child. About three-fourths of these couples were not married at the time of the birth. The survey, when weighted, is nationally representative of nonmarital births in cities of more than two hundred thousand people. Both parents were surveyed soon after the child's birth and again when their child reached ages twelve, thirty-six, and sixty months. Hereafter referred to as the Fragile Families Study.

12. These unpublished figures, compiled by Marcia Carlson, are for mothers responding to the survey whose annual income was below the federal poverty line. For a description of the sample as a whole, see "Is Marriage a Viable Alternative for Fragile Families?" Fragile Families Research Brief 9 (Princeton, NJ: Center for Child Wellbeing, Princeton University, June 2002).

13. Sharon Lerner, "Bush's Marriage Proposal," *Village Voice*, May 1–7, 2002; Diane Glass, "Do We Need Stronger Family Values?" *Atlanta Journal and Constitution*, July 31, 2003; "Quick Hit" (editorial), *San Jose Mercury News*, September 19, 2003; Elizabeth Bauchner, "Bush Marriage Initiative Robs Billions from the Needy," *Women's eNews*, September 10, 2003 (www.womensenews.org); "The Left's Marriage Problem," *Washington Post*, April 5, 2002, A22.

14. Ellwood and Jencks (2001).

15. Even those who marry may not remain so; more than 40 percent of first marriages now end in divorce, and subsequent marriages dissolve at an even higher rate (Bramlett and Mosher 2001).

16. See U.S. Census Bureau (2002) and earlier reports, as well as Ellwood and Jencks (2001).

17. Wilson (1987).

18. See Licht (1999); Burt and Davies (1982).

19. Quoted in Bissinger (1998, 70).

20. Licht (1999, 54–55).

21. Its heavy reliance on the production of nondurables (e.g., foods such as soup and ice cream) made it more vulnerable than most other cities to the larger wave of deindustrialization in the 1970s, as these products were the most susceptible to competition from abroad (Adams et al. 1991).

22. Black men were almost entirely excluded from the city's industrial economy and worked overwhelmingly in domestic service or unskilled labor. As late as the early 1940s, most "name" manufacturing firms (e.g., the Budd Company, Bendix, Cramps Shipyard, Baldwin Locomotive Works, the Crown Can Com-

pany, and the Quaker Lace Company) did not have a single black employee (Licht 1999, 43–52).

23. See Adams et al (1991); Madden and Stull (1990).

24. Webb (2000).

25. Authors' calculations from 1990 census data.

26. Annie E. Casey Foundation (2001).

27. Weigley (1982, 363).

28. For more on the Cramps Shipyards, see Harris (2000). In 1998, these neighborhoods became the target of the Philadelphia Police Department's Operation Sunrise, which drove drug arrest rates to record levels. But in 2002, the problem remained chronic enough to motivate a second campaign, Operation Safe Streets, which has flooded the neighborhood with uniformed police (Moran, Fleming, and Salisbury 2002).

29. The naval yard stayed open to refurbish, repair, and store naval ships until 1996, but with a drastically reduced workforce (Dorwart and Wolf 2001).

30. Women and nonwhites now occasionally appear in the parade as well. In addition to the string bands, there are three other divisions in the Mummers Parade: the Fancy Brigades, the Comics, and the Fancies. See *Strut*, a documentary film on the Mummers. More information about the mummers is available at the *Strut* website: http://www.strutthemovie.com/mummery-links.php.

31. Berson (1966).

32. Annie E. Casey Foundation (2000).

33. The exact figures, collected at only two points in time, are $7.20 in 1998 and $8.60 in 2002. See Michalopolous et al. (2003). Note that not all of those who left welfare for work worked full time.

34. Just over 7 percent of those doubled up with relatives or friends also had a boyfriend living with them. In total, 30 percent lived with a boyfriend and 22 percent with a boyfriend alone. See appendix A for more details.

35. All mothers' reported incomes were below the poverty line for a family of four, and all had at least one minor child living with them. All were currently single, but a relatively small number had been married.

CHAPTER 1: "BEFORE WE HAD A BABY . . ."

1. The social conditions of this neighborhood are dramatized in fictional form in Lopez (1994).

2. Philadelphia Metropolitan Planning Commission (2001, A–39).

3. Unpublished figures calculated by Stephanie J. Ventura. National Center

for Health Statistics are cited in Terry-Humen, Manlove, and Moore (2001). See also Ventura and Bachrach (2000).

4. Our focus is on the role of children and marriage in the lives of low-income single mothers, not fathers. This is an obvious limitation to the study. To remedy this problem in part, we occasionally draw from a preliminary analysis of a qualitative study of the views and experiences of low-income noncustodial fathers in Philadelphia and two other cities conducted by Kathryn Edin, Timothy Nelson, and Laura Lein. See Nelson, Clampet-Lundquist, and Edin (2002).

5. As the social networks of our respondents tend to be quite geographically restricted, many of these youth have known—or at least known of—each other since childhood.

6. Mincy (2004).

7. Between 1979 and 1999 the employment and earnings of young men with no more than a high school degree declined markedly (see Richer et al. 2003). Women who dropped out of high school have also lost ground over time, but female high school graduates now fare slightly better than they did in the late 1970s, yet when working full time earn only $459 per week—well beyond the $323 per week for high school dropouts but far from the $809 a college graduate earns. See U.S. Department of Labor (2003).

8. Fully two-thirds of our mothers say that talk of shared children occurred early in their courtship and preceded pregnancy. Though some couples had talked only in generalities, about four in ten say they and their children's fathers had discussed the subject in detail, including some of those who were extremely young at the time of conception, like Antonia.

9. Hannerz (1969) observed this "culture of distrust" more than forty years ago. See also Rainwater (1970) and Furstenberg (2001).

10. The term *relational poverty* was coined by Kaplan (1997).

11. While the number of unplanned births among the middle class is quite high as well (Musick 2002), the class differences are still significant. The highest rate of unplanned pregnancies is for teenagers: 78 percent (Henshaw 1998).

12. Approximately 15 percent of our sample began their most recent pregnancy in this way.

13. A teen having sex without contraception has a 90 percent chance of becoming pregnant within a year. See Harlap, Kost, and Forrest (1991, 36, fig. 5.4).

14. Despite the lack of clear planning and the opposition to abortion described later in this chapter, poor women usually do stop with two or sometimes three children. African Americans without a college degree have a total fertility rate between 2.2 and 2.4, whereas less-educated whites have between 2.0 and 2.1

children on average over their lifetimes. In fact, the number of children they bear over their life course is only a fraction of a child higher than for most middle-class women (the rates for more educated whites and blacks are between 1.6 and 1.8); see Yang and Morgan (2002).

15. Despite the fact that many of our Puerto Ricans and whites are from Catholic backgrounds, none claimed any religious or moral objections to birth control. Many obtain birth control at these same family planning establishments.

16. Ongoing condom use suggests a suspicion that the other partner may still be sexually involved with others and could potentially transmit AIDS or another disease.

17. Luker (1996) points to survey data showing that the irregular use of contraception is often a precursor to early childbearing. She interprets these data to mean that young women may have difficulty negotiating birth control and other sexual matters in new or non-monogamous relationships. Our findings contradict this interpretation; many of the women we interviewed said they started using contraception erratically only *after* they were in a stable, romantic relationship. Mincy et al. (2003) provide support for this view.

18. Mothers were asked about their reaction to the news that they were pregnant with children they then decided to have. Those who chose abortion instead might have been far less happy with the news.

19. Luker (1984) reviews a considerable body of evidence showing that social class, religion, and education all play important roles in how women interpret abortion.

20. Luker (1996, 154) reviews the literature on adolescent pregnancy outcomes by education. See also Leibowitz, Eisen, and Chow (1986).

21. Opposition to abortion used to be higher among the less educated, but now the opposite is true. See Martin and Parashar (2003) and Szafran and Clagett (1987).

22. Only one in five American youth leave their teens without having had sexual intercourse. See Moore, Driscoll, and Lindberg (1998, 11).

23. Ellwood, Wilde, and Batchelder (2003).

24. Ibid.; Anderson, Binder, and Krause (2002); and Dex et al. (1996).

CHAPTER 2: "WHEN I GOT PREGNANT . . ."

1. Nelson, Clampet-Lundquist, and Edin (2002).

2. Elijah Anderson's work (1989; 1991) offers a perspective on these young families in inner-city Philadelphia.

3. Timothy J. Nelson and Kathryn Edin, unpublished analysis of 180 low-income noncustodial fathers in Philadelphia.

4. Carolyn and Philip Cowan (1995; 1987) have found that the birth of the first child is a period of considerable difficulty for middle-class married couples.

5. Nelson and Edin (see n. 3 above).

6. Ibid.

7. Men in these neighborhoods commonly "step off" from their financial responsibilities as fathers and face social censure for doing so. Men often rationalize their behavior by blaming the child's mother for acting as a gatekeeper and prohibiting them access to their children. Another rationalization men employ is to claim the child's mother uses his money for her own needs, and not for the child. In some cases, these complaints are probably legitimate. See Nelson, Clampet-Lundquist, and Edin (2002).

8. See McLanahan et al. (2003).

9. Unmarried fathers who are employed are more likely to marry the child's mother within twelve months of the birth and are less likely to break up (Carlson, McLanahan, and England 2004).

10. Kaplan (1997) emphasizes how teen mothers' own mothers react with disappointment at the news of a daughter's pregnancy and argues that the community neither encourages nor celebrates early childbearing. We agree but believe her account downplays the degree to which many prospective grandmothers offer emotional support and practical aid to their pregnant daughters.

11. Nelson, Clampet-Lundquist, and Edin (2002).

12. Nelson and Edin (see n. 3 above).

13. Ibid.

14. Myers (2002).

15. Low-income noncustodial fathers routinely report that their child's mother denies them visitation (Miller and Knox 2001).

CHAPTER 3: HOW DOES THE DREAM DIE?

1. These unpublished figures, compiled by Marcia Carlson, are for survey respondents whose annual income was below the federal poverty line. For a description of the union formation and dissolution rates for the sample as a whole twelve months after the child's birth, see Center for Research on Child Wellbeing/Social Indicators Survey Center (2003). Though mothers expect that the relationship between the father and their child will continue even after the couple parts, this seldom happens. Once a poor, unwed couple's relationship dissolves,

few fathers continue to provide economic or emotional support to their children. In time, many fathers disappear from their children's lives completely. For a review of the literature on low-income fathers and father involvement, see Nelson (2004).

2. For an excellent review of the literature on family structure, see Ellwood and Jencks (2001).

3. For Philadelphia employment trends during this period, see Michalopolous et al. (2003). The labor force participation rates of black men aged 20–24 declined from 71 percent in 1989 to 59 percent in 2000, with almost all of the change during the last half of the 1990s (Offner and Holzer 2002). However, the labor force participation rate of never-married mothers stayed roughly steady from the late 1970s to the end of the 1980s (around 79 percent) and had increased to 89 percent by 2000 (unpublished tabulations of Bureau of Labor Statistics data by Gary Burtless).

4. Timothy Nelson and Kathryn Edin, unpublished analysis of qualitative interviews with 180 low-income noncustodial fathers from these same Philadelphia neighborhoods.

5. For the perspective of low-income noncustodial fathers drawn from these same neighborhoods, see Nelson, Clampet-Lundquist, and Edin (2002).

6. For an account of how crime and incarceration among low-income noncustodial fathers affect their relationships with their unmarried partners and children, see Edin, Nelson, and Paranal (2004).

7. Rates of illicit drug use are much lower among girls and women than among boys and men. In addition, the rate is much lower for pregnant women than for nonpregnant women (U.S. Department of Health and Human Services 2003).

8. For further confirmation on this point, see Edin and Lein (1997).

9. For the perspective of low-income noncustodial fathers drawn from these same neighborhoods, see Nelson, Clampet-Lundquist, and Edin (2002).

10. Income differentials among parents are the best predictors of an out-of-home placement (Lindsey 1991, 1994).

11. An audit study of entry-level employers suggests that a felony conviction hurts the prospects of black and white job seekers alike (Pager 2003).

12. Blunts are hollowed-out cigars filled with marijuana and sometimes laced with cocaine.

13. Reed (2004) finds these attitudes among a sample of unmarried new parents—both mothers and fathers.

14. Laumann and his colleagues (2004) argue that the lack of commitment

implied by cohabitation is likely responsible for the higher rates of jealousy, infidelity, and violence in cohabiting than in marital relationships.

15. Bumpass and Lu (2000).

16. For an analysis of how the poor view cohabitation and its normative expectations, see Reed (2004). For views of cohabitation among a more mixed-income sample, see Manning and Smock (2003).

17. For figures on these eight neighborhoods, see appendix A. Sex ratios are out of balance in all neighborhoods but PennsPort, which is largely white. North Camden's female-to-male ratio is the reverse of the others because the Camden County Jail is located in this neighborhood.

18. For a discussion on infidelity among moderate- and low-income unmarried parents, see Edin, England, and Linnenberg (2003). For the population as a whole, see Laumann et al. (1994).

19. See Tolman and Raphael (2000) and Kurz (1995, 1998, 1999). For the impact of infidelity on marital relationships in a sample of mostly working-class couples, see Kurz (1995).

20. Edin and Lein (1997) found that boyfriends are a major source of economic support for low-wage working mothers.

21. Some studies (e.g., Gelles and Cornell 1990) do show that women are more likely than men to hit or slap their partners, but men presumably inflict far more serious injuries.

22. We noted another difference between the groups that might explain this pattern: while the Puerto Rican and white victims of domestic abuse often stay in a relationship for years in spite of the beatings, sometimes only ending them when children seem to be at risk as well, most African American victims make a quick and clean break when a pattern of violent behavior emerges—sometimes after a single incident. If the duration of the abuse is shorter, mothers may be less likely to report it.

23. Laumann et al. (1994, 102–3, table 6) find that blacks and, to a lesser degree, Hispanics have more sexual partners within a given year than whites.

24. For rates of nonmarital childbearing by age, see Ventura and Bachrach (2000).

25. Nelson and Edin, unpublished analysis of low-income noncustodial fathers.

26. Ibid.

27. See "Barriers to Marriage among Fragile Families," Fragile Families Research Brief no. 16 (Center for Research on Child Wellbeing, Princeton University, 2003). Available at http://crcw.princeton.edu/files/briefs/Research Brief16.pdf.

28. This gender difference in problem behaviors is also seen in surveys with very high response rates among both new unmarried mothers and new unmarried fathers. In fact, the mothers' response rates are higher than those of the fathers, suggesting that the figures could underestimate the gender difference. See the source cited in the preceding note.

CHAPTER 4: WHAT MARRIAGE MEANS

1. These data are drawn from the Fragile Families and Child Wellbeing Study. See "Is Marriage a Viable Alternative for Fragile Families?" Fragile Families Research Brief no. 9 (Princeton, NJ: Center for Child Wellbeing, Princeton University, 2002).

2. Marriage rates among unmarried parents in the Fragile Families and Child Wellbeing Study, up to the time when their child turns three, have been calculated from seven of twenty cities for the authors by Marcia Carlson (unpublished calculations). However, most mothers with a nonmarital birth do marry by age forty: 82 percent of white women, 62 percent of Hispanics, and 59 percent of African Americans (Graefe and Lichter 2002). Of those with a first nonmarital birth, 21 percent of white mothers, 18 percent of Hispanics, and 19 percent for African Americans are not marrying until they are between thirty and forty. Fewer marriages occur at those later ages for women who did not have a nonmarital first birth (9 percent for whites, 7 percent for Hispanics, and 17 percent for African Americans). See also Lichter and Graefe (2001).

3. Axinn and Thornton (2000).

4. Two qualitative analyses of low-income women find that childbearing and marriage are seen as largely independent events. See Edin (2000) and Gibson, Edin, and McLanahan (2004).

5. A large literature shows the positive effects of both African American and white men's earnings and employment on marriage; see Lichter, LeClere, and McLaughlin (1991); Manning and Smock (1995); Lloyd and South (1996); Oppenheimer et al. (1997); Sweeney (2002); and Blau, Kahn, and Waldfogel (2002). Two studies show that African American women may place more emphasis on men's earnings for transitions into marriage than white women; see Bulcroft and Bulcroft (1993) and Tucker (2000).

6. Eighty-two percent of white women with a nonmarital birth will marry, as opposed to 89 percent of those who did not have a nonmarital birth. The corresponding percentages for Hispanics are 62 versus 93 percent, and for African Americans, 59 versus 76 percent. See Graefe and Lichter (2002).

7. While studies of the population as a whole find contradictory evidence as to whether women's employment or earnings encourage entries into marriage, the results are more uniformly positive for low-income and minority populations. For results showing the positive effect on African American marriage rates, see Schultz (1994); Sweeney (2002); and Raley (1996). For mainland Puerto Ricans, see Landale and Forste (1991). For low-income women, see McLaughlin and Lichter (1997). However, these studies do not control for men's earnings, and women's earnings may be a proxy for their partner's economic status, at least in part.

8. Edin (2000).

9. The economic standard these low-income, single mothers have is similar to but more modest than that for a more mixed-income group of new, unmarried parents; see Gibson, Edin, and McLanahan (2004).

10. Edin (2000).

11. In a qualitative study of new, unmarried parents, Waller and Peters (2003) also find that the fear of divorce is a barrier to marriage. Historically the less-educated have been more resistant to the notion of divorce than the more-educated, but most analyses now show that differences have declined (or have even reversed)—driven by a more rapid change in the social acceptability of divorce among the less advantaged. See Martin and Parashar (2003). However, the large majority of Americans in all educational groups still expect their own marriages to endure for a lifetime (Sayer, Wright, and Edin 2003).

12. In the neighborhood where Chelsea grew up, young people have devised a unique solution to the problem of wanting to make a public commitment without risking divorce. They treat engagement as a middle ground that represents some level of loyalty beyond dating, but not a pledge to remain united for life. This white, eighteen-year-old mother of two, ages two and three, says, "I don't want to get legally married, never, never. I don't think its worth it, because I know I'm gonna wind up getting divorced. But I would like to have an engagement ring. After three and a half years, I think I should get some kind of commitment like that! I just feel as though I've been with him for a long time, and I have his daughter now . . . my other daughter is like his daughter . . . why not get engaged?"

13. See Gibson, Edin, and McLanahan (2004).

14. Carlson, McLanahan, and England (2004) also find that mistrust depresses entry into marriage for new, unmarried parents.

15. We did not ask systematically about whether our respondents had received a proposal of marriage in the past, so we cannot estimate the prevalence.

In the cases we refer to here, this information was shared as part of a more general relationship history, or in response to questions we asked about views regarding the desirability of marriage or plans regarding marriage.

16. A number of scholars have noted the high rates of mistrust between men and women who are low income or members of racial or ethnic minority groups; see Patterson (1998); Cherlin (2000); Edin (2000); and Edin, England, and Linnenberg (2003).

17. Mincy (2002). One analysis shows that the father's other children hurt chances for marriage, while the effect of the mother's other children is not significant. See Carlson, McLanahan, and England (2004).

18. Axinn and Thornton (2000).

19. For an analysis showing similar racial and ethnic differences that use the National Survey of Families and Households, see Carter (2003). Another study finds that African American and white youth place a similarly high value on marriage (Brown 2001).

20. Surveys show that multiple-partner fertility is actually much higher among African Americans than other groups, and that African Americans are actually less likely to stay with their children's fathers after a nonmarital birth (Mincy 2000; Carlson, McLanahan, and England 2004). However, our sample was drawn only from those living in high-poverty neighborhoods. Across the nation, few whites, and fewer Hispanics than African Americans, live in such neighborhoods (Jargowsky 1997). Thus, these neighborhoods may capture an especially disadvantaged group of whites and Puerto Ricans.

21. For more evidence on this point, see Landale and Fennelly (1992). See also Landale (1994), Landale and Hauan (1996), Manning and Landale (1996).

22. See Ellwood and Jencks (2002), Moffitt (2000), and Oppenheimer (2000).

CHAPTER 5: LABOR OF LOVE

1. Lareau (2003).

2. Lareau (2003) also found few race differences within class groups in parenting philosophies.

3. Luttrell (2003) also documents the prevalence of the phrase "being there" among unmarried and pregnant, mostly low-income, African American, white, and Mexican American teens. Safety and material provision were central to what "being there" constituted for these girls.

4. Class differences in childrearing patterns have been well documented. See Kohn (1959, 1963) and Lareau (2003).

5. Lareau (2003), Hays (1996), and MacMahon (1995).

6. Unpublished figures calculated by Marcia Carlson from the Fragile Families and Child Wellbeing Study. They are for all unmarried mothers in the survey sample and the fathers of their children (not just those with first births) who reported annual incomes below the federal poverty threshold.

7. The importance of cleanliness to lower- and working-class women's demonstrations of respectability has been noted by others. See Kefalas (2003), Collins (1990), Steedman (1987), and Oakley (1974). For a discussion of how teens use their children's appearance to establish competency as mothers, see Higginson (1998).

8. Anderson (1999).

9. Lareau (2003) discusses how frankly working-class and poor parents talk with their children about their financial constraints.

10. This has been the main motive for the move to school uniforms. See Ritter (1998) and Wilkins (1999).

11. Many others have discussed how parents in dangerous neighborhoods protect their children. The most commonly used tactics are extensive monitoring and isolation of children within the home, often severely restricting or prohibiting their interaction with neighborhood peers. See Lareau (2003); Rosier (2000); Cook and Fine (1995); Furstenberg (1993); Garbarino, Kostelny, and Dubrow (1991); and Jarrett (1997). However, isolation can have seriously detrimental effects on children's development and may provoke violence or aggression. See Garbarino, Kostelny, and Dubrow (1991) and Franklin and Boyd-Franklin (2001).

12. Lareau (2003).

13. On the particularly high value that low-income African American families place on children's educational attainment, see MacLeod (1987); Slaughter and Epps (1987); Alexander and Entwisle (1988); and Stevenson, Chen, and Uttal (1990).

14. Lareau (2000).

15. Kozol (1992) documents Camden's troubled schools.

16. Lareau (2000) shows how class affects parents' interaction with teachers and their views of education in general.

17. The increase in employment rates among never-married mothers, for example, was nearly 20 percent during the 1990s, with almost all of the increase in the last half of the decade (unpublished Bureau of Labor Statistics tabulations by Gary Burtless). For employment trends in Philadelphia for women living in disadvantaged neighborhoods, see Michalopoulos et al. (2003).

18. Former welfare recipients also have trouble monitoring their children's homework when they begin full-time work (Clampet-Lundquist and Edin 2004).

19. Feelings of powerlessness play a significant role in shaping the parenting strategies of low-income parents. See Rosier (2000), Willis (1981), and Collins (1991).

20. Anderson (1999) discusses the boundary at work between "street" and "decent" families.

21. As these mothers had no custodial children, they were not included in our sample.

22. In Philadelphia, many experts question the reliability of statistics for the Department of Human Services. However, the 2003 Report for Philadelphia Safe and Sound included the following numbers on cases of abuse and neglect: 1,336 "child protective service cases" (for reports of nonaccidental physical or mental injury, sexual abuse or sexual exploitation, and serious physical neglect that endangers a child's life or development or impairs a child's functioning) and 3,830 "general protective service cases" (for reports of neglect or potential harm, with no apparent physical injuries to the child). During this same period there were 7,840 "dependent placements" and 1,608 "delinquent placements." In 2002, 6,007 young people were sent to the Youth Study Center (a facility for juvenile offenders in Philadelphia). See *Report Card 2003: The Well-Being of Children and Youth in Philadelphia* (Philadelphia: Philadelphia Safe and Sound, 2003). Also see Appell (1998) for discussions of state interventions with poor mothers through foster care.

23. Hays (1996) describes the child-centered, emotionally intense, and resource-rich approach to mothering typical of the middle class. For a historical account of how the social meaning of children has evolved, see Zelizer (1994).

24. Lareau (2003).

CHAPTER 6: HOW MOTHERHOOD CHANGED MY LIFE

1. Much has been written about the state's efforts to regulate the fertility patterns of lower-class and minority women. See Jencks and Edin (1995), Roberts (1998), Hays (2003), and Solinger (2001). See Gordon (1994) for an analysis of the historical evolution of the marginalization of single mothers and welfare programs in the United States.

2. See Luttrell (2003) for similar views among working- and lower-class women.

3. Manlove (1998) found that a substantial proportion of teen mothers who

drop out of school were already disengaged from school and had dropped out *prior to* pregnancy. Almost 60 percent of teen mothers had dropped out at some point between eighth and twelfth grades. More than a quarter of these teen mothers (28 percent) dropped out before they were pregnant. A nearly equal number (30 percent) dropped out after becoming pregnant, and the remaining 42 percent stayed in school.

4. By perceived low costs, we mean forgone opportunities for an education or career—what economists call *opportunity costs*.

5. The poor, the less-educated, those living in poor neighborhoods, and those raised in single-parent households tend to have far fewer friendships than their more advantaged counterparts. See Fernandez and Harris (1992); Hogan, Hao, and Parish (1990); Marks and McLanahan (1993); McLanahan and Sandefur (1994); and Rankin and Quane (2000).

6. This does not mean that all low-income women come from dysfunctional homes. However, a large number of the women we talked to spoke of unsettled and troubled childhoods.

7. We are not claiming that these mothers got pregnant *because* they sought validation, purpose, order, or companionship. Retrospective accounts such as these cannot be used to advance such claims. However, in the social contexts of these disadvantaged neighborhoods, it is hard to imagine that young childless girls are not influenced, at least to some degree, by the self-proclaimed transformations motherhood has wrought in the lives of so many peers, older siblings, and friends.

8. Studies of Mexican girl gangs in Los Angeles find that having a child serves as a turning point for young women, who may leave the gangs, reconnect with family, and desist from her criminal activities (Moore and Hagedorn 1996).

9. Benjamin (1988), based on personal communication with Mark Jacobs, June 2002.

CONCLUSION: MAKING SENSE OF
SINGLE MOTHERHOOD

1. Elijah Anderson's similar approach reveals a great deal about the sexual and romantic relationships of very young, inner-city African-Americans in Philadelphia, many of whom are not yet parents. See Anderson (1990, 1999).

2. Attempts to reach Antonia Rodriguez were unsuccessful. When we saw the couple last, they had plans to sell the house and move to the suburbs, which they may have done. Millie Acevedo is still living in West Kensington with the man

she met after the father of her three children left. Her daily schedule left no time for a reinterview: she's working full-time, attending college full-time, and is now the custodian of two more children, bringing the total to five.

3. See appendix A, table 2, for exact sex ratios for each neighborhood.

4. Hrdy (1999) offers an evolutionary account of motherhood from a feminist perspective and argues that relying on one man who can offer economic support is a reasonable reproductive strategy. However, when dependable male providers are not available, women may prefer a network of female kin and more than one man.

5. Becker (1991).

6. See Oppenheimer (1988), Aassve (2003), Goldscheider and Waite (1991), and Ruggles (1997).

7. Murray (1984).

8. Wilson (1987) and Wilson and Neckerman (1986).

9. Ellwood and Jencks (2002) review this literature in depth. They find that while area and micro cross-section results show a negative relationship between female labor market opportunities and the local marriage rate, hazard models typically show a positive or insignificant effect of women's employment opportunities on marriage. Both kinds of studies find positive effects of men's labor market opportunities or employment on marriage. Using cross-sectional data and considering the high- and low-wage strata of the U.S. population separately, Moffitt (2000) finds evidence that, for the high-wage strata, increasing women's employment and earnings may account for some of the decline, or delay, in marriage, but this does not appear to be true for the low-wage strata.

10. The relationship between women's employment and marriage is, as Moffitt (2000) warns, very different for the high- and low-wage segments of the population. When low-income and disadvantaged minority groups are considered separately, the relationship between female wages and employment is usually positive. Lichter et al. (1992) and McLaughlin and Lichter (1997) look exclusively at poor women and find that employment increases their entry into marriage. Olsen and Farkas (1990) find that for black female teens in an antipoverty program, those in cities with better employment opportunities were more likely to both cohabit and marry, though this study did not differentiate the employment opportunities for women and men. Sweeney (2002) found positive effects of women's earnings for both blacks and whites. Raley (1996: 980–81) finds that women's full-time employment had a stronger positive effect on marriage among blacks than whites. Finally, Landale and Forste (1991) find positive effects of women's education on marriage among teen Puerto Rican women living in the United States.

11. Exact figures for declines in the real value of welfare are available from McLanahan (1994). Though it is clear that the more recent time trend cannot be explained by the expansion of the welfare state, studies examining effects of state or year variation in benefit levels have often shown negative effects on marriage, but they are often small and sometimes nonsignificant for blacks (see Moffitt 1994, 1998, 2001).

12. Ellwood and Jencks (2001).

13. This literature is reviewed by Ellwood and Jencks (2001). See also Jencks (1992) and Wood (1995).

14. Thornton and Young-DeMarco (2001); see also Axinn and Thornton (2000).

15. Harding and Jencks (2000).

16. Thornton and Young-DeMarco (2001).

17. There are very few class differences among women or men in terms of attitudes toward sex, cohabitation, and childbearing. A large majority of Americans in all educational groups now say that having premarital sex and living together is okay. Regardless of their education, more than half of all Americans agree that it is advisable to live together before marriage. For the middle class and the poor alike, only about half now believe nonmarital childbearing is immoral. Hardly anyone in any educational category now believes married couples ought to have children or that children are the purpose of marriage. Nor do they believe that a couple should get married just to legitimate a birth Finally, both the middle class and the poor now strongly reject the idea that parents who don't get along should stay together for the sake of the children. For patterns of sexual activity by class, see Laumann et al. (1994). For class differences in attitudes, see Sayer, Wright, and Edin (2003).

18. Veroff, Douvan, and Kulka (1981).

19. Cherlin (2004).

20. Danziger and Gottschalk (1995); Oliver and Shapiro (1997).

21. Daly and Valetta (2000).

22. Goldin (1995). Goldin and Katz (2002) argue that this cultural change was made possible, in part, by the introduction of the pill.

23. Thornton and Young-DeMarco (2001).

24. Taylor, Tucker, and Mitchell-Kernan (1999). Blee and Tickamyer (1995) find that for white men, economic factors are positively related to egalitarian views.

25. These notions fit with bargaining theory; see Lundberg and Pollack (1996).

26. Sayer, Wright, and Edin (2003).

27. Ibid.

28. Graefe and Lichter (2002) find that having a child outside of marriage diminishes the chance for future marriage and increases one's risk of divorce, and that these results differ in magnitude by race and ethnicity. Still, most women in all groups (regardless of marital status at the time of the birth or of race or ethnicity) do marry eventually. There is no evidence showing that the negative effects of nonmarital childbearing on marriage and marital stability are due to other observed or unobserved characteristics of unmarried and married mothers. This potential "cost" is one that the poor are apparently willing to risk, as the reward of a child apparently outweighs it.

29. Manlove (1998) finds that girls who become mothers in their teens no longer always find it necessary to drop out of school and that a substantial share of teen mothers (42 percent) never drop out at all. Of those who do, nearly half have already left school by the time they become pregnant. This leaves a small group, about a quarter of all girls with a school-age birth, who drop out during pregnancy or after giving birth.

30. Ellwood, Wilde, and Batchelder (2003).

31. Recent analyses show that a young woman's background characteristics, not the advent of birth, explain most of what formerly looked like a deleterious effect of early childbearing on the mother's life in a variety of domains. See Hotz, McElroy, and Sanders (1997); Hoffman (1998); Geronimus (1997); Kunz (2002); and Kalil and Kunz (2002).

32. McLanahan (2004).

33. Yang and Morgan (2002).

34. When their families have reached the desired size, usually two children, most poor women do use contraception, disproportionately choosing tubal ligation over condoms, birth control pills, Norplant, or Depo-Provera shots they use when they're younger. For age and marital status as a factor in condom use, see Bankole, Darroch, and Singh (1995). On the relationship between age, marital status, and other demographic attributes for sterilization, see Godecker, Thomson, and Bumpass (2001). Koray and Payn (2000) discuss the role of demographic characteristics in predicting the use of injectibles and implants.

35. See also Waller and Peters (2003). Sayer, Wright, and Edin (2003) find large class differences in the proportion of Americans who agree to the statement "There are few good or happy marriages these days" (the poor are more likely to agree). See also Martin and Parashar (2003).

36. The poorly educated are more than three times as likely to believe that there are few good or happy marriages these days than are college graduates, all else held constant. See Sayer, Wright, and Edin (2003).

74. African American workers have about twice the rate of white unemployment. See ibid. (98–99).

APPENDIX A: CITY, NEIGHBORHOOD, AND FAMILY
CHARACTERISTICS AND RESEARCH METHODS

1. Berube and Frey (2002).

2. As defined by Wilson (1987).

3. As table 2 shows, by 2000 PennsPort no longer had 20 percent of its family households headed by single-parent families; still, the rate was close, at 16 percent.

4. For a map showing the concentration of poverty in Philadelphia in 1990 as well as the concentration of child poverty by race, see Michalopolous et al. (2003: 160, fig. 6.2).

5. The number of persons living in tracts with very high poverty concentration is lower in both East and South Camden, which border more affluent suburbs. The other predominantly black neighborhoods had two to three times the numbers of persons living in highly concentrated poverty.

6. Note that, among the employed, white females were much more likely to be earning less than $10,000 per year than their employed male counterparts. The gap was much smaller, though still significant, among employed females and males in our largely black and Puerto Rican communities.

7. Burkhart (2004).

8. Ketkar and Peterson (2000).

9. See Yang and Morgan (2002). High school dropouts had a higher rate of total lifetime fertility than did graduates until 1990 (Rindfuss, Morgan, and Offutt 1996). These figures are not yet available for the 1990s.

10. Michalopolous et al. (2003).

11. We conducted more intensive fieldwork in East Camden and Kensington, as we explain in the introduction.

12. In addition, we have retained entire transcripts in their uncoded form, so that coders and analysts can read them for context.

REFERENCES

Aassve, Arnstein. 2003. "The Impact of Economic Resources on Premarital Childbearing and Subsequent Marriage among Young American Women." *Demography* 40: 105–26.

Acs, Gregory, and Pamela Loprest. 2001. "Synthesis Report of the Findings from ASPE's 'Leavers' Grants." Washington, DC: U.S. Department of Health and Human Services.

——— and Sandi Nelson. 2001. " 'Honey, I'm Home': Changes in Living Arrangements in the Late 1990s." New Federalism Project Policy Brief B-38. Washington, DC: Urban Institute Press.

Adams, Carolyn, David Bartlet, David Elesh, Ira Goldstein, Nancy Kleniewski, and William Yancey. 1991. *Philadelphia: Neighborhoods, Division, and Conflict in a Postindustrial City.* Philadelphia, PA: Temple University Press.

Alexander, Karl L., and Doris R. Entwisle. 1988. *Achievement in the First Two Years of School: Patterns and Processes.* Chicago: University of Chicago Press.

Anderson, Deborah, Melissa Binder, and Kate Krause. 2002. "The Motherhood Wage Penalty: Which Mothers Pay It and Why?" *American Economic Review* 92: 354–58.

Anderson, Elijah. 1989. "Sex Codes and Family Life among Poor Inner-City Youth." *Annals of the American Academy of Political and Social Science* 501: 59–78

———. 1990. *Streetwise: Race, Class, and Change in an Urban Community.* Chicago: University of Chicago Press.

———. 1991. "Neighborhood Effects on Teenage Pregnancy." In *The Urban Underclass,* ed. Christopher Jencks and Paul E. Peterson, 375–98. Washington, DC: Brookings Institution.

———. 1999. *Code of the Street: Decency, Violence, and the Moral Life of the Inner City.* New York: W. W. Norton.

Annie E. Casey Foundation. 2000. *A Path Forward for Camden: A Report Commissioned for the City of Camden and Its Constituents.* Baltimore, MD: Annie E. Casey Foundation.

———. 2001. *City Kids Count: Data on the Wellbeing of Children in Large Cities.* Baltimore, MD: Annie E. Casey Foundation.

Appell, Annette R. 1998. "On Fixing Bad Mothers and Saving their Children." In *"Bad Mothers": The Politics of Blame in Twentieth-Century America,* ed. Molly Ladd-Taylor and Lauri Umansky, 356–80. New York: New York University Press.

Axinn, William G., and Arland Thornton. 1996. "The Influence of Parents' Marital Dissolutions on Children's Attitudes toward Family Formation." *Demography* 33: 66–81.

———. 2000. "The Transformation in the Meaning of Marriage." In *The Ties That Bind: Perspectives on Marriage and Cohabitation,* ed. Linda J. Waite, 147–65. New York: Aldine de Gruyter.

Baker, Andrea. 2004. *Double Click: Romance and Commitment of Online Couples.* Cresskill, NJ: Hampton Press.

Bankole, Akinrinola, Jacqueline E. Darroch, and Susheela Singh. 1995. "Determinants of Trends of Condom Use in the US: 1980–1995." *Family Planning Perspectives* 31: 264–71.

Becker, Gary S. 1991. *A Treatise on the Family.* Chicago: University of Chicago Press.

Benjamin, Jessica. 1988. *Bonds of Love: Psychoanalysis, Feminism, and the Problem of Domination.* New York: Pantheon.

Berson, Lenora E. 1966. *Case Study of a Riot: The Philadelphia Story.* New York: American Jewish Committee, Institute of Human Relations Press.

Berube, Alan, and William H. Frey. 2002. *A Decade of Mixed Blessings: Urban and Suburban Poverty in Census 2000.* Washington, DC: Brookings Institution.

Bissinger, Buzz. 1998. *A Prayer for the City.* New York: Vintage.

Blau, Francine D., Lawrence M. Kahn, and Jane Waldfogel. 2002. "Understanding Young Women's Marriage Decisions: The Role of Labor and Marriage Market Conditions." *Industrial and Labor Relations Review* 53: 624–47.

Blee, Kathleen M., and Ann R. Tickamyer. 1995. "Racial Differences in Men's Attitudes about Women's Gender Roles." *Journal of Marriage and the Family* 57: 21–30.

Bouchet, Stacey, Theodora Ooms, and Mary Parke. 2004. *Beyond Marriage Li-*

censes: Efforts in States to Strengthen Marriage and Two-Parent Families, A State-by-State Snapshot. Washington, DC: Center for Law and Social Policy.

Bradbury Thomas N., Frank D. Fincham, and Steven R. H. Beach. 2000. "Research on the Nature and Determinants of Marital Satisfaction: A Decade in Review." *Journal of Marriage and the Family* 62: 964–80.

Bramlett, Matthew D., and William T. Mosher. 2001. "First Marriage Dissolution, Divorce, and Remarriage: United States." *Advance Data from Vital and Health Statistics.* No. 323. Hyattsville, MD: National Center for Health Statistics.

Brown, Brett V. 2001. "Youth Attitudes on Family, Work, and Community Service: Implications for Welfare Reform." Working Paper A-47. Washington, DC: Urban Institute Press.

Bulcroft, Richard A., and Kris A. Bulcroft. 1993. "Race Differences and Attitudinal and Motivational Factors in the Decision to Marry." *Journal of Marriage and the Family* 55: 338–55.

Bumpass, Larry, and Hsien-Hen Lu. 2000. "Trends in Cohabitation and Implications for Children's Family Contexts in the United States." *Population Studies* 54: 29–41.

Burkhart, Michael T. 2004. "Saturday Court Sessions Clear Cases: Program Lowers Camden County Jail's Weekend Population." *Camden Courier-Post,* January 4.

Burt, Nathaniel, and Wallace E. Davies. 1982. "The Iron Age, 1876–1905." In *Philadelphia: A 300-Year History*, ed. Russell F. Wiegley, 471–523. New York: W. W. Norton.

Carlson, Marcia, Sara McLanahan, and Paula England. Forthcoming. "Union Formation in Fragile Families." *Demography.*

Carter, Wendy Y. 2003. "Attitudes toward Pre-Marital Sex, Non-Marital Childbearing, and Marriage among Blacks and Whites." NSFH Working Paper 61. Madison, WI: Center for Demography and Ecology, University of Wisconsin, Madison.

Case, Anne C., I-Fen Lin, and Sara S. McLanahan. 2001. "Educational Attainment of Siblings in Stepfamilies." *Evolution and Human Behavior* 22: 269–89.

Center for Research on Child Wellbeing/Social Indicators Survey Center. 2003. "Union Formation and Dissolution in Fragile Families." Fragile Families Research Brief #14. Princeton, NJ: Center for Research on Child Wellbeing, Princeton University.

Cherlin, Andrew J. 2000. "Toward a New Home Socioeconomics of Union Formation." In *The Ties That Bind: Perspectives on Marriage and Cohabitation*, ed. Linda J. Waite, 126–44. Berlin and New York: Aldine de Gruyter.

———. Forthcoming. "The Deinstitutionalization of Marriage." *Journal of Marriage and the Family*.

Child Trends. 2002. "Facts at a Glance 2002: Annual Newsletter on Teen Pregnancy." No. 2002–50.

Clampet-Lundquist, Susan, and Kathryn Edin. 2004. "Making a Way out of No Way: How Low-Income Single Mothers Meet Basic Family Needs while Moving from Welfare to Work." In *Work-Family Challenges for Low-Income Workers and Their Children*, ed. Alan Booth and Nan Crouter, 203–41. Mahwah, NJ: Lawrence Erlbaum Associates.

Clark-Kauffman, Elizabeth, Mirella Landriscina, and Kathryn Edin. 2004. "How Poor Single Mothers Parent Children in Early, Middle, and Later Childhood." Evanston, IL: Institute for Policy Research, Northwestern University.

Collins, Patricia Hill. 1991. "The Meaning of Motherhood in Black Culture and Black Mother-Daughter Relationships." In *Double Stitch: Black Women Write about Mothers and Daughters*, ed. Patricia Bell-Scott, 42–60. Boston: Beacon Press.

Collins, Randall. 1990. "Women and the Production of Status Cultures." In *Cultivating Differences: Symbolic Differences and the Making of Inequality*, ed. Michele Lamont and Marcel Fournier, 213–31. Chicago: University of Chicago Press.

Cook, Donelda A., and Michelle Fine. 1995. " 'Motherwit': Childrearing Lessons from African-American Mothers of Low Income." In *Children and Families "At Promise": Deconstructing the Discourse of Risk*, ed. Beth Blue Swadener and Sally Lubeck, 118–42. Albany, NY: SUNY Press.

Cooksey, Elizabeth C. 1997. "Consequences of Young Mothers' Marital Histories for Children's Cognitive Development." *Journal of Marriage and the Family* 59: 245–61.

Cowan, Carolyn P., and Philip A. Cowan. 1987. "Men's Involvement in Parenthood: Identifying the Antecedents and Understanding the Barriers." In *Men's Transitions to Parenthood: Longitudinal Studies of Early Family Experience*, ed. Phyllis W. Berman and Frank A. Pedersen, 145–74. Hillsdale, NJ: Lawrence Erlbaum Associates.

———. 1995. "Interventions to Ease the Transition to Parenthood: Why They Are Needed and What They Can Do." *Family Relations* 44: 412–23.

Daly, Mary, and Robert Valletta. 2000. "Inequality and Poverty in the United States: The Effects of Changing Family Behavior and Rising Wage Dispersion." Working Paper 2000–06. San Francisco: CA: Federal Research Bank of San Francisco.

Danziger, Sheldon, and Peter Gottschalk. 1995. *America Unequal.* New York: Russell Sage Foundation; Cambridge, MA: Harvard University Press.

Dex, Shirley, Heather Joshi, Andrew McCulloch, and Susan Macran. 1996. "Women's Employment Transitions around Childbearing." Working Paper #1408. London: Center for Economic Policy Research.

Dorwart, Jeffery M., and Jean K. Wolf. 2001. *Philadelphia Navy Yard: From the Birth of the U.S. Navy to the Nuclear Age.* Philadelphia: University of Pennsylvania Press.

Dupree, Allan, and Wendell Primus. 2001. "Declining Share of Children Lived with Single Mothers During the Late 1990s: Substantial Differences by Race and Income." Washington, DC: Center on Budget and Policy Priorities.

Edin, Kathryn. 2000. "How Low-Income Single Mothers Talk About Marriage." *Social Problems* 47: 112–33.

———, Paula England, and Kathryn Linnenberg. 2003. "Love and Distrust among Unmarried Parents." Paper presented at symposium entitled Marriage and Family Formation among Low-Income Couples: What Do We Know from Research? Ann Arbor, MI: National Poverty Center.

——— and Laura Lein. 1997. *Making Ends Meet: How Low-Income Single Mothers Survive Welfare and Low-Wage Work.* New York: Russell Sage Foundation.

———, Timothy J. Nelson, and Rechelle Paranal. 2004. "Fatherhood and Incarceration as Potential Turning Points in the Criminal Careers of Unskilled Men." In *Imprisoning America: The Social Effects of Mass Incarceration*, ed. Mary Patillo, David Haproff, and Bruce Western, 46–75. New York: Russell Sage Foundation.

Ellwood, David T., and Christopher Jencks. 2001. "The Spread of Single-Parent Families in the United States since 1960." Cambridge, MA: John F. Kennedy School of Government, Harvard University.

———. 2002. "The Growing Differences in Family Structure: What Do We Know? Where Do We Look for Answers?" Cambridge, MA: John F. Kennedy School of Government, Harvard University.

———, Ty Wilde, and Lilly Batchelder. 2003. "The Impact of Childbearing on Wages of Women of Differing Skills." Paper presented to the MacArthur Network on the Family and the Economy. Jackson Hole, WY, August.

Fernandez, Roberto, and David Harris. 1992. "Social Isolation and the Underclass." In *Drugs, Crime, and Social Isolation*, ed. Adele W. Harrell and George E. Peterson, 257–93. Washington DC: Urban Institute Press.

Franklin, Anderson. J., and Nancy Boyd-Franklin. 2001. "A Psychoeducational Perspective on Black Parenting." In *Black Children: Social, Educational, and*

Parental Environments, ed. Harriette Pipes McAdoo, 194–210. Newbury Park, CA: Sage.

Frey, William H., Bill Abresch, and Jonathan Yeasting. 2001. *America by the Numbers: A Field Guide to the U.S. Population.* New York: New Press.

Furstenberg, Frank. 1993. "How Families Manage Risk and Opportunity in Dangerous Neighborhoods." In *Sociology and the Public Agenda*, ed. William J. Wilson, 231–58. Newbury Park, CA: Sage.

———. 2001. "The Fading Dream: Prospects for Marriage in the Inner City." In *Problem of the Century: Racial Stratification in the United States*, ed. Elijah Anderson and Douglas S. Massey, 224–46. New York: Russell Sage Foundation.

Garbarino, James, Kathleen Kostelny, and Nancy Dubrow. 1991. "What Children Can Tell Us About Living in Danger." *American Psychologist* 46: 376–83.

Gelles, Richard J., and Claire Pedrick Cornell. 1990. *Intimate Violence in Families.* Newberry Park, CA: Sage.

Gennetian, Lisa A., and Virginia Knox. 2003. "Staying Single: The Effects of Welfare Reform Policies on Marriage and Cohabitation." The Next Generation Working Paper Series. No. 13. New York: Manpower Demonstration Research Corporation.

——— and C. Miller. 2000. "Encouraging the Formation and Maintenance of Two-Parent Families: Experimental Evidence on Welfare Reform." New York: Manpower Demonstration Research Corporation.

Geronimus, Arlene T. 1997. "Teenage Childbearing and Personal Responsibility: An Alternative View." *Political Science Quarterly* 112: 405–30.

——— and Sanders Korenmann. 2002. "The Socioeconomic Consequences of Teen Childbearing Reconsidered." *Quarterly Journal of Economics* 107: 1187–1214.

Gibson, Christina, Kathryn Edin, and Sara McLanahan. 2004. "High Hopes but Even Higher Expectations: The Retreat from Marriage among Low-Income Couples." Working Paper #2003–06-FF. Princeton, NJ: Center for Research on Child Wellbeing, Princeton University.

Godecker, Amy L., Elizabeth Thomson, and Larry L. Bumpass. 2001. "Union Status, Marital History, and Female Sterilization in the United States." *Family Planning Perspectives* 33: 35–49.

Goldin, Claudia. 1995. "Career and Family: College Women Look to the Past." Working Paper #5188. National Bureau of Economic Research.

——— and Lawrence F. Katz. 2002. "The Power of the Pill: Oral Contraceptives and Women's Career and Marriage Decisions." *Journal of Political Economy* 110: 730–70.

Goldscheider, Frances K., and Linda J. Waite. 1991. *New Families, No Families? The Transformation of the American Home*. Berkeley and Los Angeles: University of California Press.

Gordon, Linda. 1994. *Pitied but Not Entitled: Single Mothers and the History of Welfare, 1890–1935*. New York: Free Press.

Graefe, Deborah R., and Daniel T. Lichter. 2002. "Marriage among Unwed Mothers: Whites, Blacks, and Hispanics Compared." *Perspectives on Sexual and Reproductive Health* 34: 286–93.

Grogger, Jeffrey. 1997. "Incarceration-Related Costs of Early Childbearing." In *Kids Having Kids: Economic Costs and Social Consequences of Teen Pregnancy*, ed. Rebecca A. Maynard, 95–143. Washington, DC: Urban Institute Press.

Hagan, John, and Alberto Palloni. 1988. "Crimes as Social Events in the Life Course: Reconceiving a Criminological Controversy." *Criminology* 26: 87–100.

Hannerz, Ulf. 1969. *Soulside: Inquiries into Ghetto Culture and Community*. New York: Columbia University Press.

Harding, David, and Christopher Jencks. 2000. "Changing Attitudes toward Premarital Sex: Cohort, Period, and Aging Effects." Cambridge, MA: John F. Kennedy School of Government, Harvard University.

Harlap, Susan, Katherine Kost, and Jaqueline Darroch Forrest. 1991. *Preventing Pregnancy, Protecting Health: A New Look at Birth Control Choices in the United States*. New York: Alan Guttmacher Institute.

Harris, Howell John. 2000. *Bloodless Victories: The Rise and Fall of the Open Shop in the Philadelphia Metal Trades, 1890–1940*. New York: Cambridge University Press.

Haveman, Robert, Barbara Wolfe, and Karen Pence. 2003. "Intergenerational Effects of Nonmarital and Early Childbearing. In *Out of Wedlock: Causes and Consequences of Nonmarital Fertility*, ed. Lawrence L. Wu and Barbara Wolfe, 287–316. New York: Russell Sage Foundation.

Hays, Sharon. 1996. *The Cultural Contradictions of Motherhood*. New Haven, CT: Yale University Press.

———. 2003. *Flat Broke with Children*. New York: Oxford University Press.

Henshaw, Stanley K. 1998. "Unintended Pregnancy in the United States." *Family Planning Perspectives* 30: 24–29.

Higginson, Joanna Gregson. 1998. "Competitive Parenting: The Culture of Teen Mothers." *Journal of Marriage and the Family*. 60: 135–49.

Hoffman, Saul. 1998. "Teenage Childbearing Is Not So Bad After All, . . . or Is It?" *Family Planning Perspectives* 30: 236–39, 243.

Hogan, Dennis P., Ling Xian Hao, and William L. Parish. 1990. "Race, Kin Networks, and Assistance to Mother-Headed Families." *Social Forces* 68: 797–812.

Hotz, V. Joseph, Susan W. McElroy, and Seth G. Sanders. 1997. "The Impacts of Teenage Childbearing on the Mothers and the Consequences of those Impacts for Government." In *Kids Having Kids: A Robin Hood Special Report on the Costs of Adolescent Childbearing*, ed. Rebecca A. Maynard, 54–94. Washington, DC: Urban Institute Press.

Hrdy, Sarah Blaffer. 1999. *Mother Nature: Maternal Instincts and How They Shape the Human Species.* New York: Ballantine Books.

Jargowsky, Paul A. 1997. *Poverty and Place: Ghettos, Barrios, and the American City.* New York: Russell Sage Foundation.

Jarrett, Robin. 1997. "African-American Family and Parenting Strategies in Impoverished Neighborhoods." *Qualitative Sociology* 20: 275–88.

Jencks, Christopher. 1992. *Rethinking Social Policy: Race, Poverty, and the Underclass.* New York: HarperCollins.

——— and Kathryn Edin. 1995. "Do Poor Women Have the Right to Bear Children?" *American Prospect* 1: 43–52.

Kalil, Ariel, and James Kunz. 2002. "Teenage Childbearing, Marital Status, and Depressive Symptoms in Later Life." *Child Development* 73: 1748–60.

Kane, Andrea, and Isabel V. Sawhill. 2003. "Preventing Early Childbearing." In *One Percent for the Kids: New Policies, Brighter Futures for America's Children*, ed. Isabel V. Sawhill. Washington, DC: Brookings Institution.

Kaplan, Elaine Bell. 1997. *Not Our Kind of Girl: Unraveling the Myths of Black Teenage Motherhood.* Berkeley and Los Angeles: University of California Press.

Kefalas, Maria. 2003. *Working-Class Heroes: Protecting Home, Community, and Nation in a Chicago Neighborhood.* Berkeley and Los Angeles: University of California Press.

Ketkar, Kesum W., and Barrie A. Peterson. 2000. *Immigrant Workers in New Jersey: A Preliminary Assessment of Available Statistics, Issues, and Policy Options.* South Orange, NJ: Seton Hall University Institute on Work.

Kitson, Gay C., and William M. Holmes. 1992. *Portrait of Divorce: Adjustment to Marital Breakdown.* New York: Guilford Press.

Kohn, Melvin. 1959. "Social Class and Parental Values." *American Journal of Sociology* 64: 337–51.

———. 1963. "Social Class and Parent-Child Relationships: An Interpretation." *American Journal of Sociology* 68: 471–80.

Koray, Susan Weirzbicki, and Betsy Payn. 2000. "Why Are U.S. Women Not

Using Long-Lasting Contraceptives?" *Family Planning Perspectives* 32: 176–91.

Kozol, Jonathan. 1992. *Savage Inequalities: Children in America's Schools.* New York: Harper Perennial.

Kunz, James. 2002. "Teen Pregnancy and Negative Life Outcomes: What Is the Relationship?" *Social Work Today* 2, no. 15.

Kurz, Demie. 1995. *For Richer, for Poorer: Mothers Confront Divorce.* New York: Routledge.

———. 1998. "Old Problems, New Directions in the Study of Violence Against Women." In *Issues in Intimate Violence*, ed. Raquel Bergen Kennedy, 197–208. Newbury Park, CA: Sage.

———. 1999. "Women, Welfare, and Domestic Violence." In *Whose Welfare?* ed. Gwendolyn Mink, 132–51. Ithaca, NY: Cornell University Press.

Landale, Nancy S. 1994. "Migration and the Latino Family: The Union Formation of Puerto Rican Women." *Demography* 31, no. 1: 133–57.

——— and Kevin Fennelly. 1992. "Informal Unions among Mainland Puerto Ricans: Cohabitation or an Alternative to Legal Marriage?" *Journal of Marriage and the Family* 54: 269–80.

——— and Renate Forste. 1991. "Patterns of Entry into Marriage and Cohabitation among Mainland Puerto Rican Women." *Demography* 28: 587–607.

——— and Susan M. Hauan. 1996. "Migration and Premarital Childbearing among Puerto Rican Women." *Demography* 33, no. 4: 429–42.

Lareau, Annette. 2000. *Home Advantage: Social Class and Parental Intervention in Elementary Education.* 2nd ed. Lanham, MD: Rowan and Littlefield.

———. 2003. *Unequal Childhoods: Class, Race, and Family Life.* Berkeley and Los Angeles: University of California Press.

Laub, John H., Daniel S. Nagin, and Robert J. Sampson. 1998. "Trajectories of Change in Criminal Offending: Good Marriages and the Desistance Process." *American Sociological Review* 63: 225–38.

——— and Robert J. Sampson. 1993. "Turning Points in the Life Course: Why Change Matters to the Study of Crime." *Criminology* 31: 301–25.

Laumann, Edward O., Stephen Ellingson, Jenna Mahay, Anthony Paik, and Yoosik Youm. 2004. *The Sexual Organization of the City.* Chicago: University of Chicago Press.

———, John H. Gagnon, Robert T. Michael, and Stuart Michaels. 1994. *The Social Organization of Sexuality: Sexual Practices in the United States.* Chicago: University of Chicago Press.

Leibowitz, Arleen, Marvin Eisen, and Winston K. Chow. 1986. "An Economic Model of Teenage Pregnancy Decision-Making." *Demography* 23: 67–77.

Levine, Judith, Harold Pollack, and Maureen E. Comfort. 2000. "Academic and Behavioral Outcomes among the Children of Young Mothers." JCPR Working Paper #193. Chicago: Joint Center for Poverty Research.

Licht, Walter. 1999. *Getting Work: Philadelphia, 1840–1950*. Philadelphia: University of Pennsylvania Press.

Lichter, Daniel T., and Deborah Roempke Graefe. 2001. "Finding a Mate? The Marital and Cohabitation Histories of Unwed Mothers." In *Out of Wedlock: Causes and Consequences of Nonmarital Fertility*, ed. Lawrence L. Wu and Barbara Wolfe, 317–43. New York: Russell Sage Foundation.

———, Felicia B. LeClere, and Diane K. McLaughlin. 1991. "Local Marriage Markets and the Marital Behavior of Black and White Women." *American Journal of Sociology* 94: 843–67.

———, Diane K. McLaughlin, George Kephart, and David J. Landry. 1992. "Race and the Retreat from Marriage: A Shortage of Marriageable Men?" *American Sociological Review* 57: 781–99.

Lindsey, Duncan. 1991. "Adequacy of Income and the Foster Care Placement Decision: Using an Odds-Ratio Approach to Examine Client Variables." *Social Work Research and Abstracts* 28: 29–36.

———. 1994. *The Welfare of Children*. New York: Oxford University Press.

Lloyd, Kim M., and Scott J. South. 1996. "Contextual Influences on Young Men's Transition to First Marriage." *Social Forces* 74: 1097–1119.

Lopez, Steve. 1994. *Third and Indiana*. New York: Viking Penguin.

Loprest, Pamela. 2003. "Fewer Welfare Leavers Employed in a Weak Economy." Washington, DC: Urban Institute Press.

Luker, Kristin. 1984. *Abortion and the Politics of Motherhood*. Berkeley and Los Angeles: University of California Press.

———. 1996. *Dubious Conceptions and the Politics of Teenage Pregnancy*. Cambridge, MA: Harvard University Press.

Lundberg, Shelly, and Robert Pollack. 1996. "Bargaining and Distribution within Marriage." *Journal of Economic Perspectives* 10: 139–58.

Luttrell, Wendy. 2003. *Pregnant Bodies, Fertile Minds: Gender, Race, and the Schooling of Pregnant Teens*. New York: Routledge.

MacLeod, Jay. 1987. *Ain't No Making It: Aspirations and Attainment in a Low-Income Neighborhood*. Boulder, CO: Westview Press.

MacMahon, Martha. 1995. *Engendering Motherhood: Identity and Self-Transformation in Women's Lives*. New York: Guilford Press.

Madden, Janice Fanning, and William J. Stull. 1990. *Post-Industrial Philadelphia: Structural Changes in the Metropolitan Economy.* Philadelphia: University of Pennsylvania Press.

Manlove, Jennifer. 1998. "The Influence of High School Dropout and School Disengagement on the Risk of School-Age Pregnancy." *Journal of Research on Adolescence* 8: 187–220.

Manning, Wendy. 2003. "Measuring and Modeling Cohabitation: New Perspectives from Qualitative Data." Unpublished manuscript.

——— and Nancy Landale. 1996. "Racial and Ethnic Differences in the Role of Cohabitation in Premarital Childbearing." *Journal of Marriage and the Family* 58: 63–77.

——— and Pamela Smock. 1995. "Why Marry? Race and the Transition to Marriage among Cohabiters." *Demography* 32: 509–20.

Markman, Howard J., Scott M. Stanley, and Susan L. Blumberg. 2001. *Fighting for Your Marriage: Positive Steps for Preventing Divorce and Preserving a Lasting Love.* New York: Jossey-Bass.

Marks, Nadine F., and Sara S. McLanahan. 1993. "Gender, Family Structure, and Social Support among Parents." *Journal of Marriage and the Family* 55: 481–93.

Martin, Steven P., and Sangeeta Parashar. 2003. "An Educational Crossover in Divorce Attitudes." Unpublished paper. College Park, MD: Maryland Population Research Center, University of Maryland.

McLanahan, Sara S. 1994. "The Consequences of Single Motherhood." *American Prospect* 5: 48–58.

———. 1997. "Parent Absence or Poverty: Which Matters More?" In *Consequences of Growing Up Poor*, ed. Greg Duncan and Jeanne Brooks-Gunn, 35–44. New York: Russell Sage Foundation.

———. 2004. "Growing Inequality in Children's Family Resources." Presidential Address. Annual Meetings of the Population Association of America. Boston, MA. April 1–3.

———, Irwin Garfinkel, Nancy Reichman, and Julian Teitler. 2000. "Unwed Parents or Fragile Families? Implications for Welfare and Child Support Policy." Working Paper #00–04. Princeton, NJ: Center for Research on Child Wellbeing, Princeton University.

———, Irwin Garfinkel, Nancy Reichman, Julian Teitler, Marcia Carlson, and Christina Norland Audigier. 2003. *The Fragile Families and Child Wellbeing Study: Baseline National Report.* Princeton, NJ: Center for Research on Child Wellbeing, Princeton University.

————— and Gary Sandefur. 1994. *Growing Up with a Single Parent: What Helps, What Hurts.* Cambridge, MA: Harvard University Press.

McLaughlin, Diane K., and Daniel T. Lichter. 1997. "Poverty and the Marital Behavior of Young Women." *Journal of Marriage and the Family* 59: 582–94.

Michalopoulos, Charles, Kathryn Edin, Barbara Fink, Mirella Landriscina, Denise Polit, Judy Polyne, Lashawn Richburg-Hayes, David Seith, and Nandita Verma. 2003. *Welfare Reform in Philadelphia: Implementation, Effects, and Experiences of Poor Families and Neighborhoods.* New York: Manpower Demonstration Research Corporation.

Miller, Cynthia, and Virginia Knox. 2001. *The Challenge of Helping Low-Income Fathers Support Their Children: Final Lessons from Parents' Fair Share.* New York: Manpower Demonstration Research Corporation.

Mincy, Ronald. 2002. "Who Should Marry Whom? The Incidence of Multiple-Partner Fertility on New Unmarried Parents." Working Paper #02–03-FF. Princeton, NJ: Center for Research on Child Wellbeing, Princeton University.

—————. 2004. "The Survey Findings." Paper presented at conference entitled Getting Married: Evolving Practical Policies for Fragile Families. New Orleans, January.

—————, Hillard Poncy, Dana Reychert, and Phil Richardson. 2003. "Fragile Families in Focus: A Look at How Never-Married, Low-Income Parents Perceive Marriage and Relationships." Paper presented at conference entitled Let's Get Married. New Orleans, December.

Moffitt, Robert A. 1994. "The Incentive Effects of the U.S. Welfare System: A Review." *Journal of Economic Literature* 30: 1–61.

—————. 1998. "The Effect of Welfare on Marriage and Fertility." In *Welfare, the Family, and Reproductive Behavior,* ed. Robert Moffitt, 50–51, 59–97. Washington, DC: National Academy Press.

—————. 2000. "Female Wages, Male Wages, and the Economic Model of Marriage: The Basic Evidence." In *The Ties That Bind: Perspectives on Marriage and Cohabitation,* ed. Linda J. Waite, 302–19. New York: Aldine de Gruyter.

—————. 2001. "Welfare Benefits and Female Headship in U.S. Time Series." In *Out of Wedlock: Causes and Consequences of Non-Marital Fertility,* ed. Lawrence L. Wu and Barbara Wolfe, 143–72. New York: Russell Sage Foundation.

Moore, Joan, and John Hagedorn. 1996. "What Happens to Girls in the Gang?" In *Gangs in America,* ed. Ron Huff, 205–20. Thousand Oaks, CA: Sage.

Moore, Kristin A., Anne Driscoll, and Laura B. Lindberg. 1998. *A Statistical Portrait of Adolescent Sex, Contraception, and Childbearing.* Washington, DC: National Campaign to Prevent Teen Pregnancy.

———— and Thomas M. Stief. 1989. "Change in Marriage and Fertility Behavior: Behavior versus Attitudes of Young Adults." Washington, DC: U.S. Department of Health and Human Services.

Moran, Robert, Leonard N. Fleming, and Stephan Salisbury. 2002. "Aiming to Take Back Drug Sites." *Philadelphia Inquirer*, May 2.

Murray, Charles. 1984. *Losing Ground: American Social Policy, 1950–1980*. New York: Basic Books.

Musick, Kelly. 2002. "Planned and Unplanned Childbearing among Unmarried Women." *Journal of Marriage and the Family* 64: 916–29.

Myers, Teresa A. 2002. "Issue Brief: State Child Support Pass-through Programs." Child Care Project Issue Brief. October 23.Washington, DC: National Conference of State Legislatures.

Nelson, Timothy J. Forthcoming. "Low-Income Fathers." *Annual Review of Sociology*.

————, Susan Clampet-Lundquist, and Kathryn Edin. 2002. "Sustaining Fragile Fatherhood: How Low-Income, Non-Custodial Fathers in Philadelphia Talk About their Families." In *The Handbook of Father Involvement: Multidisciplinary Perspectives*, ed. Catherine Tamis-LeMonda and Natasha Cabrera, 525–53. Mahwah, NJ: Lawrence Erlbaum Associates.

Oakley, Ann. 1974. *Housewife*. London: Allen Lane.

Offner, Paul, and Harry Holzer. 2002. "Left Behind in the Labor Market: Recent Employment Trends among Young Black Men." Washington, DC: Brookings Center on Urban and Metropolitan Policy.

Oliver, Melvin L., and Thomas M. Shapiro. 1997. *Black Wealth, White Wealth: A New Perspective on Racial Inequality*. New York: Routledge.

Olsen, Randall J., and George Farkas. 1990. "The Effect of Economic Opportunity and Family Background on Adolescent Cohabitation and Childbearing among Low-Income Blacks." *Journal of Labor Economics* 8: 341–62.

Oppenheimer, Valerie Kincaid. 1988. "A Theory of Marriage Timing." *American Journal of Sociology* 94: 563–91.

————. 2000. "The Continuing Importance of Men's Economic Position in Marriage Formation." In *The Ties That Bind: Perspectives on Cohabitation and Marriage*, ed. Linda J. Waite, 283–301. New York: Aldine de Gruyter.

————. 2002. "Cohabiting and Marriage Formation during Young Men's Career Development Process." *Demography* 40: 127–49.

————, Matthijs Kalmijn, and Nelson Lim. 1997. "Men's Career Development and Marriage Timing During a Period of Rising Inequality." *Demography* 34: 311–30.

Oropesa, R. S., and Bridget K. Gorman. 2000. "Ethnicity, Immigration, and Beliefs about Marriage as a 'Tie that Binds.' " In *The Ties That Bind: Perspectives on Marriage and Cohabitation*, ed. Linda J. Waite, 188–211. New York: Aldine de Gruyter.

Pager, Devah. 2003. "The Mark of a Criminal Record." *American Sociological Review* 66: 542–67.

Parke, Mary. 2003. "Are Married Parents Really Better for Children? What Research Says About the Effects of Family Structure on Child Well-Being." Policy Brief 3, Couples and Marriage Series. Washington, DC: Center for Law and Social Policy.

Patterson, Orlando. 1998. *Rituals of Blood: Consequences of Slavery in Two American Centuries*. Washington, DC: Civitas/Counterpoint.

Philadelphia Metropolitan Planning Commission. 2001. "Philadelphia Neighborhood Profiles." Philadelphia: Philadelphia Metropolitan Planning Commission, p. A-39.

Rainwater, Lee. 1970. *Behind Ghetto Walls: Black Families in a Federal Slum*. Chicago: Aldine.

Raley, R. Kelly. 1996. "A Shortage of Marriageable Men: A Note on the Role of Cohabitation in Black-White Differences in Marriage Rates." *American Sociological Review* 61: 973–83.

Rankin, Bruce H., and James M. Quane. 2000. "Neighborhood Poverty and the Social Isolation of Inner-City African American Families." *Social Forces* 79: 139–64.

Reed, Joanna. 2004. "Meanings of Marriage and Cohabitation for Unmarried Couples with Children." Unpublished ms. Department of Sociology, Northwestern University.

Richer, Elise, Abbey Frank, Mark Greenberg, Steve Savner, and Vicky Turetsky. 2003. "Boom Times a Bust: Declining Employment among Less-Educated Young Men." Publication 03-49. Washington DC: Center for Law and Social Policy.

Rindfuss, Ronald R., S. Philip Morgan, and Kate Offutt. 1996. "Education and the Changing Age Pattern of American Fertility: 1963–89." *Demography* 33: 277–90.

Ritter, John. 1998. "Uniforms Changing Culture of the Nation's Classrooms." *USA TODAY*, October 15.

Roberts, Dorothy. 1999. "Welfare's Ban on Poor Motherhood." In *Whose Welfare?* ed. Gwendolyn Mink, 152–70. Ithaca, NY: Cornell University Press.

Rosier, Katherine Brown. 2000. *Mothering Inner-City Children: The Early School Years*. New Brunswick, NJ: Rutgers University Press.

Ruggles, Steven. 1997. "The Rise of Divorce and Separation in the United States, 1880–1990." *Demography* 34: 455–66.

Sampson, Robert J., and John H. Laub. 1990. "Crime and Deviance over the Life Course: The Salience of Adult Social Bonds." *American Sociological Review* 55: 609–27.

———. 1993. *Crime in the Making: Pathways and Turning Points through Life*. Cambridge, MA: Harvard University Press.

Sayer, Liana C., Nathan Wright, and Kathryn Edin. 2003. "Class Differences in Family Attitudes." Unpublished ms. Ohio State University.

Schultz, T. Paul. 1994. "Marital Status and Fertility in the United States." *Journal of Human Resources* 29: 637–69.

Slaughter, Diana T., and Edgar Epps. 1987. "The Home Environment and Academic Achievement of Black Children and Youth: An Overview." In *Black Families: Interdisciplinary Perspectives*, ed. Harold E. Cheatham and James B. Stewart, 111–30. New Brunswick, NJ: Transaction.

Solinger, Rickie. 2001. *Beggars and Choosers: How the Politics of Choice Shapes Adoption, Abortion, and Welfare in the United States*. New York: Hill and Wang.

Spanier, Graham B., and Linda Thompson. 1984. *Parting: The Aftermath of Separation and Divorce*. Beverly Hills, CA: Sage.

Stanley, Scott M. 2001. "Making the Case for Premarital Education." *Family Relations* 50: 272–80.

———, Howard J. Markman, and S. Whitton. 2002. "Communication, Conflict, and Commitment: Insights on the Foundations of Relationship Success from a National Survey." *Family Process* 41: 659–75.

Steedman, Carolyn Kay. 1987. *Landscape for a Good Woman: A Story of Two Lives*. New Brunswick, NJ: Rutgers University Press.

Stevenson, Harold W., Chuansheng Chen, and David H. Uttal. 1990. "Beliefs and Achievement: A Study of Black, White, and Hispanic Children." *Child Development* 61: 508–23.

Sweeney, Megan M. 2002. "Two Decades of Family Change: The Shifting Economic Foundations of Marriage." *American Sociological Review* 67: 132–47.

Szafran, Robert F., and Arthur F. Clagett. 1987. "Variable Predictors of Attitudes toward the Legalization of Abortion." *Social Indicators Research* 20: 271–90.

Taylor, Pamela L., M. Belinda Tucker, and Claudia Mitchell-Kernan. 1999.

"Ethnic Variations in Perceptions of Men's Provider Role." *Psychology of Women Quarterly* 23: 741–61.

Terry-Humen, Elizabeth, Jennifer Manlove, and Kristen Moore. 2001. "Births Outside of Marriage: Perceptions versus Reality." ChildTrends Research Brief. Available at www.childtrendsdatabank.org//indicators/75Unmarried-Births.cfm.

Thornton, Arland, and Linda Young-DeMarco. 2001. "Four Decades of Attitudes toward Family Issues in the United States: The 1960s through the 1990s." *Journal of Marriage and the Family* 64: 1009–37.

Tolman, Richard M., and Jody Raphael. 2000. "A Review of Research on Welfare and Domestic Violence." *Journal of Social Issues* 56: 655–82.

Tucker, Belinda M. 2000. "Marital Values and Expectations in Context: Results from a Twenty-one-City Survey." In *The Ties That Bind: Perspectives on Cohabitation and Marriage*, ed. Linda J. Waite, 166–87. New York: Aldine de Gruyter.

—— and Claudia Mitchell-Kernan. 1995. *The Decline in Marriage among African Americans*. New York: Russell Sage Foundation.

Turley, Ruth N. 2003. "Are Children of Young Mothers Disadvantaged Because of Their Mother's Age or Family Background?" *Child Development* 74: 463–74.

U.S. Census Bureau. 2002. "Children's Living Arrangements and Characteristics." Annual Demographic Supplement to the March 2002 Current Population Survey. Current Population Reports, Series P20–547. Washington, DC: U.S. Government Printing Office.

U.S. Department of Health and Human Services, Office of Applied Studies. 2003. "2002 National Survey on Drug Use and Health (NSDUH)." Washington, DC: U.S. Government Printing Office.

U.S. Department of Labor, Bureau of Labor Statistics. 2003. "Highlights of Women's Earnings in 2002." Report 972. Washington, DC: U.S. Government Printing Office. September.

Ventura, Stephanie J., and Christine A. Bachrach. 2000. "Nonmarital Childbearing in the United States, 1940–1999." *National Vital Statistics Reports* 48, no. 16. Washington, DC: National Center for Health Statistics.

Veroff, Joseph, Elizabeth Douvan, and Richard A. Kulka. 1981. *The Inner American: A Self-Portrait from 1957 to 1976*. New York: Basic Books.

Vleminckx, Koen, and Timothy Smeeding, eds. 2003. *Child Well-Being, Child Poverty, and Child Policy in Modern Nations: What Do We Know?* Tonawanda, NY: University of Toronto Press.

Waite, Linda, and Maggie Gallagher. 2001. *The Case for Marriage: Why Married People Are Happier, Healthier, and Better Off Financially.* New York: Broadway Books.

Waller, Maureen, and Elizabeth Peters. 2003. "Perceptions of Divorce as a Barrier to Marriage." Paper presented at symposium entitled Marriage and Family Formation among Low-Income Couples: What Do We Know from Research? Washington, DC, October.

Wallerstein, J. S., and J. B. Kelly. 1980. "Effects of Divorce on the Visiting Father-Child Relationship." *American Journal of Psychiatry* 137: 1534–39.

Warr, Mark. 1998. "Life Course Transitions and Desistance from Crime." *Criminology* 36: 183–216.

Webb, David A. 2000. *Vital Statistics Report 2000: City of Philadelphia.* Philadelphia, PA: Philadelphia Department of Public Health.

Weigley, Russell F. 1982. "The Border City in Civil War." In *Philadelphia: A 300-Year History*, ed. Russell F. Weigley. New York: W. W. Norton.

Wilkins, Julia. 1999. "School Uniforms." *Humanist* 59.

Willis, Paul E. 1981. *Learning to Labour: How Working-Class Kids Get Working-Class Jobs.* New York: Columbia University Press.

Wilson, William Julius. 1987. *The Truly Disadvantaged: The Inner City, the Underclass, and Public Policy.* Chicago: University of Chicago Press.

——— and Kathryn Neckerman. 1986. "Poverty and Family Structure: The Widening Gap between Evidence and Public Policy Issues." In *Fighting Poverty: What Works and What Doesn't*, ed. Sheldon Danziger and Daniel H. Weinberg, 232–59. Cambridge, MA: Harvard University Press.

Wood, Robert G. 1995. "Marriage Rates and Marriageable Men: A Test of the Wilson Hypothesis." *Journal of Human Resources* 30: 163–93.

Wu, Lawrence L., Larry L. Bumpass, and Kelly Musick. 2001. "Historical and Life-Course Trajectories of Nonmarital Childbearing." In *Out of Wedlock: Causes and Consequences of Nonmarital Fertility*, ed. Lawrence L. Wu and Barbara Wolfe, 3–48. New York: Russell Sage Foundation.

Yang, Tang, and S. Philip Morgan. 2002. "How Big are Educational and Racial Fertility Differentials in the U.S.?" Paper presented at the Annual Meetings of the Population Association of America, May 8–10, Atlanta, GA.

Zelizer, Viviana A. 1994. *Pricing the Priceless Child: The Changing Social Value of Children.* Princeton, NJ: Princeton University Press.

INDEX

abandonment: during pregnancy, 56, 62; of children, 162

abortion, 43–47, 51, 93, 142, 252n14, 253nn18, 19, 21; boyfriends' insistence on, 51, 54–56, 60, 68–69; parents' attitude toward, 65, 66, 68

abused children, 162, 173–74, 261n22

Acevedo, Millie, 54–56, 58, 60, 119–20, 150–51, 160–61, 160, 168–70, 172, 262n2

adoption, giving children up for, 120, 142, 143; attitudes toward, 45, 47, 66

African Americans, 13, 14, 16–24, 97–98, 100–101, 187–89, 191–93, 211–13, 216, 237, 250n22, 259n20, 266nn49, 50; criminal behavior among, 82, 83, 86–87, 212; demographic and social characteristics of, 233–36; domestic violence among, 98, 256n22; dreams of life partnership by, 103; drug and alcohol abuse among, 87–89, 98, 212; emotional responses to birth by, 61–64; family's response to daughter's pregnancy among, 66–68; fertility rate of, 252n14; financial conflicts among, 75–77, 79; good mothering by, 33, 138–43, 145, 148–52, 155–56, 159, 160, 259n3; incarceration among, 85–86, 98, 212; income and family characteristics of, 226, 228–29; infidelity among, 73–74, 91–93, 256n23; meaning of marriage for, 109–15, 117–19, 123–33, 208, 212–13, 257nn2, 5, 6, 259n19, 263n10; planned pregnancies of, 33–37; poverty rate for, 225–27, 230; pregnancy experiences of, 50–55, 57, 59; prospective male partners of, 99; response to conception by, 42–46; romantic relationships of, 31, 262n1; sample selection of, 238; transforming influence of motherhood on, 172–77, 179–82; unplanned pregnancies of, 37–40

after-school programs, 154–55; for at-risk teenagers, 217

AIDS, 94, 253n16

alcohol abuse, 44, 127, 217; domestic violence and, 96, 97; motherhood as redemption from, 180, 181, 184, 196; relationship failure due to, 81, 87–90, 97, 98, 101, 102, 203, 212, 214

Anderson, Elijah, 261n20, 262n1

domestic violence, 120, 169, 182, 217, 256nn21, 22; during pregnancy, 55, 56, 59, 61, 64, 69; relationship failure due to, 75, 94–98, 101, 203, 212, 214; and reluctance to marry, 126, 127, 131

drug abuse, 39, 44, 106, 127, 217, 255nn7, 12; cautioning children about, 157–58; losing children to foster care due to, 143–44, 162–63; motherhood as redemption from, 172, 180–81, 184, 196; relationship failure due to, 75, 84, 87–90, 95, 97–99, 101, 102, 189–91, 203, 214

drug dealing, 15, 27, 81–85, 101, 103, 148, 162–63, 251n28

Earned Income Tax Credit, 154

economic independence, female, 9, 108, 111–14, 190, 195, 203–4, 258n7; changes in family formation attributed to, 197–99

education, 260n16; achieving, 187, 192, 193; instilling value of, 139, 151–56, 158–59, 178–79, 192; level of, 2, 25, 207

Ellwood, David T., 249n4, 263n9, 265n43

engagement, 258n12

England, Paula, 258n12

family formation, changes in, 197–99; economic inequalities and, 201–2; redefinition of marriage and, 199–201

family of origin: response to pregnancy of, 64–68, 254n10; troubled relationship with, see home life, troubled

Farkas, George, 263n10

Federal Housing Administration, 18

feminism, 171, 201, 263n4

fertility rates, 206, 252n14

financial security, 114–16, 257n5, 258n9

Forste, Renate, 263n10

foster care, losing children to, 84, 143, 162–63, 261n22

Fragile Families and Child Wellbeing Study, 3, 249nn5, 7, 250nn11, 12, 257n2, 260n6

France, two-parent households in, 213

Friends (sitcom), 207–8

Gelles, Richard J., 256n21

gender roles, change in attitudes toward, 203

Germany, two-parent households in, 213

Geronimus, Arlene T., 266n43

good mothering, 9–10, 138–67, 210–11; bad mothering versus, 161–64, 173–74; "being there" and, 140–44, 167, 210, 259n3; confidence in, 33; education and, 151–55, 260n16; in face of problems, 157–61; instilling values and, 155–57; neighborhood influences and, 149–52, 157, 166, 167, 260n11; providing for children and, 146–49; social value of, 41, 43, 177; supervision and, 144–46

Graefe, Deborah R., 265n28

Grant, William T., Foundation, 19

gun violence, 20

Hays, Sharon, 261n23

Hewlett, Sylvia Ann, 1

high school: dropping out of, 2, 25, 28, 48–49, 180, 194, 195, 227, 249n2, 252n7, 262n3, 265n29, 266n40; rate of nonmarital births and, 207

Hispanics, 13, 14, 211–13, 256n23, 257nn2, 6, 259n3; income and family characteristics of, 226, 228–29; poverty rate for, 225–27; see also Puerto Ricans

HIV, 163; see also AIDS

home life, troubled, 10, 28, 33–34, 174, 175, 180–82, 262n6

homework, supervision of, 154–55

homicide, 139; drug-related, 83; incarceration for, 86, 120

Horn, Wade, 214

Hrdy, Sarah Blaffer, 263n4

incarceration, 2, 23–24, 59, 112, 120, 157, 196, 217, 255n11; and decline in male marriageable pool, 199; for failure to pay child support, 70; relationship failure and, 75, 83–87, 97, 194, 212, 214

income level, 2, 24

inequality, growth in, 201–2

infertility, 1–2

infidelity, 107, 217; domestic violence and guilt over, 97; during pregnancy, 58, 69, 72, 73, 93, 105, 127; relationship failure due to, 75, 90–94, 97–99, 101, 203, 212, 214; and reluctance to marry, 127–28, 131

interviews, 238–39, 241–47; coding of transcripts of, 239–40

Jencks, Christopher, 249n4, 263n9

Jews, 16

job loss, 13, 15, 20, 21, 75, 76

Kaplan, Elaine Bell, 254n10

Koray, Susan Weirzbicki, 265n34

Korenmann, Sanders, 266n43

Landale, Nancy S., 263n10

Lareau, Annette, 260nn9, 16, 266n46

Latinos. *See* Hispanics; Puerto Ricans

Laumann, Edward O., 255n14, 256n23

Lein, Laura, 256n20

Lichter, Daniel T., 263n10, 265n28

lifetime partnership, ideal of, 74, 103

Lin, I-Fen, 267n58

Losing Ground (Murray), 198

Luker, Kristin, 44, 253nn17, 19, 20

Luttrell, Wendy, 259n3

male marriageable pool, decline in, 197–200, 209, 216

Manlove, Jennifer, 261n3

marriage, 8–9, 73, 104–37, 257nn2, 4, 258n15, 259n17, 265n28; causes of retreat from, 197–99; delaying, 121–25, 188–89, 193, 202, 209; diversity in views on, 131–33; economic independence and, 111–14, 199, 203–4, 258n7, 263nn9, 10; fear of possessiveness in, 117–19; financial security requirements for, 114–17, 202–3, 257n5, 258n9; government policies on, 213–19; as lifetime commitment, 119–21; in moral hierarchy, 207–10; personhood and, 135, 201; racial differences in patterns of, 211–13; redefinition of, 199–201; reluctance about, 8–9, 73, 107–8, 216; standards for relationship worthy of, 128–31, 188, 191, 197, 200, 217–18; timing of, 109–11; trust and, 125–28, 258n14, 259n16

Match.com, 208

McLanahan, Sara S., 206, 258n12, 267n58

McLaughlin, Diane K., 263n10

mental abuse, 96

Mexican Americans, 262n8

middle class, 170, 180, 218; attitude toward abortion of, 44–45; childrearing attitudes and practices of, 139–41, 149, 155, 158, 166, 183, 206, 210–11, 261n23, 266n46; domestic violence among, 101; education in, 152, 155; fertility rates of, 253n14; infidelity in, 101; investigations by Child Protective Services of, 84; meaning of marriage for, 109, 111, 135, 200–204, 207–9; notions of commitment of, 90, 91; opportunities of, 46, 99, 205, 206; postponing childbearing in, 48, 164, 165, 208, 209, 249n2; preparations for childbearing of, 142; prospective male partners in, 99; reaction to early pregnancy among, 47; remarriage in, 215; self-indulgence of, 147; unplanned pregnancies in, 252n11

Midvale Steel Corporation, 12

Moffitt, Robert A., 263nn9, 10

money, conflicts over, 76–81, 101; infidelity and, 93, 94; mistrust and, 127

motherhood, 169–85; emotional rewards of, 174–77; as motivation, 172–74; social rewards of, 177–79; transforming influence of, 179–82, 184, 195–96, 262n7; as turning point, 170–72, 262n8; *see also* good mothering

Mummers Parade, 16, 78, 104, 251n30

Murray, Charles, 198

National Longitudinal Survey of Children, 266n50

neglected children, 162, 261n22

New York Shipbuilding Company, 20

Olsen, Randall J., 263n10

opportunity costs, 205, 262n4

paternity, denial of, 51, 52, 54–56, 60–63, 68; child support avoidance and, 69–70

Payn, Betsy, 265n34

personhood, marriage and, 135, 201

Peters, Elizabeth, 258n11

Philadelphia: Department of Human Services, 261n22; economic history of, 11–19, 250nn21, 22, 251n29; income and family characteristics in, 226, 228–29, 231–32; Police Department, 251n28; poverty rate in, 225–27, 230–31

physical abuse. *See* domestic violence

Planned Parenthood, 29, 38

possessiveness, 117–19; during pregnancy, 59

pregnancy, 7, 50–70; being there during, 142, 166; families' responses to, 64–68, 254n10; infidelity during, 58, 69, 72, 73, 93, 105, 127, 189; marriages due to, 123; relationships during, 51–60, 68–69, 72, 106, 126, 169, 187–88, 209; *see also* conception

premarital counseling, 214

prison. *See* incarceration

promiscuity, 180, 181; *see also* infidelity

Protestants, 16

Puerto Ricans, 16, 20, 24, 211–13, 226, 237, 239, 253n15, 259n20; child support for, 69–70; criminal behavior among, 83–85; demographic and social characteristics of, 233–36; domestic violence among, 94–96, 98, 212, 256n22; drug abuse among, 98, 212; emotional response to birth by, 62–63; family's response to daughter's pregnancy among, 66, 68; financial conflicts among, 76, 77; good mothering by, 33, 143–45, 150–51, 153, 156–61, 211; income and family characteristics of, 231–32; infidelity of, 91–92; meaning of marriage for, 112–13, 116–19, 121–22, 125, 128, 130, 132–33, 212, 263n10; planned pregnancies by, 33; poverty rate for, 226, 230; pregnancy experiences of, 54–59; response to conception by, 42–43; romantic relationships of, 27–30; sample selection of, 238; transforming influence of motherhood on, 168–70, 172, 174–75, 177–81; unplanned pregnancies of, 37, 38, 40–42

Quaker Lace Company, 251n22

racial and ethnic differences, 211–13; *see also* African Americans; Puerto Ricans; whites

Raley, R. Kelly, 263n10

RCA Victor, 20
redemption, motherhood as, 10–11,
    168–89
Reed, Joanna, 255n13
relational poverty, 34, 174–75, 262n5
relationship failure, 8, 71–103, 169,
    188, 254n1; criminal behavior and,
    72, 75, 81–87, 97, 98, 101, 102, 194,
    203, 212, 214; domestic violence
    and, 75, 93–98, 101, 203, 212, 214;
    drug and alcohol addiction and, 75,
    84, 87–90, 95, 97–99, 101, 102,
    189–91, 203, 214; financial factors
    in, 75–81; infidelity and, 75, 90–94,
    97–99, 101, 203, 212, 214; racial dif-
    ferences in, 212
relationship-skills training, 214
religious faith, 119–20, 156
riots, 19
Rodriguez, Antonia, 6, 7, 27–31, 40, 43,
    48–49, 51, 53, 59, 68, 99, 102,
    132–34, 262n2
romantic relationships, 7, 27–49, 125,
    262n1; accidental conception and,
    37–42; dreams of shared children
    in, 29–32, 54, 252n8; emotional re-
    wards of motherhood versus, 175,
    176; impact of pregnancy on,
    51–60; planned conception and,
    33–37
Rutgers University, 156

sample selection, 236–38
San Jose Mercury, 4
Sandefur, Gary, 267n58
Sayer, Liana C., 265n35, 266n44
Schmidt, Christian, 12
school. See education
service-sector jobs, 25
sexual abuse, 181
sexual activity, promiscuous, 180, 181;
    see also infidelity
sexually transmitted diseases, 94,
    253n16

sexual revolution, 200–201, 203, 264n17
shotgun weddings, 107
social isolation, 34, 239; see also rela-
    tional poverty
Spain, two-parent households in, 213
"speaker-listener" techniques, 214
spending habits, conflicts over, 77–81,
    101
Stetson hats, 12
Sweden, two-parent households in, 213
Sweeney, Megan M., 263n10

teenage childbearing, 3, 7, 20, 23, 25;
    declining rate of, 206; frequency of,
    30; programs to reduce, 217; roman-
    tic relationships and, 28
Temple University, 16, 156
Thornton, Arland, 266nn44, 49
Time (magazine), 1, 2
Treatise on the Family (Becker), 197
Truly Disadvantaged, The (Wilson),
    198
trust, low levels of, 34, 259n16; reluc-
    tance to marry and, 125–28, 258n14;
    sexual, 59, 73

unemployment, 2, 28, 216, 219, 227,
    255n3; changes in family formation
    attributed to, 198, 199; criminal be-
    havior and, 83, 85–87, 98; economic
    decline and, 13, 19; relationship fail-
    ure and, 75–77
U.S. Naval Shipyard, 12, 16

Vallas, Deena, 8, 104–9, 112–13, 117,
    130–31, 134, 189–91, 197, 199,
    202–4, 207, 211
values, instilling, 155–57
verbal abuse, 96
Veterans Administration, 18–19
Victor Talking Record Company, 12
Village Voice, 4
violence, 27; drug-related, 83, 97; gun,
    20; see also domestic violence

Waller, Maureen, 258n11

Washington, Mahkiya, 7, 50–54, 57, 63–64, 66, 73, 99, 102, 133, 147, 187–89, 197, 199, 202–4, 211

Washington Post, 4

Watkins, Dominique, 138–42, 191–93, 197, 203, 204, 211, 217

weddings, 107, 109, 111, 112, 115–17, 202

welfare, 24, 25, 70, 143, 178, 185, 197, 208, 266; change in family formation attributed to, 198, 199, 264n11; women leaving, 154, 216, 219

whites, 13–14, 22–24, 74, 189–91, 193–96, 211–13, 237, 238, 253n15, 259n20; alcohol and drug addiction among, 88–90, 98, 212; criminal behavior among, 82; demographic and social characteristics of, 233–36; domestic violence among, 94, 96–98, 182, 212, 256n22; emotional responses to birth by, 61–64; exodus to suburbs by, 13, 20; family's response to daughter's pregnancy among, 64–67; fertility rate of, 252n14; financial conflicts among, 77–79; good mothering by, 140, 142, 145–51, 154–57, 159, 161–63,

259n3; income and family characteristics of, 228–29, 231–32; infidelity among, 71–73, 256n23; meaning of marriage for, 104–10, 113–16, 119–22, 126, 128–34, 207, 212–13, 257nn2, 5, 6, 258n12, 259n19, 263n10; middle-class, *see* middle class; planned pregnancies of, 33–36; poverty rate for, 225–27, 230; pregnancy experiences of, 55, 56, 69; prospective male partners of, 98–100; response to conception by, 43–46; romantic relationships of, 30–31; sample selection of, 238; transforming influence of motherhood on, 171–82; unplanned pregnancies of, 37–39

Wilde, Ty, 266n43

Wilson, William Julius, 198, 199, 216

Winfrey, Oprah, 164

Women's eNews, 4

workforce participation, female, 198; by single mothers, 154, 255n3, 260n17, 261n18

World War II, 16

Wright, Nathan, 265n35, 366n44

Young-DeMarco, Linda, 266n44

INDEXER: Ruth Elwell
COMPOSITOR: Binghamton Valley Composition
TEXT: 10/15 Janson
DISPLAY: Interstate
PRINTER AND BINDER: Maple-Vail Manufacturing Group